ILEIA READINGS IN SUSTAINABLE AGRICULTURE

Let Farmers Judge

Experiences in Assessing the Sustainability of Agriculture

Edited by Wim Hiemstra, Coen Reijntjes
and Erik van der Werf

INTERMEDIATE TECHNOLOGY PUBLICATIONS 1992

Published by Intermediate Technology Publications
103/105 Southampton Row, London WC1B 4HH, UK

A CIP catalogue record for this book is available from the British Library

ISBN 1 85339 149 2

1766225

Printed by Antony Rowe, Bumper's Farm, Chippenham, Wiltshire SN14 5QA, UK.

Contents

Preface

Mrs Christine Karuru owns a 9-acre farm in Mangu village, about an hour's drive northeast of Nairobi, in the central Kenyan highlands. Population pressure is high, and continuous cropping has led to depletion and deterioration of the land resource. In Christine's words, 'Ordinary farming has failed so obviously in this area'.

That is why Christine decided to turn her farm into an organic farm. She learned about the necessary practices from KIOF, the Kenyan Institute of Organic Farming. Now she has succeeded in introducing composting, the recycling of nutrients, the use of liquid manure, crop diversification, double digging, crop rotation, natural pesticides, mulching and the use of leguminous trees. She is even being asked to educate other farmers in the area interested in taking up organic farming.

But is her farm *more* sustainable or *less* sustainable than it was before? What *is* sustainability, and *what* is sustainable—the farm, the watershed, the natural resource base, the crop or livestock production system, or the livelihood of Christine and her family? In other words, how can sustainability best be assessed?

The need for sustainable agriculture is now generally accepted, but the discussion of what sustainability means is still confused. Detailed comparative analyses of the sustainablity of different systems and practices are few, and the methodology for conducting such analyses remains to be developed and standardized.

It was in response to this situation that ILEIA organized, in December 1990, an international workshop on Assessing the Effectiveness of Low-external-input Farming Techniques. The main theme of the workshop was how to assess techniques for managing soil fertility—a problem central to the pursuit of sustainable agriculture. A literature search was made, publications on different technologies and on various aspects of environmental economics were studied, and members of the ILEIA network offered their views in a baseline paper. Twenty-eight people from different backgrounds—farming, policy making, research, development—and different countries were invited to share their experiences at the workshop. The results were edited and, together with other relevant articles, published in a special issue of the ILEIA Newsletter (1 and 2, 1991).

This reader is a follow-up to that workshop. It is a collection of papers on the theme of assessing sustainability in agriculture. The collection is divided into four parts. Following an introductory theme paper (Part I), the papers in Part II discuss the conceptual framework for assessment. Part III examines specific methodological issues, with the emphasis on farmers' assessment criteria. Part IV contains case studies comparing the performance of environmentally friendly farming practices and systems with that of conventional (high-external-input) agriculture.

The objective of this reader is to keep the non-specialist in agricultural economics informed about the current debate on how to assess sustainability and the effectiveness of low-external-input agriculture. Its title, *Let Farmers Judge*, reflects an important conclusion that emerged as the book took shape—that only if farmers themselves are centrally involved in assessments will such assessments be realistic. It is easy for scientists and others to imagine they understand farmers' criteria for evaluating new practices and systems. Time and again, however, rates of adoption suggest that they did not, or did so only partially. The 'paired' papers in this book illustrate this theme potently.

We hope this reader will create some understanding, not only of the difficulties but also of the rewards, of economic and social analysis of low-external-input and sustainable agriculture. Several papers reflect a sense of wonder and admiration on the part of their authors, as they discover the resourcefulness of the traditional practioners of low-external-input agriculture—the so-called 'resource-poor' farmers of developing countries—and the beauty of the systems they have developed and perfected over the centuries. This book should stimulate field workers to develop participatory approaches to technology development and assessment. It should also provide food for thought for policy makers, who will find in it much convincing evidence of the viability of low-external-input systems which, in so many ways, are capable of outperforming conventional 'modern' systems.

Your own experiences in assessing the effectiveness of low-external-input farming systems and practices, and your comments on this reader, will be very welcome, and may eventually be used in other ILEIA publications.

Wim Hiemstra, Coen Reijntjes and Erik van der Werf (editors)

ILEIA
P.O. Box 64
3830 AB Leusden
The Netherlands

Acknowledgements

This book would not have been possible without the help of many people outside ILEIA. We extend our thanks in paticular to:
• The farmers, field workers and researchers who shared their experiences and insights with us, either in writing or in discussion;
• The authors and publishers who gave their permission to use their material, most of which has been published previously;
• Mr Kees Zijderveld, of Partners in Agricultural and Rural Development (PARDEC), Wageningen; Ms Anne Stanneveld of MATRIX consultants in development management, Utrecht; and Ms Neertje van de Geest, previously with the Royal Tropical Institute, Amsterdam. These Dutch agricultural economists assisted in selecting the articles and in commenting on the editorial.
• Ms Ellen Radstake, Ms Suzanne Gosman, Ms Lyanne Alons and Ms Marian de Boer, for their administrative and secretarial assistance;
• Mr Simon Chater and Ms Kerry Smith of Hawson Farm, Buckfastleigh, UK, for editing the articles and making them camera-ready for the publisher;
• Mr Erik van de Werf, for the photographs appearing on the front cover and as an introduction to Part II. The front cover shows Mr Tangaswamy, an Indian farmer, admiring a heavy jackfruit on his ecological farm in Pudikottai, Tamil Nadu, Southern India.
•Mr Laurens van Veldhuizen, for the photograph of Christine Karuru; Mr. Kees Manintveld, for that of Mrs. Balomtesi Ngongorego and Mr Hilario Padilla, for that of the Bontoc rice terraces.

PART ONE:

Measuring Sustainability

Mrs Christine Karuru is an organic farmer in Kenya. She feeds her cows with Napier Grass, fodder from leguminous trees and 'organic waste' from the garden. To what extent does her farm provide an example of a sustainable production system? *Photo: Laurens van Velthuizen*

Measuring Sustainability: Issues and Alternatives

Larry W. Harrington

Introduction

Sustainability has been defined and characterized in vastly different ways—from the resilience of individual agro-ecosystems to food security in the face of global climate change. Approaches to measuring sustainability are heavily conditioned by how the word sustainability itself is understood. Some general issues are nevertheless common across all possible approaches.

General Issues

Predicting the future

Measuring sustainability implies drawing conclusions, or at least stating probabilities, about future events. When an agro-ecologist warns of agro-ecosystem breakdown as a system becomes less diversified, he or she is making a forecast. Similarly, when farmers' cultural practices are portrayed as unsustainable, predictions are implicitly being made about future levels of soil depth and fertility and crop productivity. More obviously, when the proponents of low-input sustainable agriculture advocate a switch to wholly renewable resources, they are making tacit assumptions about the future availability and prices of agricultural inputs.

All forecasts contain uncertainty, but some are more uncertain than others. Forecasts about the future effects of soil erosion on crop yields are probably more reliable than those about regional changes in temperature and rainfall due to global warming. The degree to which sustainability can be measured depends greatly on the ability of analysts to predict the future accurately.

Time frame

The problems of measuring sustainability are exacerbated by the different time frames that apply to different sustainability issues. Some problems are best studied over the medium term, within a time frame of 5 to 20 years. These include problems such as soil nutrient depletion, the build-up of weeds, pests and diseases, rapid soil erosion, and so on.

Other problems are best studied over a longer time frame of 20 to 100 years. These include slower forms of land degradation, such as erosion, salinization or desertification, and some of the changes expected in the external environment, such as the initial effects of global warming. Still other problems are best 'studied' (if the word still makes sense in this context) over very long time frames of 100 to 1000 years and beyond. These include questions concerning the 'ultimate' sustainability of agriculture.

State versus control variables

In some approaches to measuring sustainability, only 'state variables' (descriptors of the quality of the environment or of specific resources) are quantified. In others, both state variables and 'control variables' (variables that directly influence the level of a state variable) are quantified. For example, the control variable 'tillage practice' influences the state variable 'soil depth remaining after erosion'. There is typically a cause-and-effect relationship between control and state variables.

When only state variables are measured, considerable doubt can remain regarding the causes of observed changes. For example, per capita food production (a state variable) may be declining. The causes, however, cannot be ascertained unless appropriate control variables are also measured. They might be rising human population, lower use of inputs, a switch to non-food cash crops, declining yields, or a combination of these and other factors. A satisfactory assessment of sustainability is likely to require the simultaneous measurement of several state and control variables, linking problems with their causes.

Continuous versus discrete measurement

There seems to be little discussion in the literature on the issue of whether variables should be measured continuously or discretely. If sustainability is thought of as discrete, then in theory at least an agro-ecosystem can be described as being either sustainable or not. Measuring sustainability comes down to ascertaining which of these two states prevails. If sustainability is seen as continuous, however, it is possible to entertain different degrees of sustainability, opening the way to comparisons between systems. Most proponents of increased quantification seem to assume that continuous measurement is possible.

Level of measurement and substitution options

It is frequently assumed that sustainability is best measured at the plot level. Sustainability is taken to mean indefinitely maintaining the productivity of a specific cropping pattern in a specific location, without incurring a deterioration in the quality and quantity of the resources devoted to its production. Yet other cropping patterns may come along that are more attractive to farmers. And it is not always necessary to insist on the sustainability of all system components: some resources may be used in excess of sustainable levels, and the overall productivity of the system maintained by substituting among resources over time (Graham-Tomasi 1990). A major issue, then, is deciding exactly what it is that we are trying to sustain.

4

Sustainability of What? Three Concepts

Sustainability and sustainable agriculture have been analysed and defined in numerous ways. Indeed, there are almost too many definitions. Most of them fall under one or more of three concepts of sustainability: the agro-ecological concept, the resource concept, and the growth concept.

Sustainable agro-ecologies

Some definitions focus on sustainability in terms of system resilience, or the ability of an agricultural system or ecology to 'maintain its productivity when subject to stress or perturbation' (Conway 1986). Sustainability in the agro-ecological sense is enhanced through system diversity. The diversity of enterprises over time and space fosters the recycling of nutrients, increased efficiency in the use of moisture, nutrients and sunlight, and the reduced incidence of weeds, pests and diseases (Altieri 1987). Modern monoculture, characterized by low levels of diversity, is viewed as highly fragile, its equilibrium being controled through the use of external inputs rather than through internal feedback mechanisms (Ingram and Swift 1989).

In this view, then, agriculture can be made more sustainable by increasing system diversity and by fostering nutrient and energy cycling (and thereby reducing the use of external inputs) through the development of suitable new farming systems (Francis 1986; Altieri 1987). Consequently, monitoring trends in system diversity and in the internal cycling of nutrients and energy is perceived as fundamental when measuring the sustainability of an agricultural system.

Sustainable resources

Other definitions of sustainability focus on the continuing availability of resources over time, especially with regard to future generations and the rights of non-human species (Batie 1989). The emphasis is on stewardship, or the proper care and protection of resources (Barker and Chapman 1988). This approach is founded on the belief that future generations have the right to an environment and a stock of renewable and non-renewable resources in no worse condition than that enjoyed by the current generation.

In theory, the efficient intertemporal use of resources can be assessed by means of cost-benefit analysis (Schmid 1989). However, intertemporal efficiency considerations can be used to rationalize the extinction of renewable resources and the exhaustion of non-renewable resources (Clark 1976). Discounting future costs and benefits involves making judgements concerning the value of current versus future consumption. Serious ethical questions arise when the current generation of human beings makes these judgements on the behalf of future generations (Batie 1989; IFPRI 1989). Moreover, it can be argued that agricultural and economic development are inherently unsustainable simply because geometric growth rates (for example, in the demand for food) are ultimately incompatible with absolute scarcities (for example, in resources, or in the capacity of the environment to absorb pollution) (Heilbroner 1980; Batie 1989).

According to this perspective, the sustainability of agriculture can best be enhanced by slowing down economic development, stabilizing human population levels, and discouraging the exploitation of natural resources (especially common property resources) (Barbier and McCracken 1988; Durning 1990). Proponents of the resource availability view, then, argue that assessments of sustainability must somehow capture the quantity and quality of natural resources expected to be available for future generations.

Sustainable growth

A third major view of sustainability focuses on the need for continued growth in agricultural productivity while maintaining the quality and quantity of the resources devoted to agriculture. It implies using renewable resources at rates lower than that at which they can be generated, emitting wastes at rates lower than those at which they can be absorbed by the environment, and optimizing the efficiency with which renewable resources are used (Barbier and McCracken 1988).

This view of sustainability takes into account predicted increases in the demand for food arising from continuing population and income growth. It is this view that has inspired the definition of sustainable agriculture proposed by the Technical Advisory Committee of the Consultative Group on International Agricultural Research (CGIAR), according to whom sustainable agriculture 'should involve the successful management of resources for agriculture to satisfy changing human needs while maintaining or enhancing the quality of the environment and conserving natural resources' (CIMMYT 1989).

Sustainable growth can be realized (and measured) at several different levels. Among them are the regional level, at which the sources of growth in agricultural productivity are compared with expected growth in the demand for agricultural products (Byerlee and Siddiq 1989; Rosegrant and Pingali 1991), and the plot level, at which changes in yields and total factor productivity are explained in terms of changes in the levels of inputs, technical change, and changes in resource quality (Lynam and Herdt 1988). Clearly, the two levels are related: the ability of food supply to keep up with growth in demand increasingly depends on solving plot-level constraints to increased yields. Here again, not all system components need be used sustainably, for one resource may be substituted for another over time. Plot-level issues can be further subdivided according to the importance of externalities or common property resources as causal factors.

Categories of Sustainability Issues

A plethora of issues are raised regularly in relation to the sustainability of agriculture. An incomplete listing of these issues might include soil erosion, global warming, salinization of irrigated areas, deforestation, deterioration of soil structure, reduction in biodiversity, exhaustion of soil nutrients, desertification, pest and disease build-up, pollution from agricultural chemicals, and reduced future availability of agricultural inputs (including fossil fuels). Many of these issues, especially those having to do with land degradation or the maintenance of soil quality, have been studied in some depth by disciplinary and subject matter specialists. Other issues, such as global warming, are relatively new fields of enquiry.

To facilitate analysis, sustainability issues can be grouped into categories. Different ways of assessing sustainability may be needed for each category.

External versus internal

External issues of sustainability are those associated with changes in farmers' external circumstances. Global warming and climate change, the availability and prices of fertilizers and other purchased inputs, and changes in global biodiversity are examples. These issues are beyond the individual farmer's control. In contrast, internal issues of sustainability are those associated directly with the farming system and the farmer's capacity to change matters.

Not all issues can be classified as either internal or external. Farm operations undoubtedly contribute (although in a relatively subordinate way) to global warming (Pretty and Conway 1989). Moreover, most internal issues are conditioned to some extent by external circumstances. Nonetheless, the distinction helps by highlighting the relative importance of farm-level decision making in addressing sustainability problems.

Reversible versus irreversible

Sustainability problems may be distinguished as reversible and irreversible. The per–manent effects of irreversible problems cause special concern. When future demand for a resource is uncertain and the effects of irreversible change are not well known, the present generation may perceive a value ('option demand') in maintaining the option to use that resource in the future (Johnston 1988). Some of the problems commonly associated with the sustainability of agriculture are not wholly irreversible. For example, soil nutrient depletion, loss of soil structure, or build-up of pests and diseases. In contrast, severe soil erosion or massive deforestation can be considered reversible only under the most optimistic—and unlikely—assumptions about future land use over very long periods.

Public health versus agricultural productivity

Some of the issues often included under the rubric of sustainable agriculture have less to do with the long-term productivity of agriculture than with the effects of agricultural practices (such as pesticide application) on public health. There is no doubt that these questions are important and that agricultural technology can or should be adjusted to address them. However, they are different from other sustainability problems in that they do not deal with threats to future food security.

Implications for Measuring Sustainability

Measuring an abstract property such as sustainability is, to say the least, challenging. It is unlikely that a single approach—equally useful regardless of the concept of sustainability or the category of problem under consideration—will ever be found. To this extent, the idea of 'measuring sustainability' has little meaning.

Measurements of the sustainability of agricultural productivity when this is threatened by external problems are likely to depend greatly on the work of disciplinary specialists outside agriculture. Within resource economics, for example, there are those who specialize in assessing the future availability and prices of natural resources (such as Chapman 1983, US Department of the Interior 1989). Agricultural field scientists would do well to monitor (without feeling compelled to duplicate) the work of these specialists. Probable farmer adaptations to increases in the prices of external inputs (adjustments in input use, shifts in enterprise mix, adoption of low-input technologies) can then be assessed. The work of specialists on global climate change and its implications for agriculture will take on a similar importance. Some studies of this issue have already been conducted (Arthur 1988; Jodha 1989), but much remains to be done.

According to the agro-ecological concept of system resilience, the measurement of sustainability depends on the development of reliable indicators of resilience and diversity that can be easily quantified. To date there has been little progress in formulating such indicators (Tisdell 1988). In contrast, following the 'sustainable growth' concept, there has been considerable work on approaches to measuring the sustainability of agricultural productivity when this is threatened by internal problems. Several approaches have been proposed, typically relying in one way or another on trends in yields or total factor productivity (state variables), with or without complementary evidence on resource degradation. Discussion of some of these approaches constitutes the rest of this paper.

Methods for Measuring Sustainable Growth

Non-quantitative approaches
Rejecting quantification. Some scientists reject the very notion that sustainability can or should be measured. For example, MacRae et al. (1989) argue that quantification tends to distort the research process, inducing researchers to choose quantifiable (but less relevant) variables at the expense of other non-quantifiable (but conceptually more important) ones. They are especially sceptical of numerical modeling of biological systems, arguing that the internal consistency of these models does not compensate for their lack of realism.

This rejection of quantification is linked to a similar rejection of 'reductionism.' It is not usually possible, MacRae et al. (1988) maintain, to analyse complex systems by examining a few variables and then applying the results over a broad area. Nor is it realistic to assume direct, single cause-and-effect relationships between factors. Given that sustainable processes are location-specific, they are difficult or impossible to quantify.

There is undoubtedly some truth in these arguments. Yet it is never possible to deal with any problem (not just sustainability problems) in all its real-world complexity. Scientists 'have to simplify to survive' (McCall and Kaplan 1985). In addition, the experience of farming systems research suggests that it is often possible to quantify and model complex biological systems without unacceptable loss of realism.

In contrast, analyses conducted without attempting quantification can lead to circular reasoning, with the relative sustainability of systems being assessed in terms of the degree to which they use practices that have been defined *a priori* as 'sustainable'. This increases the probability of self-deception and virtually eliminates the ability to compare different systems rigorously, examine sustainability-productivity trade-offs, or gauge the progress made towards specific goals.

Directional measurements. Most proponents of sustainable agriculture would probably not agree that measuring sustainability is utterly impossible, and that trying to measure it is a bad idea. Many, however, would be content with 'directional' measurements. A directional measurement is one that measures only the direction of change in the sustainability of a system, not the magnitude of that change.

Directional measurements are most attractive when it is felt that a proportional relationship exists between control and state variables. The assumption is that the sustainability of an agro-ecosystem is changed in rough proportion to changes in those practices felt to most strongly influence the system's future productivity (and/or its ability to deal with stresses and perturbations). For example, an agro-ecosystem suffering from gradually declining levels of soil nutrients is thought to become more sustainable in rough proportion to the amount of nutrients that, through appropriate interventions, can be generated or recycled within the system or applied from external sources. Insofar as the levels of these nutrients are increased, the system is assumed to become more sustainable.

Note that, in this approach, current levels of sustainability need not be measured. In fact, cardinal units of measurement are unnecessary. It is assumed that sustainability is a continuous, not a discrete, variable, but that measuring levels of sustainability in cardinal terms is unnecessary. If the assumption of proportionality between control and state variables is incorrect, of course, this approach can be thoroughly misleading.

Quantitative approaches
Purpose. Suitable methods of quantification are necessary in order for researchers to answer questions such as the following:
- Is System A sustainable or not?
- Is System A becoming more or less sustainable over time?

- Is System A more or less sustainable than System B?
- By what percent is System A more sustainable than System B?
- Is the relative sustainability of System A with respect to System B increasing or decreasing over time?
- What are the trade-offs between longer term sustainability and current levels of productivity of System A?
- Is the current productivity of System A more or less sensitive than that of System B to technical changes aimed at enhancing sustainability?

All the quantitative approaches discussed below have trend analysis in common. In trend analysis, time series data from the recent past are used to forecast the near future. The trends for specific state variables, such as output, yields, total factor productivity or per capita production, are assessed. The main aim of the analysis is to measure the extent to which a system has already become less sustainable. The questions are: which variables best capture a change in sustainability? Do some variables confound trends in system sustainability with other factors? Which variables are easy and economical to use?

Aggregate trends in output and yields. There is an understandable temptation to measure system sustainability in terms of trends in production and/or yields. These trends can be assessed through published data at the aggregate level. For example, when maize yields show a decline over time, researchers become apprehensive about the possible degradation of the resources devoted to maize production.

The drawback of this approach is that problems of sustainability can be present—and worsening—even when published data indicate a rising trend in output and yields. Similarly, they may be entirely absent despite data showing declining trends. Changes in aggregate output or yields may be due to other factors, such as changes in the quantity or quality of inputs used, or in the mix of enterprises selected by farmers (Harrington et al. 1990). For example, yields of a crop may appear to be declining over time simply because more attractive crops have replaced it in the more favorable production environments. Researchers must be especially careful of these confounding effects. On the whole it is unwise to assume that the productivity of a particular crop or enterprise over time is an adequate proxy for trends in system productivity or sustainability.

Total factor productivity. Lynam and Herdt (1988) suggest that sustainability be measured in terms of trends in total factor productivity (TFP). Thus:

(1) TFP = O / I

where O is the total value of all outputs and I is the total value of all inputs. A sustainable system would feature a positive trend in TFP.

Monteith (n.d.) notes, however, that the 'total value of all inputs' can be a somewhat arbitrary quantity, having diverse components whose relative value may be hard to assess.

A declining trend in TFP (as defined above) might be due to resource degradation or to declining product prices and higher input prices caused by gradual shifts in government policy. This approach takes no account of changes in the quality of the agricultural resource base and does not separate the technical factors that may be causing an observed decline in TFP. Measuring the total value of the outputs and inputs used in a farming system is likely to be expensive, since measurement is needed several times during the year (to minimize recall error), for a reasonably large number of farmers (to minimize sampling error), over an indefinite number of years.

Finally, Monteith notes that this approach focuses on sustainability at the plot level, avoiding assessment at the regional level. Rising TFP may mean little if population is increasing faster. Similarly, past gains in TFP may be misleading if made at the expense of system resilience or in ways that ultimately degrade farmers' resources. 'Turning points' in trends have always been the bane of those who would predict the future on the basis of the past.

Trends in per capita production. Monteith (n.d.) argues that, to be sustainable, a system should maintain per capita benefit levels from year to year (and in principle from generation to generation) and should not itself deteriorate as a consequence of being used. He summarizes this in the following rule: A system is sustainable over a defined period if outputs do not decrease when inputs are not increased.'

This rule has much to recommend it. However, it can be tested only in systems in which farmers use the same cropping patterns and associated livestock enterprises year after year on the same fields without increasing input levels. These conditions are sometimes found in subsistence systems with few opportunities for enterprise diversification or the use of external inputs, to which the rule seems best to apply.

With input levels held constant, per capita production is a function of yields, harvested area, and population density, where yield changes are driven by 'sustainability' factors (resource quality), not by varying input levels or land use shifts. Thus:

$$(2)\ C = Y\ (A/P)$$

where C = per capita production, Y = yield per unit area, A = harvested area, and P = population density. By differentiating with respect to time, percentage changes become additive in the following manner:

$$(3)\ (dC/dt)/C = (dY/dt)/Y + (dA/dt)/A - (dP/dt)/P$$

where $(dC/dt)/C$ is the percentage change in per capita production with a small increment in time. In other words, the percentage increase in per capita production is the sum of the percentage increase in harvested area and the percentage increase in yields, less the percentage increase in population density.

For example, if yields are growing at 3.1% per year, with harvested area declining at 0.2% per year, and population increasing at 2% per year, then per capita production is increasing by 3.1 + (– 0.2) – 2.0 = 0.9% per year. Note that this approach assumes that parameter values do not vary over time.

Because this approach defines sustainability as the maintenance of per capita net benefits from year to year (net benefits vary in direct proportion to gross benefits because inputs are held constant), declining trends in per capita production are used to identify sustainability issues. However, this approach, like the previous two approaches, provides little information on the technical dimensions of any decline in the quality of the agricultural resource base—the root causes of unsustainability.

This approach could be applied to whole systems. However, given the need to measure harvested area and yield, its use in enterprise-specific analyses seems virtually inevitable. Indeed, Monteith himself uses enterprise-specific examples in his paper. This increases the danger of confounding yield declines caused by resource degradation with those caused by other factors, such as movement of a commodity from one land type to another.

Finally, the feasiblity of this approach hinges on whether input levels are held constant. In controlled trials, they can be, but on the farm they are usually found to vary. An approach that cannot assess the sustainability of systems in which both outputs and inputs are increasing does not seem terribly helpful.

TFP revisited. An acceptable method of quantifying sustainability should be capable of distinguishing between: (1) yield changes due to changes in levels of purchased inputs (movements along a production function), (2) increases in total factor productivity due to technological change (for example, upward shifts in the production function due to the adoption of an improved variety, or to earlier planting), and (3) reductions in total factor productivity due to resource degradation (for example, downward shifts in the production function due to nutrient depletion). Case (3) might be reflected in stagnant yields despite continuously increasing input levels, or yield reductions given constant input levels.

The TFP approach, which has been widely used for measuring the effects of techno-logical change, can be be made more useful by linking it to a production function. TFP has been defined in many different ways. Samuelson and Nordhaus (1985), for example, use the following:

(4) $TFP = Q - S_L(L) - S_K(K)$

where TFP = total factor productivity (percentage change per year), Q = output growth rate (percentage per year), L = labour input growth rate (percentage per year), K = capital input growth rate (percentage per year), S_L = (constant) labour factor share, and S_K = (constant) capital factor share.

As defined here, TFP is a residual after accounting for the effects of increased input levels on output. As noted above, it confounds the positive effects of technological change and the negative effects of resource degradation. If it were possible to identify shifts in the production function attributable to technological change, the new residual after subtracting these would reflect the effect of resource degradation on productivity.

A farmer monitoring program recently begun in Nepal by the National Agricultural Research Center, the International Maize and Wheat Improvement Center, and the International Rice Research Institute takes this approach to measuring sustainability. A farmer panel is monitored by local research and extension workers twice per year. Input and output data are obtained, along with information on field-level productivity problems and assessments of resource quality. Yields and TFP are then explained (through a set of recursive regressions) in terms of changes in input levels, technological change, and changes in resource quality (with weather information included to reduce unexplained variability). This project is still at an early stage of development. However, like the 'trends in per capita production' approach, this approach focuses on the plot level, not the regional level. It says nothing about the race between rising demand on the one hand and productivity growth on the other.

Yield trends in relation to inputs applied. Not everyone likes the idea of estimating TFP. Direct estimation of the contribution of different factors to yield increase might be a less complex approach.

Cardwell (1982), for example, estimated the relative contributions of a number of factors, both positive and negative, affecting Minnesota maize yields from the 1930s to the present. Each factor was assessed separately. First, the contribution of a particular factor in kg/ha or kg/ha/year was estimated synthetically. The area and numbers of years over which the factor had been effective were used to estimate its current year contribution to yield change, which was then expressed as a percentage of the current yield.

Cardwell found that the switch from open-pollinated varieties to hybrids, improved weed control through herbicide use, increased plant densities and earlier planting accounted for most of the increase in yields. An increase in nitrogen fertilizer use also accounted for part of the yield increase, but much of this was merely a substitute for lower levels of manure and reduced levels of N from mineralized organic matter. Soil erosion was found to have reduced yield potential by 8% over the 50-year time horizon studied.

Byerlee and Siddiq (1989) used a more elaborate variation on this approach in their assessment of sources of growth in wheat production and yields in the Pakistan Punjab. They identified three major sources of growth: increased irrigated area relative to rainfed area, adoption of high-yielding varieties (HYVs) in both irrigated and rainfed areas, and increased HYV yields in irrigated areas. They also identified factors tending to depress yields: earlier planting, declining groundwater quality and increased field salinization, an increase in problem weeds, and lower fertilizer efficiency. Secondary factors were also included and measured. For example, the increase in irrigated wheat area was found to be partly due to a shift in cropping patterns, with farmers moving the crop from rainfed to irrigated areas.

This approach is powerful. It measures trends in both state and control variables, takes into account both land type changes and cropping pattern changes, assesses changes in input use levels, and identifies both positive and negative factors affecting yields. The approach enables researchers to predict future events more confidently.

At this level of disaggregation, for example, it becomes clear that some of the past sources of yield increase (notably, the adoption of HYVs) have been fully used and can no longer support further growth. It may also be found that some of the negative factors (such as salinity) are increasing in importance, threatening future productive capacity. By integrating all these factors into a single model, a powerful tool is forged for assessing yield and production growth over the near future. The figures can then be compared with expected changes in demand, to develop regional-level assessments of sustainability.

A disadvantage of this approach is that it is extremely data-intensive. It requires a combination of time series data from secondary sources and micro-level data from farm surveys and from on-farm and on-station experiments. In many cases these data will not be available and the approach will be unusable without a substantial investment in data generation. Moreover, the approach is even more difficult to apply to complex farming systems, at the level of the system rather than the commodity. The example given, focusing on wheat in the context of a relatively simple system, is already somewhat elaborate.

Finally, this approach, like all the others, interprets sustainability in terms of efficiency, not resilience, and shows little sensitivity to the virtues of diversity as a solution to sustainability problems. That is, the principles of agro-ecology seem to have little place, either in the analysis or in the conclusions.

Linear programming. When trend analysis is used to forecast the near future on the basis of information about the recent past, linear programming can be used to simulate possible future events given parametric changes in farmers' access to land and other assets. If farmers can choose between several activities that have different effects on sustainability, the conditions determining their choice become interesting.

One recent study examined this very question (Hildebrand and Ashraf 1989). Several alternative cropping activities were assessed, with some of them assumed to have more beneficial carry-over effects than others. Farm size was parametrically reduced to reflect likely changes arising from population pressure. An estimate was made of the minimum farm size needed to meet family food requirements, while maintaining soil fertility through fallow, alley cropping or fertilizer application strategies. Not surprisingly, it was found that minimum allowable farm sizes were larger when soil fertility maintenance depended on traditional fallowing and alley cropping activities. Activities featuring the use of chemical fertilizer allowed farm sizes to decline much further without reducing soil fertility below critical levels. The results highlighted a trade-off between fertilizer application and bush fallow area. However, it was not possible to compare the sustainability of different strategies, due to a lack of time series data.

References

Altieri, M. 1987. *Agroecology: The scientific basis of alternative agriculture.* Boulder, Colorado: Westview Press.

Arthur, L. 1988. The greenhouse effect and the Canadian prairies: Simulation of future economic impacts. In: *Natural resource and environmental policy analysis: Cases in applied economics.* Boulder, Colorado: Westview Press.

Barbier, E. and J. McCracken. 1988. *Glossary of selected terms in sustainable economic development.* IIED Gatekeeper Series SA7. IIED, London.

Barker, R. and D. Chapman. 1988. The economics of sustainable agricultural systems in developing countries. Agricultural Economics Working Paper 88-13. Cornell University, Ithaca, New York.

Batie, S.S. 1989. Sustainable development: Challenges to the profession of agricultural economics. Presidential Address, AAEA Summer Meeting, Baton Rouge, La., July 3-August 2.

Byerlee, D. and A. Siddiq. 1989. Sources of increased wheat production and yields in Pakistan's irrigated Punjab, 1965-2000. CIMMYT Economics Working Paper 90/04. International Maize and Wheat Improvement Center, Mexico City.

Cardwell, V. B. 1982. Fifty years of Minnesota corn production: Sources of yield increase. *Agronomy Journal* 74 (November-December).

Chapman, D. 1983. Energy resources and energy corporations. Ithaca, New York: Cornell University Press.

CIMMYT. 1989. Toward the 21st century: Strategic issues and the operational strategies of CIMMYT. Mexico City.

Clark, C. 1976. *Mathematical bioeconomics.* New York: John Wiley.

Conway, G. 1986. Agroecosystem analysis for research and development. Bangkok, Thailand: Winrock International.

Durning, A. 1990. How much is enough? *World Watch* 3 (6). Washington D.C.

Francis, C. 1986. Resource-efficient systems for Third World farmers. Seminar presentation, Kansas State University, Manhattan, April.

Graham-Tomasi, T. 1991. Sustainability: Concepts and implications for agricultural research policy. In: Pardey, Roseboom and Anderson (eds), *Agricultural resource policy: International quantitative perspectives.* New York: Cambridge University Press.

Harrington, L., P. Hobbs, T. Pokhrel, B. Sharma, S. Fujisaka and C. Lightfoot. 1990. The rice-wheat pattern in the Nepal Terai: Issues in the identification and definition of sustainability problems. *Journal of Farming Systems Research-Extension* 1(2):1-27.

Heilbroner, R. 1980. *An inquiry into the human prospect.* New York: Norton.

Hildebrand, P. and M. Ashraf. 1989. Agricultural sustainability as an operational criterion. Paper presented at the Ninth Annual Farming Systems Research-Extension Symposium, Fayetteville, Arkansas, October 9-12.

IFPRI. 1989. Environmental policy for agricultural sustainability: An IFPRI research thrust for the 1990s. Unpublished draft. Washington, D.C.

Ingram, J. and M. Swift. 1989. Sustainability of cereal-legume intercrops in relation to management of soil organic matter and nutrient cycling. Paper presented at the Intercropping Conference, Lilongwe, Malawi, January.

Jodha, N. 1989. Potential strategies for adapting to greenhouse warming: Perspectives from the developing world. In: N. Rosenberg et al. (eds), *Greenhouse warming: Abatement and adaptation.* Washington, D.C.: Resources for the Future.

Johnston, G. 1988. The role of economics in natural resource and environmental policy analysis. In: *Natural resource and environmental policy analysis: Cases in applied economics.* Boulder, Colorado: Westview Press.

Lynam, J. and R. Herdt. 1988. Sense and sensibility: Sustainability as an objective in international agricultural research. Paper presented at the CIP-Rockefeller Conference on Farmers and Food Systems, Lima, Peru.

MacCrae, R., S. Hill, J. Henning and G. Mehuys. 1989. Agricultural science and sustainable agriculture: A review of the existing scientific barriers to sustainable food production and potential solutions. *Biological Agriculture and Horticulture* 6:173-219.

McCall, M., and R. Kaplan. 1985. *Whatever it takes: Decision-makers at work.* Englewood Cliffs, New Jersey: Prentice-Hall.

Monteith, J. (ed.). n.d. Can sustainability be quantified? Conference Paper No. 538. International Crop Research Institute for the Semi-Arid Tropics. Submitted.

Pretty, J. and G. Conway. 1989. *Agriculture as a global polluter.* IIED Gatekeeper Series No. SA11. International Institute for Environment and Development, London.

Rosegrant, M. and P. Pingali. 1991. Sustaining rice productivity growth in Asia: A policy perspective. Social Science Division Paper No. 91-01. International Rice Research Institute, Los Banos, the Philippines.

Samuelson, P. and W. Nordhaus. 1985. *Economics.* New York: McGraw Hill.

Schmid, A. 1989. *Benefit-cost analysis: A political economy approach.* Boulder, Colorado: Westview Press.

Tisdell, C. 1988. Sustainable development: Differing perspectives of ecologists and economists, and relevance to LDCs. *World Development* 16 (3):373-384.

US Department of the Interior. 1989. Estimates of undiscovered conventional oil and gas resources in the United States. U.S. Government Printing Office, Washington, D.C.

Source

First published in the *Journal of Farming Systems Reserch-Extension* 3 (1), 1992. Reprinted by kind permission of the author and the publisher.

Address

Larry Harrington, CIMMYT Economics Programmme Asia, P.O. Box 9-188 Bangkhen, Bangkok 10900, Thailand.

PART TWO:

What Criteria to Use?

Farmers transplanting rice on the ecological farm of Mr Tangaswamy, in Sendangudi, Pudukkottai, Tamil Nadu, South India. In a study of the transition experiences of twelve ecological farmers in this area, environmental and sustainability considerations, alongside those of health and food quality, were most frequently mentioned as reasons for making the change. *Photo: Erik van der Werf*

The Costs of Change in Plant Protection

J.C. Zadoks

Introduction

The topic of this paper is plant protection in the worlds of today and tomorrow.

On a global scale there need be no shortage of food (Buringh et al. 1975; Mellor and Paulino 1986; Parikh and Rabár 1981). On a regional scale, hunger is a reality. Usually, hunger is the sequel to factors such as human strife, civil war, poor pricing policies, lack of purchasing power, or lack of equity (FAO 1981; Sen 1981). Rarely, nowadays, is hunger due to the failure of plant protection. Plant protection has, then, been rather successful. Its very success has led to severe criticism.

Leaders in the field used to defend plant protection by quoting statistics—preferably a single, global figure—on the world's losses of food, feed, fibre and fuel due to pests, diseases and weeds. I consider a global figure to be meaningless for two reasons. The first reason is political. Despite serious crop losses there is no global food shortage today, nor will there be in the near future. The problem is access to food, which is a problem of equity. The second reason is technical. We have no yardstick by which to measure crop losses adequately, because we have no criteria for determining optimum, as opposed to maximum, potential yield. For similar reasons I also doubt the meaning of relative figures breaking down global losses. Loosely quoted figures usually go back to the pioneer work of Cramer (1967), depicted in Figure 1. My view is that we should not quote losses, real or imaginary, but instead focus on the advantages of changing our whole approach to plant protection (Schulten 1988; Zadoks 1981 and 1991).

In this paper I will discuss the mission of plant protection as I see it. I will indicate the changes needed and the price to be paid for those changes. The flow of my argument will be punctuated by two digressions, one on production situations and their relevance for pesticide use, and one on pesticides themselves.

Digression 1: Production Situations

Agricultural production is governed by three types of production factors—yield-determining factors, yield-limiting factors and yield-reducing factors (Rabbinge and De Wit 1989). Yield-determining factors such as soil and sunshine govern the level of potential production. Often, this potential can not be realized because of yield- limiting factors such as the lack of water, nitrogen or phosphorus. Again, the attainable yield

Figure 1 Value (%) of world crop production and losses caused by insects, diseases and weeds

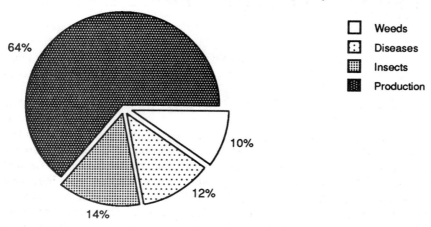

Source: Cramer (1967)

(Zadoks and Schein 1979) may not be harvested because of yield-reducing factors, such as floods, pests, diseases or weeds. Crop protection deals with the yield-reducing factors, with due consideration of yield-limiting factors.

Further consideration of yield-limiting factors leads to the recognition of four different production situations (Figure 2]. The first situation is exemplified by wheat yields of 10 t/ha or more, occurring where there are no constraints. This is found occasionally in northwest Europe. The fourth situation is typified by the Sahelian zone in Africa or by northeastern Brazil where, at times, the farmer hardly produces enough seed for next year's crop.

These production situations are relevant to crop protection. In situation 1, it pays to eliminate yield reducing factors by applying a high level of external inputs. This has been

Figure 2 Four crop production situations

Situation			Growth rate (kg/ha/day)
HEIA:	1	No limitations	250 ▲
	2	Water limited	|
	3	Water + N limited	|
LEIA:	4	Water + N + P limited	10

Source: De Wit (1982)

one of the principles of the Green Revolution. Discussing plant protection at international congresses, we talk mostly about production situation 1, indicated in the figure as HEIA, high-external-input agriculture, with petrol, mechanization, resistance breeding, seed treatment, fertilizers, pesticides and knowledge as the inputs. We choose to ignore the other half of the agricultural world, characterized by low-external-input agriculture (LEIA), low either by choice, as in organic farming, or because of poverty, as in production situation 4.

For many years the economics of crop protection have been seen in a rosy light. They dealt with the gross margin of the crop and the increase in farm income, but not with the environment of the farm and its surroundings. Unfortunately, what is profitable to one may be damaging to others. Such is the case with many pesticides in HEIA, where it is estimated that only 1% of the active ingredient applied to the crop reaches the site of action (Pimentel et al. 1991). The remaining 99% pollute the soil, water and air. They have effects beyond the farm gate—the so-called external effects or externalities of agriculture. These externalities can be demonstrated and, sometimes, measured (Loevinsohn 1987; Pimentel et al. 1980). Here we come face to face with the Green Revolution's 'second generation' of problems.

Obviously, the externalities have a value, since people who can afford to do so tend to pay for health and happiness, for clean water, fresh air and healthy food. There is a value, but no price, as there is no market where we can bargain for health and happiness. In the USA, Pimentel et al. (1991) tried to estimate the social and environmental costs of pesticide use (Figure 3). Their figure approaches US$ 1 billion per year. To extrapolate to the world level, I suggest multiplying this figure by 100.

Figure 3 Social and environmental costs of pesticide use in the USA

Damage	Cost (US$ millions)
Human poisoning	250
Reduced natural enemies and pesticide resistance	300
Honey bee poisoning	150
Pollution control	150
Other	105
Total	955

Source: Pimentel et al. (1991)

The Mission of Plant Protection

Definition

I see the mission of crop protection over the next decade as being *to reduce the quantity and to improve the quality of external inputs, and of pesticides specifically, in order to promote sustainability, to safeguard food production, and to improve both food production methods and food quality.*

The political pressure is high. In several countries, a vociferous public refuses to accept the present situation. As an example, take the European Community standard for drinking water and its sources. It is 0.1 µg of any pesticide per litre of water, or 0.1 part per billion (Roberts 1989). The logic behind the European Community Directive is simply this: drinking water should be free of pesticides. Thus, the standard has been set at the technical limits of chemical analysis. Toxicology tells us that the standard is far higher than scientifically warranted. But the logic here is not of a scientific nature; it is political logic. The costs of purifying drinking water, which have now become one of the externalities of agricultural practices, are so enormous that the only reasonable solution is to change those practices. Hence my mission statement says 'to *reduce* the quantity of external inputs ...'.

This new mission of plant protection carries both benefits and costs. These will be illustrated by four examples—two drawn from developed and two from developing countries, all four from HEIA. They mark the transition from HEIA to high-external-input sustainable agriculture (HEISA).

Four examples

The Netherlands. The first example comes from The Netherlands. This country is said to be the world's second largest exporter of agricultural produce. As the country is small, such exports can only be achieved by using at a very high level of external inputs. For pesticides this is 20 kg of active ingredient per hectare per year, pastures excluded (Anonymus 1990). The Multi-Year Plan for Crop Protection (Anonymus 1990), ratified by Cabinet in June 1991, seeks a radical change according to the following principles:
- Reduced dependence on chemical pesticides
- Reduced emissions of chemical pesticides to the environment.

The target was to reduce the overall volume of active ingredients used by 50% over a period of 10 years (1990-2000). This included a reduction of 80% in the use of soil disinfectants. The costs of change have been estimated at roughly Dfl. 1 billion (US$ 0.5 billion) per year over the 10-year period, or 6% of the added value produced annually by agriculture. The question then arose, who would pay the bill? Growers only, consumers too, or all tax payers together? The Dutch answer is that the growers will have to pay. The government will limit the taxpayer's contribution to 10% at the most. Because of the overriding need of governments within the European Community to curry favour with the consumer, the latter will not have to pay. The happy few, who can afford to demand a more

22

sustainable and ethical production of their food, will accelerate the change at moderate costs to themselves.

United States. The second example comes from the USA. For all the major crops grown in that country, change is being introduced in the form of integrated pest management (IPM).

Early economic analyses of the effect of change are for the most part optimistic. The effect in budgetary terms is said to be neutral. Inputs in the form of pesticides will decrease, inputs in the form of knowledge and management will increase. A recent and thorough analysis by Pimentel et al. (1991) states that total production will not go down, and will become more sustainable. Growers' incomes will be stable or even higher, while social and environmental losses will decrease considerably. As a result, public expenditure may well be reduced. The consumer price of food will rise by no more than 1%.

Brazil. The third example comes from Brazil, a major soybean producer. During the past 20 years the value of soybean production has risen from zero to US$ 52 million. EMBRAPA, the Brazilian agricultural research organization, introduced IPM in the late 1970s (Moscardi and Cerrea Ferreira 1985). Savings by farmers are said to have amounted to some US$ 3 billion by 1990. Cumulative savings on the use of pesticides have exceeded the costs of project implementation, a remarkable success (Figure 4). The project has saved scarce foreign currency, reducing imports by some US$ 2 billion . This reduction does, of course, represent a loss to the pesticides industry. Roughly one half of this loss is incurred within Brazil, the other half in other countries.

South-East Asia. The fourth example comes from the Intercountry Program for the Development and Application of Integrated Pest Control in Rice in South and South-East Asia, organized by the Food and Agriculture Organization (FAO). Integrated pest control (IPC), in FAO parlance, is equivalent to the term integrated pest management (IPM) used elsewhere. Under the programme some 100 million farmers are to be trained in IPM. About 400 000 have already been trained. After training, the number of pesticide applications per crop goes down (Figure 5), while crop yields rise (Figure 6). In the Philippines, the internal rate of return to one project (roughly speaking, the annual profit to farmers on the money invested by donors) was estimated at 40%, a very high value. In Indonesia, there are also benefits at national level because pesticide imports have been cut back. In the long run even the consumer benefits, since the price of rice is kept low.

A Tentative Conclusion

These four examples lead to a tentative conclusion. When the added value produced by agriculture is high, as in the Netherlands, external imputs (among which pesticides) are

Figure 4 Economic impact of IPM in soybean

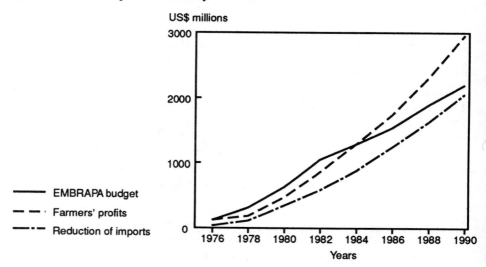

Figure 5 Number of insecticide applications per season for rice grown using different pest control practices in Indonesia

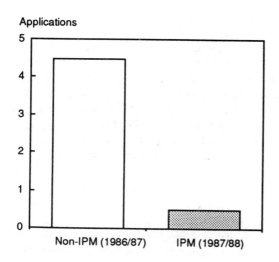

Figure 6 Yields (t/ha) of rice grown using different pest control practices in Indonesia

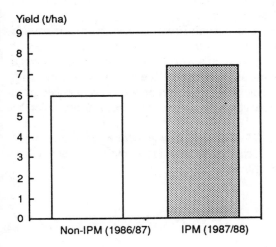

relatively cheap, with the result that dependence on pesticides tends to become excessive. The costs of change towards a more sustainable form of production, involving a drastic reduction of externalities, are then high indeed, such that making the change will be painful. When the added value produced by agriculture is low, as in South-East Asian rice farming, overdependence on pesticides can be averted and externalities reduced more easily, since the change is profitable for rice farmers. In all four examples there will be drastic change, but in none will the consumer pay the price of change.

Digression 2: Pesticides

The examples discussed above come from areas with good production situations (1 or 2), where pesticides are an important input; HEIA areas, in short. My plea is to change HEIA into HEISA. The inputs will remain high but they will change in nature, with more resistance breeding, genetic engineering, seed technology, spray technology, disease and pest forecasting, biological control and, most important, knowledge. The change to HEISA represents a challenge to both scientists and farmers. But I have met many farmers, from the well educated to the illiterate, in both developed and developing countries, who like the idea of that challenge and are willing to respond to it.

But what about LEIA, in which pesticides are little used, or used not at all? What about production situations where the environment is fragile and local food supplies are inadequate? The traditional answer is to expand the area farmed, cultivating increasingly marginal soils. These degrade and erode rapidly, and soon have to be abandoned. This traditional response is not sustainable. To improve matters, more external inputs may well be needed, and among them pesticides (mainly herbicides), used in conjunction with other technologies. This is the pesticides paradox of LEISA.

Pesticides are here to stay. They are needed, not only in emergencies but also in routine applications. Pesticide efficiency, expressed as kg of marketable commodity per kg of active ingredient used, can be much improved on a world-wide scale, but this needs a substantial research effort. As the volume of research conducted grows or shrinks with the number of pesticide producers in business, the steady reduction in that number gives cause for concern. I fear that the search for new active ingredients may slacken under the pressure of today's public opinion.

We will continue to need pesticides. We will need new and better (less poisonous) formulations, targeted for specific circumstances, to be used sparingly and knowledgeably, in accordance with sustainability criteria.

Conclusions

I come to the following conclusions:
• The mission of plant protection must change radically, discarding present practices with their high level of externalities and adopting new ones in accordance with sustainability criteria
• The change may be costly to growers in some instances, but will be profitable in most cases
• The change will be economically neutral for the consumer
• The change will benefit the tax payer of the future
• The change will demand great efforts from the pesticides industry, in terms of research, and the adoption of new codes of practice.

Finally, I suspect we may need *more* pesticides for sustainable agriculture at low external input levels.

My hope is that a more innovative approach to plant protection will soon develop. This may well lead to somewhat lower crop yields, but it will also lead to much lower levels of pesticide use than today (Figure 7), 'making the Green Revolution greener' (Swaminathan 1990).

References
Anonymous. 1990. Meerjarenplan Gewasbescherming. Beleidsvoornemen. The Hague, Ministry of Agriculture, Nature Conservation and Fisheries.
Buringh, P., H.D.J. Van Heemst and G.J. Staring. 1975. Computation of the absolute maximum food production of the world. Department of Tropical Soil Science, Wageningen Agricultural University.

Figure 7 Plant protection pathways

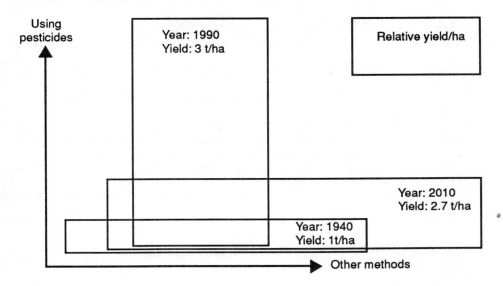

Cramer, H.H. 1967. Plant protection and world crop production. Pflanzenschutz-Nachrichten Bayer 20: 1-524.

De Wit, C.T. 1982. La productivité des pâturages Sahéliens. In: F.T.W. Penning de Vries and M.A. Djiteye (eds), La productivité des pâturages Sahéliens: Une étude des sols, des végétations et de l'exploitation de cette ressource naturelle. Wageningen, PUDOC Agricultural Research Report No. 918.

FAO. 1981. *Agriculture: Toward 2000*. Rome.

Loevinsohn, M.F. 1987. Insecticide use and increased mortality in rural central Luzon, Philippines. *The Lancet*, June 13: 1359-1362.

Mellor, J.W. and L. Paulino. 1986. Food production needs in a consumption perspective. In: M.S. Swaminathan and S.K. Sinha (eds), *Global aspects of food production*. Oxford, Tycooly.

Moscardi, F. and B.S. Cerrea Ferreira. 1985. Biological control of soybean caterpillars. In: R. Shibles (ed.), *World Soybean Research Conference III: Proceedings*. Boulder, Colorado: Westview Press.

Parikh, K.S. and F. Rabár. 1981. Food problems and policies: Present and future, local and global. In: K.S. Parikh and F. Rabár (eds), Food for all in a sustainable world: The IIASA food and agriculture program. Laxenburg (Austria), IIASA.

Pimentel, D. et al. 1980. Environmental and social costs of pesticides: A preliminary assessment. *Oikos* 34: 125-140.

Pimentel, D. et al. 1991. Environmental and economic impacts of reducing U.S. agricultural pesticide use. In: D. Pimentel (ed.), CRC handbook of pesticide management in agriculture, Vol. I. Baton Rouge, CRC.

Rabbinge, R. and C.T. de Wit. 1989. Systems, models and simulation. In: R. Rabbinge, S.A. Ward and H.H. van Laar (eds), Simulation and systems management in crop protection. Wageningen, PUDOC.

Roberts, T. 1989. Pesticides in drinking water. GIFAB Bulletin 15 (3).

Schulten, G.G.M. 1988. FAO's experiences with crop loss assessment. *Insect Science and its Application* 9: 763-767.

Sen, A. 1981. *Poverty and famines: An essay on entitlement and deprivation.* Oxford, Clarendon Press.

Swaminathan, M.S. 1990. The Green Revolution and small-farm agriculture. CIMMYT 1990 Annual Report, Mexico City.

Zadoks, J.C. 1981. Crop losses today, profit tomorrow: An approach to quantifying production constraints and to measuring progress. In: L. Chiarappa (ed), *Crop loss assessment methods,* Supplement 3, Commonwealth Agricultural Bureaux, Farnham Royal (UK).

Zadoks, J.C. 1991. A hundred and more years of plant protection in the Netherlands. *Netherlands Journal of Plant Pathology* 97: 3-24.

Zadoks, J.C. and R.D. Schein. 1979. *Epidemiology and plant disease management.* Oxford University Press, New York.

Source

First published in the *Journal of Crop Protection in the Tropics,* August 1992. Reprinted by kind permission of the publisher and author.

Address

J.C. Zadocks, Department of Plant Pathology, Wageningen Agricultural University, P.O.Box 8025, 6700 EE Wageningen, The Netherlands.

Lessons from the Mantaro Valley Project, Peru

Douglas E. Horton

Introduction: Research Phases

This paper concentrates on the major results of the four research activities listed in the original proposal for the Mantaro Valley Project: literature review; baseline survey of ecology and agriculture; single and multiple-visit producer surveys; and on-farm potato experiments.

Literature review
The Mantaro Valley is one of the most intensively studied regions in the highlands of Peru, and potatoes are its major crop. A great deal of biological research has been conducted on potatoes in the valley over the years, and several classics of Peruvian social science literature are based on fieldwork there. However, the literature provides surprisingly few empirical data on farmers' actual (as opposed to recommended) production and postharvest technologies, or on the performance of new technologies under representative farming conditions (Werge 1977; Mayer 1979). Hence it was found to be of little direct use for identifying farmers' production problems and selecting technologies for on-farm testing. Nevertheless, maps, regional statistics and general studies of the region's geography and agriculture were quite useful for planning surveys.

Baseline survey
Based on 2 months of fieldwork in the valley and a review of topographical maps, aerial photographs, census figures and published reports, Mayer (1979) produced land-use maps and a descriptive analysis of the valley's agriculture. Major agro-ecological zones, subzones and types of producers were defined. The results of this informal survey were later used for planning and executing more formal surveys and on-farm experiments.

Single- and multiple-visit surveys
Based on Mayer's (1979) findings, two formal questionnaire-type surveys were used to generate detailed information on potato production and use. In September 1977, some 260 farmers were interviewed at points randomly selected throughout the valley (Franco et al. 1979). From October of the same year until June 1978, a series of weekly visits were made to a subset of 53 producers (Horton et al. 1980). Information generated from the single-visit survey was used to refine the agro-ecological zonation and quantify important

aspects of potato production and use (for example, average farm size, crop mix, market orientation, and use of traditional and modern inputs). The multiple-visit survey, observations, and direct field measurements provided a check for estimates obtained from the single-visit survey and generated information on production costs, returns, and technical aspects of crop production and postharvest practices.

On-farm experiments
A number of technologies were evaluated in experiments conducted on farm. The production constraints team, which tested a number of inputs and packages under a range of conditions, conducted 30 farm-level experiments in Mantaro Valley during the 1978/79 crop year and 35 in 1979/80. The postharvest team, which experimented with fewer variables and placed strong emphasis on frequent interaction with farmer collaborators, conducted four experiments in 1978/79, six in 1979/80, and six in 1980/81. For the reasons outlined below, the team researching seed systems conducted experiments on the Peruvian coast and in the highlands of Equador and Colombia rather than in Mantaro Valley.

Research Results

The Mantaro Valley Project generated a wealth of empirical information, both technical and socio-economic, on Andean potato agriculture. The research demonstrated how land use and agricultural technology are influenced by two key factors—ecology and farm type—beyond the immediate control of farmers. It also provided new perspectives on four concepts that are central to the philosophy of the research and technology transfer programme of the International Potato Center (CIP) and, in fact, to most agricultural research and development programmes. These are the concepts of the small-scale farmer, the technological package, improved seed, and technology transfer.

Agro-ecological zones
The valley's cropland can be divided into three agro-ecological zones: the relatively flat land of the 'low zone' along the Mantaro River, the sloping land of the 'intermediate zone' and the more steeply sloping fields of the 'high zone'. Of the valley's 150 000 ha of cropland, approximately 50% is in the low zone, 40% in the intermediate zone, and 10% in the high zone.

Cropping is most intensive in the low zone, particularly on irrigated fields. A wide range of food crops is grown, the most important of which is maize. As one climbs into the intermediate and high zones, fewer and fewer crops can be grown and fallow becomes more important in the rotation cycle. In the high zone, a large proportion of the land is permanent natural pasture.

In the high zone, where only the hardiest of plants survive the cold and frost, potatoes are the dominant crop (Figure 1). However, nearly 90% of the valley's potatoes are produced in the low zone and on the eastern slopes of the intermediate zone.

Figure 1 Percentage of cropland in food crops by agro-ecological zone in the Mantaro Valley

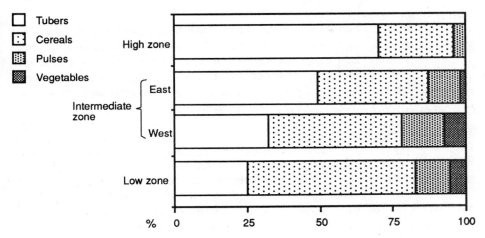

Source: Franco et al. (1979)

Types of farms

Small farms, which are in the majority throughout the valley, occupy every possible ecological environment. In contrast, large farms are found primarily in the low zone, where they occupy the valley's best cropland, and in the grazing lands of the high-altitude tableland (*puna*).

Nearly every farmer in Mantaro Valley produces potatoes, but most produce them on less than 1 ha of land. The bulk of Potato production is concentrated on a few large farms. Ten percent of the valley's farmers produce over half the potatoes and an even higher percentage of the marketed output. Moreover, in recent years the degree of concentration of potato production on large farms has increased. High production costs and risks are forcing small-scale farmers to reduce planting, whereas large-scale growers, with their greater willingness to take risks and their more advantageous financial and marketing arrangements, are expanding the area cultivated to supply the growing coastal markets with seed and consumption potatoes.

The small-scale farmer

Many agricultural research and development programmes assume, explicitly or implicitly, that small-scale farmers are isolated from input and commodity markets and are

31

particularly resistant to change. In the Mantaro Valley Project, it was assumed that small-scale potato producers grew mainly native varieties for home consumption and that they applied little or no fertilizer or pesticides. Surveys indicated that, although such traditional, subsistence-oriented small-scale farmers can be found, they are by no means the norm.

Market integration
Although nearly all farmers in the intermediate and high zones are small scale, the smallest in the valley were found in the low zone. These farmers are subsistence oriented in the sense that they keep a large proportion of their potato harvest for home consumption. They purchase most inputs, however, including labour, and most of them have off-farm jobs. They are, in essence, part-time farmers who are well integrated into the cash economy.

Use of purchased inputs
In the low zone, fertilizer and pesticide application rates were found to be surprisingly high—often exceeding recommended levels. Even small-scale farmers applied, on average, over 100 kg N/ha (Table 1). In the intermediate and high zones, many small-scale farmers applied less of both inputs, for two reasons. First, because the probability of crop loss from hail or frost is extremely high, farmers minimize financial risks by keeping their use of purchased inputs to a minimum. The second reason is that, because two-thirds of the zone's potatoes are planted after fallow, they require little fertilizer application and pest control. It is clear that the use of purchased inputs is not determined by culture, lack of knowledge or lack of input supplies, because the same farmers who used less fertilizer and pesticide in the high zone applied more on their fields at lower elevations.

Table 1 Use of chemical fertilizers, pesticides and fallow

	Low zone			Intermediate zone	High zone
	Large farms	Medium farms	Small farms		
Percentage of potato fields with:					
Chemical N fertilizer	100	95	83	74	28
Pesticide	89	63	80	90	54
N application rate (kg/ha)	212	124	108	85	148
Fields planted after fallow (%)	0	8	6	52	67

Sources: Franco et al. (1979); Horton et al. (1980)

Use of hybrid and native varieties by small-scale farmers

Nearly all farmers, both large- and small-scale, grow hybrid varieties in the low zone, whereas most farmers in the high zone grow native varieties (Figure 2). Native (bitter and non-bitter) potatoes are grown at high altitudes because traditional producers prefer their culinary qualities (Carney 1980). These potatoes are extremely well adapted to the production conditions of the high Andes.

Figure 2 Cultivation of modern and native potato varieties by agro-ecological zone in Mantaro Valley

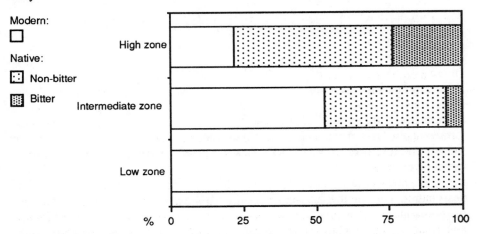

Note: bitter native potatoes are not consumed directly but are processed into *chuño*
Source: Franco et al. (1979)

With present technology, hybrid varieties have a considerable yield advantage over native varieties in the low zone. This is not always the case, however, in higher zones (Table 2). Traditional varieties are highly resistant to frost and hail and produce reasonably well with low applications of chemical fertilizer and pesticides (Brush et al. 1981). Their use allows farmers to minimize losses in an environment characterized by frequent crop failure. In addition, native varieties are now considered a luxury item in urban areas and fetch a higher market price than hybrid varieties. Thus, in areas where native varieties yield the same or more than hybrid varieties—as they do in the intermediate zone—many farmers derive a substantial cash income from marketing native potatoes.

Potatoes play an important role in the diet of rural households in the high zone due to limited cropping alternatives and the absence of retail food markets in these thinly populated areas. Because native varieties store well, farmers can keep them for home

Table 2 Average yields and producer scores[1] for modern and native potato varieties

	Low zone		Intermediate and high zones		
	Hybrid varieties	Native varieties	Hybrid varieties	Native varieties	
				Non-bitter	Bitter
Average yield (t/ha)	5.7	3.7	4.8	4.7	4.9
Producer scores:					
Cooking quality	87	96	76	95	67
Market price	76	84	82	87	58
Yield	80	68	82	73	85
Pest resistance	59	46	66	46	85
Frost resistance	49	35	49	43	91
Storability	65	72	69	85	84

1. Scores ranged from 0-100. A score of zero would indicate that all producers considered the variety 'bad'. A score of 100 would indicate that all producers considered the variety 'good'
Source: Franco et al. (1979)

consumption practically year round, from one harvest to the next. Night frost and sunny days after harvest provide excellent natural conditions for transforming inedible bitter potatoes into *chuño* (Werge 1979; Christiansen 1977). This dehydrated potato product plays a special role in the diet of this zone. Light in weight, it can easily be carried by herders during their seasonal migration to the high-altitude pastures. Also, because it can be stored for years, it provides them with a degree of food security in this uncertain environment.

Economics of small farm production systems
Table 3 illustrates how a 'traditional' low-input system can offer producers economic advantages over a 'modern' higher input system. In the intermediate and high zones, the *ticpa* system, employing native varieties, no tillage prior to planting, hand power (using the *chaquitaclla* or Andean plough) for all cultivation and harvest operations, and very little chemical fertilizer and pesticides, was found to produce a higher net return than the *barbecho* system, which employed hybrid varieties, tractor power, and high levels of inputs. The yields associated with the *ticpa* system were about 20% less than those associated with the *barbecho* system, but the net return over direct input costs was higher in the *ticpa* system. Not only did the native varieties produced have a higher cash value at market, but also—equally, or perhaps even more, important—only about one-third of

Table 3 Yields, costs and returns in two potato production systems in the intermediate and high zones

	Barbecho system[1] (N = 8)	Ticpa system[2] (N = 9)
Yield (t/ha)	9.4	7.3
Total returns (US$/ha)	1102	1030
Direct input costs (US$/ha)		
Seed	278	235
Labour	186	218
Pesticides	67	14
Tractor/oxen	64	0
Chemical fertilizer	62	18
Manure	15	59
Total	672	544
Purchased	316	114
Gross margin (US$/ha)		
Return to direct inputs	430	486
Return to purchased inputs	786	916

1. Hybrid varieties grown; tractor used for plowing
2. Native varieties grown with no tillage before planting; all cultivation done by hand
Source: Horton et al. (1980)

the value of purchased inputs was used compared with the *barbecho* system. Hence, the *ticpa* system exposed farmers to relatively little financial risk.

These empirical findings stood in sharp contradiction to the assumptions of many CIP scientists and development experts working in the Andes. They helped destroy the myth that traditionalism among farmers is a major barrier to the transfer of technology.

The technological package approach to agricultural extension
Belief in technological packages is widespread in the development community. Based on the principle of the synergetic interaction of inputs and on a superficial analysis of the 'seed-fertilizer revolution' of the 1960s and 70s, many development experts and policymakers have concluded that agricultural improvement requires that farmers adopt what may sometimes be quite complex technological packages.

When CIP's work on agronomic constraints began in 1978, it was thought that many small-scale farming practices were so rudimentary that a complete package of improvements would be needed to substantially increase yields and economic returns. Hence, a package approach was used for evaluating recommended technologies under farmers' conditions. In consultation with local production specialists, three packages were designed. A 'low-cost' package was designed to increase yields and net returns without increasing costs and financial risks, while 'medium-' and 'high-cost' packages were designed to increase yields and net returns more significantly, but at higher costs—and risks—to the farmer. Each package included three recommended components, the effects of which were believed to be complementary: improved seed, fertilizer application and pest control. The levels and cost of these components varied between the three packages.

The on-farm trials and subsequent evaluation of farmer adoption revealed four problems with the technological package approach: results were poorer than expected; an optimal package could not be identified; one key element of the packages performed poorly; and farmers did not adopt the packages.

On average, the high-cost package increased yields by 50-60% over the farmers' current level, the medium-cost package increased yields by 20-30%, and the low-cost package yielded about the same as the farmers' established technology (Table 4). These results were disappointing to production specialists, who had expected a doubling or tripling of yields.

Experimental results varied widely across farms. In the intermediate zone, farmers' yields ranged from less than 5 t/ha to nearly 30 t/ha, while the packages yielded from about 5 t/ha to more than 40 t/ha. These diverse yield levels reflected variations in soil fertility and weather conditions within the zone, coupled with differences in farmers' management practices (for example, variety used; tillage and rotation). Clearly, no single package represented an economic optimum under the diverse farming conditions found even within this single agro-ecological zone.

This illustrates the risk of determining farmer recommendations on the basis of average results of on-farm trials. Such averages may mask an extremely high degree of variability. In this context, it is interesting to note that in conventional statistical terms the average yields of the medium- and high-cost packages were significantly higher than the average farmers' yield (at the 5% level of significance).

As noted earlier, one of the justifications for the package approach is the generally accepted agronomic principle that the combined effect on yield of several improved practices applied together is greater than the sum of the effects of each applied alone. The results of the on-farm trials in Mantaro Valley illustrate how misleading this principle can be. In the experiments, the combined effect on yield of recommended seed, fertilizer application and insect control was slightly greater than the sum of the effects of each individual practice. However, economic analysis showed that the adoption of either insect control or fertilizer application alone offered farmers considerably higher rates of return than adoption of the complete package (Table 4).

Table 4 Average increase in yield and cost and net benefit/cost ratio of technological packages and single factors[1]

	Increase in yield (%)	Increase in cost (US$/ha)	Benefit/cost ratio
Technological packages:			
1978/79 (N = 11):			
Low cost	1	48	−0.9[2]
Medium cost	17	165	0.7
High cost	53	252	3.1
1979/80 (N = 20):			
Low cost	8	10	20.2
Medium cost	32	306	2.2
High cost	59	457	2.8
Single factors:			
Insect control (N = 5)	16	48	7.1
Fertilizer (N = 4)	17	70	4.0
Improved seed (N = 5)	17	223	−0.2[2]

1. Average increases in yield and cost are expressed in relation to the farmer's technology (control treatment) for each experiment. Cost-benefit ratio is defined as (change in net returns–change in cost)/change in cost
2. Cost-benefit ratio is negative because cost increased but net returns decreased
Source: Franco et al. (1980, 1981)

The packages had one very weak component—the so-called improved seed—the use of which actually reduced net farm earnings. Interestingly, most production specialists considered this component to be the most important one of the packages. Assumptions about the relative importance of production constraints and the economic viability of alternative technologies thus proved to be incorrect. Surveys conducted after the experiments indicate that, although farmers are now using certain recommended practices, they have not adopted the complete technological packages.

The concept of improved seed
Poor seed quality has been identified by many agricultural experts as the most critical factor limiting crop yields in developing countries. Seed quality is considered to be a more

serious problem with potatoes than with most other crops due to the transmission of virus diseases in seed tubers.

Mantaro Valley farmers often consume or sell their largest potatoes and keep smaller tubers for seed. Production specialists fault this practice on the grounds that planting small tubers increases the spread of virus diseases and reduces yields. It is generally believed that if small-scale farmers would use certified or 'improved' seed they could substantially increase their yield and income.

Yet surveys and on-farm experiments indicate that farmers' seed is not as bad as it is generally assumed to be, and that for most farmers the use of the 'improved' seed currently available is uneconomical. The data show that yield-reducing virus diseases are not as common as previously thought. There are two important reasons for this. First, farmers' native varieties are not as severely affected by yield-reducing virus diseases as are most modern varieties. Second, farmers' seed management practices tend to minimize the spread of viruses.

Over the centuries, Andean farmers have developed sophisticated informal seed dissemination networks and management practices to cope with local diseases, including viruses. Farmers seldom plant seed tubers harvested from one crop in the same field the next year. Instead, they plant their seed in another of their own fields or exchange the seed with their neighbours. Farmers generally select the fields from which they will keep seed on the basis of the vigour and yield of the crop and the appearance of harvested tubers. When they consider the seed stock to have degenerated, they consume or sell the harvest and acquire new seed. In the low zone, where virus infection is greatest, farmers replace their seed stock more often than do farmers in the higher zones. Farmers also know where to acquire good seed: from higher areas where virus infection is lower (Monares 1981).

In the on-farm experiments, the use of improved seed increased yields on average by 15-20%. However, due to its high cost, it reduced farmers' net returns below the level obtained when using their own seed.

The technology transfer paradigm

In the conventional research-technology transfer paradigm, new agricultural technology is developed by researchers in laboratories and experimental stations and then 'transferred' via extension services to farmers, who are seen as passive recipients (Whyte 1981). Sweeping optimistic statements have been made concerning the amount of superior technology that is 'on the shelf', awaiting transfer to needy farmers in developing countries.

On the assumption that developed countries and research centres have generated a large stock of appropriate technology, international development agencies are now looking for ways to speed up the transfer of research results to farmers. The Training and Visit extension system, promoted by the World Bank and implemented in over 50 developing countries, is based on the view that the extension of known practices, with little or no local testing, can substantially and rapidly increase farmers' yields.

In the Mantaro Valley Project, two things became abundantly clear: first, there was little technology that could be transferred directly to farmers without local refinement or adaptive research; and second, farmers are not passive recipients of recommended technologies but active researchers and developers in their own right. In contrast to the optimism concerning the transferability of superior technology stands the failure of many extension programmes and the disrespect shown by many farmers for extension agents who, in the farmers' view, offer little or no technology that is viable under current farming conditions.

No extension campaign was conducted within the framework of the Mantaro Valley Project. However, many farmers showed interest in the research and began applying on their own farms some of the practices being tested by their neighbours. A 1982 survey indicated that very few of the farmers who tested technological packages adopted them in their entirety, but that more than half the farmers reported taking advantage of one or more of the component technologies. In general, they adopted low-cost practices, such as the use of diffused-light seed storage, the selection of healthy seed, and improved insect-control measures. Very few began using costly certified seed or recommended fertilizer application levels (Table 5).

In most cases farmers did not *adopt* the practices tested, but rather *adapted* them to suit their specific needs. The most striking illustration of farmer adaptation was that of

Table 5 Percentage of farmers adopting the packages and practices tested on their farms

	Adopted (%)	Not adopted (%)	No. of observations
Technological packages	12	88	24
Seed management practices:			
Diffused-light storage	58	42	19
Planting one large tuber per hill	36	64	28
Selecting healthy seed	56	44	18
Using certified seed	20	80	15
Fertilizer practices:			
Recommended levels	17	83	30
Split N application	29	71	31
Insect control measures:			
Foliar application	43	57	30
Soil application	60	40	30

diffused-light seed storage. This technique, which involves exposing stored seed potatoes to indirect sunlight to retard sprout elongation and green the skin, was tested on a number of farms by the postharvest team. In 16 trials, the average yield increase resulting from storing seed in diffused light, rather than in the dark stores traditionally used by farmers, was 20% (Booth et al. 1983). These authors note that 'farmers did not copy the model store but began applying the principle of diffused-light storage in a wide range of innovative ways.' In most cases, rather than building an elaborate new store, they simply modified their existing one. As a physical entity or precise recommendation, the technology was not transferred to farmers. Instead, farmers understanding the principle applied it in ways that suited their needs. Similar kinds of adaptation have been observed in a number of other countries (Rhoades et al. 1983; Potts 1983).

References

Booth, R.H., R.L. Shaw and A.T. Yupanqui. 1983. Use of natural diffused light for the storage of tuber seeds. In: Research for the Potato in the Year 200. Lima, International Potato Center.

Brush, S.B., H.J. Carney and Z. Huaman. 1981. Dynamics of Andean potato agriculture. *Economic Botany* 35 (11): 70-88.

Carney, A.J. 1980. Diversity, distribution and peasant selection of indigenous potato varieties in the Mantaro Valley, Cama, Peru: A biocultural evolutional process. Lima, International Potato Center.

Christiansen, J.A. 1977. *The utilization of bitter potatoes to improve food production in the high-altitude tropics.* Ithaca, New York: Cornell University.

Franco, E., D. Horton and F. Tardieu. 1979. Producción y utilización de la papa en el Valle del Mantaro, Perú: Resultados de la encuesta agro-económica de visita unica. Working document, Social Sciences Department. Lima, International Potato Center.

Franco, E., D. Horton, R. Cortbaoui, F. Tardieu and L. Tomassini. 1980. Evaluacíon agro-económica de ensayos conducidos en campos de agricultores en el Valle del Mantaro (Perú), campaña1978/79. Working document, Social Sciences Department. Lima, International Potato Center.

Franco, E., D. Horton, R. Cortbaoui, L. Tomassini and F. Tardieu. 1981. Evaluacíon agro-económica de ensayos conducidos en campos de agricultores en el Valle del Mantaro (Perú), campaña1979/80.

Horton, D., F. Tardieu, M. Benavides, L. Tomassini and P. Accatino. 1980. Tecnología de la produccíon de papa en el Valle del Mantaro, Perú: Resultados de una encuesta agro-económica de visita múltiple. Working document, Social Sciences Department. Lima, International Potato Center.

Mayer, E. 1979. Land use in the Andes: Ecology and agriculture in the Mantaro Valley of Peru, with special reference to potatoes. Lima, International Potato Center.

Monares, A. 1981. *The potato seed system in the Andean Region: The case of Peru.* Ithaca, New York: Cornell University.

Potts, M. 1983. Potato technology transfer in the Philippines: The development of the 'Optimizing Potato Productivity' approach in Benguet and Mountain Provinces. Lima, International Potato Center.

Rhoades, R., R.H. Booth and M.J. Potts. 1983. Farmer acceptance of improved potato storage practices in developing countries. *Outlook on Agriculture* 11 (1).

Werge, R.W. 1977. Socio-economic aspects of the production and utilization of potatoes in Peru: A bibliography. Lima, International Potato Center.

Werge, R.W. 1979. Potato processing in the central highlands of Peru. *Ecology of Food and Nutrition* 7: 229-234.

Whyte, W.F. 1981. Participatory approaches to agricultural research and development: A state-of-the-art paper. Ithaca, New York: Cornell University.

Source

Excerpted from *Social Scientists in Agricultural Research: Lessons from the Mantaro Valley Project, Peru,* published 1984 by IDRC, Ottawa. Reprinted by kind permission of the author and the publisher.

Address

Douglas Horton, ISNAR, P.O. Box 93375, 2509 AJ The Hague, The Netherlands.

Soil Erosion? That's Not How We See the Problem!

Christine Pahlman

Introduction

The reasons for increased pressure on upland and highland areas in South-East Asia are complex. The demand for food and other basic needs of a growing population and the shift from subsistence to a market economy are partly responsible. They have led to more intensive cultivation of marginal sloping land, and to the instability or, in some cases, the breakdown of the traditional swidden systems of agriculture. Fallow periods have shortened, and increasingly land is being cultivated again before the soil has fully recovered.

In Thailand, soil degradation is one of the most devastating consequences of intensified farming. Upland soils tend to be of moderate to low fertility and highly susceptible to erosion. In 1980 it was estimated that 33% of the country's total land area was moderately to severely eroded, particularly on upland slopes. Indications are that the extent and degree of erosion have increased since then.

Dependance on Land for Survival

Although it can be argued that a significant proportion of the sloping lands of northern Thailand are too steep and poorly structured to be suitable for any form of agriculture, it is probably neither realistic nor acceptable to prohibit farming in these areas—land on which hundreds of thousands of people depend for their survival. For this reason there is an urgent need to develop sustainable agricultural systems appropriate for upland communities—systems capable of supporting the inhabitants whilst conserving soil and other natural resources.

Much work has been and is being directed towards developing more sustainable farming practices for sloping land. Promising and potentially appropriate methods, including various agroforestry systems such as alley cropping, have been developed. Nevertheless, the rate of farmer adoption of these practices remains notably low and, in northern Thailand, is still insufficient to have any real impact on the situation. This suggests a disparity between the perceptions of researchers and development workers on the one hand and those of farmers on the other. While researchers may perceive soil erosion as a major problem, the low adoption rate of soil conservation practices suggests that farmers perceive their problems quite differently, or perhaps cannot adopt these innovations for reasons not well understood by others.

Farmers' Perceptions of Sustainability

To develop an understanding of how upland farmers perceive their problems and the sustainability of their production systems, a group of 240 farmers from eight villages of Nan Province in northern Thailand were interviewed. Farmers were selected on the basis that they were farming mostly rainfed upland areas and derived most of their food and income from these activities. Questions were answered mostly by household heads, usually males, although other family members often contributed.

It was found that a typical farmer has little if any formal education, is farming an area of less than 1.8 ha located more than 2 km from the house, and has an annual household income of less than US$ 400. The main crops grown are glutinous upland rice, maize and groundnut in the wet season and mung beans in the dry season. Cultivating fields in rows up and down the slope and burning crop residues are standard practices. The dry season is characterized by widespread burning of fields, fires being lit and then left to run their course largely uncontrolled. Fields lie bare, exposed to the impact of the hot tropical sun during the dry season and the highly erosive monsoonal rains at the beginning of the wet season.

Most farmers were unaware of soil erosion, or thought it not serious enough to require action. Alternatively, they were unaware of what they could do about soil erosion and/ or were unable to adopt soil conservation strategies due to shortages of cash and labour.

Despite general recognition among the research and extension community that soil erosion is a critical problem in northern Thailand, only 1 farmer out of the 240 questioned spontaneously mentioned soil erosion when asked generally about major farming problems. Instead, the primary concerns of farmers were weeds, insect pests and the shortage of water. When specifically questioned on the incidence of soil erosion on their fields, 43% said there was none, 34% acknowledged a moderate degree of erosion, and only 23% said there was substantial erosion.

Lack of New Land

Despite the seemingly low awareness and concern about soil erosion, declining soil quality/fertility was recognized as a problem by most of those questioned. According to the farmers, the major reason for the decline in soil quality is the lack of new land to clear, making it necessary to practise more continuous farming, reducing the length and frequency of fallow periods. It became clear that farmers are well aware of the soil degradation that results from continuous slash-and-burn cycles on a single piece of land. To them, it is like a law of nature: 'Fallows are necessary to rest the soil; without fallows, the soil eventually dies.' Many farmers therefore do not see the problem so much in terms of farming practices, but rather as lack of land, making fallowing and soil regeneration impossible.

Farmers' views on five potential soil conservation measures (integration of trees, contour farming, bench terraces, alley cropping and rock/log barriers) were sought. Farmers regarded the integration of trees, particularly 'economic' trees such as fruit trees, to be both the most effective and suitable.

Although tree crops are already widely used, and the majority of farmers are aware of their beneficial effects on soil quality, soil conservation as such does not seem to be a major incentive to plant trees. Some 141 of the 200 farmers growing or interested in growing fruit trees said this was for economic reasons, whereas only 10 said it was to control soil erosion.

Food and Income Needs

Farmers also spoke of the value of growing tree crops to suppress weed growth (their major farming concern) and to offset the effects of deforestation, including declining infiltration of water and dwindling supplies of timber and forest food resources. The study confirmed the importance of developing and extending soil conservation techniques that have a direct and clear relevance to the food and income needs of farmers, and do not just address environmental concerns.

In the view of the farmers interviewed, the main constraints to integrating tree crops into their fields (in order of importance) are lack of resources/funds, lack of water, the possible reduction in yields of their field crops, and security problems associated with protecting trees and their produce from uncontrolled fires, and from theft and damage.

Land Tenure Makes No Difference

Fifty per cent of farmers' fields were farmed without any form of legal title. Only a few were covered by what is considered to be highly secure legal tenure.

Conservation literature has generally argued that secure land tenure is a necessary precondition for the adoption of long-term sustainable farming practices. It is therefore highly interesting that 69% of farmers interviewed thought that land tenure made no difference to farming practices and did not rule out the establishment of permanent tree crops. Of the farmers who had already planted fruit trees, 40% did not have any legal form of land tenure and only 6% had highly secure tenure. Some farmers even went so far as to say that planting fruit trees was a way for them to make their claim to the land more secure.

Conservation Farming Approaches

In the sample group, there were two examples—one an individual farmer (Nai Anorak Seetabut) and one a village community (Ban Giw Muang)—of people who have actively sought and developed ways of farming more sustainably and, in this regard, were not typical of the interviewed farmers. Their success provides some insights into the technologies and processes that may be appropriate for more sustainable farming in the upland areas.

Nai Anorak Seetabut

Nai Anorak Seetabut is a young, hard-working and thoughtful farmer who recently acquired a 2-/ha plot of degraded upland through a government land reform programme. His own experiences and observations had led him to believe that a continuous cycle of slash-and-burn farming with annual crops would inevitably lead to soil degradation and decreased productivity. He therefore sought to develop a diversified and integrated farming system incorporating perennial tree crops, food crops throughout the year for family consumption, cash crops for monetary income, low use of external inputs, and the recycling (rather than the burning) of crop residues. Having witnessed many fellow villagers fall into a downward spiral of debt and hardship, Nai Anorak wanted to develop his farm without borrowing money.

With training and advice from local extension personnel, Nai Anorak started experimenting with different cover crops and began propagating fruit trees and planting them in between various field crops. In recognition of his commitment and interest in conservation farming, Nai Anorak was selected as a 'model farmer' by a local agricultural project. This meant that he received modest technical and material support for developing his farm in return for trying out new crops and technologies and helping to extend successful ones to other farmers. So far, he has experimented and attained moderate success with alley cropping, growing wheat as a supplementary dry-season crop, digging fish ponds, and raising fish and pigs.

Within 4 years, Nai Anorak and his family have transformed 2 ha of relatively unproductive deforested and degraded sloping land into a diversified and integrated farm incorporating tree crops, field crops, animals and conservation structures. This has been done with a lot of hard work, few external inputs and little capital investment. It is a system which Nai Anorak believes will produce enough food and income to support his family throughout the year.

Ban Giw Muang

The farming approach of villagers in Ban Giw Muang could be described as unique for the uplands of northern Thailand. The majority of farmers in the village have not only been integrating fruit trees into their fields for several years, but have also been contour farming as opposed to cultivating up and down the slope as is the norm in northern Thailand. Villagers were exposed to the concept of contour farming by local extension workers, and a few farmers experimented with the technique. More and more villagers adopted the technique when they realized that it produced better crop yields and reduced soil loss. The village headman explained that, when maize is planted up and down the steep slopes around the village, the field can be cropped for only 1 year, after which the soil is so degraded that it must be fallowed for 3 years. Contour farming, on the other hand, enables fields to be farmed for 2 successive years before it is necessary to fallow.

Farmer-to-farmer extension was also the means by which the integration of fruit trees has become so popular in Ban Giw Muang. One of the villagers had perceived the economic and conservation benefits of growing trees amidst field crops and, with the assistance of a local conservation-minded monk, he began experimenting with tree species. Interest amongst villagers quickly spread.

Planting fruit trees on their fields presents many challenges to these farmers. So far, they have grown trees mostly on fields close to the village, which allows greater protection from uncontrolled fires, damage by animals and theft by other villagers. The farmers have had to cut grass and dig around the trees in the hope of creating a firebreak. The village headman envisages that the threat from fires will reduce in future as more and more farmers start to grow trees in their fields.

Recently, becoming increasingly concerned about the effects of deforestation in their area, Ban Giw Muang villagers joined together to protect remaining forest close to the village. A community forestry area was proclaimed and a blessing ceremony was held. A small shrine was erected by local Buddhist monks to bless and sanctify the area.

In addition to protecting existing forest, the villagers are also planting tree seedlings in the school and temple grounds, along roads and in other public areas. Although a local development worker supported and was involved in these activities, the main initiative came from the villagers themselves.

Selling Conservation

Progress towards more sustainable farming practices involves both identifying appropriate practices and the process of developing and extending them. This study provided some useful insights into the characteristics of appropriate practices, as well as some ideas on how to ensure more widespread adoption.

Appropriate farming practices for the upland farming communities of northern Thailand are those which:

- Address immediate, short-term needs for food and income
- Are based on existing practices, i.e. modify rather than replace them
- Diversify farming practices and systems
- Minimize capital/resource requirements and the use of external inputs
- Provide acceptable economic returns
- Can be implemented with existing labour.

The participation of the whole community is crucial to the development and extension of appropriate practices. Farmer experimentation and farmer-to-farmer extension are especially valuable because they encourage the promotion of only those practices that are seen as appropriate by local people. To achieve sustainable land use in the upland areas, emphasis must be placed on practices which meet other needs—notably the demand for food and income. There is no point in trying to 'sell' sustainable farming practices on the grounds of conservation alone, when the farmers themselves see their problems differently.

Reference

Srikhajon, M. et al. 1980. Soil erosion in Thailand. Department of Land Development, Bangkok, Thailand.

Source

First published 1991 in *ILEIA Newsletter* 1 and 2, under the title 'Assessing low-external-input farming techniques: Report of a workshop.'

Address

Christine Pahlman, P.O. Box 3517, Vientiane, Laos PDR.

On-farm Research and Household Economics

Allan Low

Introduction

Although there is in theory a close relationship between the two new philosophies of farming systems research and household economics, this relationship has not been sufficiently recognized or adequately developed in practice. This paper focuses on the need to orient on-farm research methodologies towards household economics concepts.

By 'on-farm research' I mean farm-level research to (1) understand farmers' circumstances, (2) generate hypotheses about how best to improve farm productivity in the near term, (3) design and test new technologies based on these hypotheses, or (4) guide station research towards the development of more relevant technologies, practices or systems.

By 'household economics' I mean the concept of household production behaviour that has its basis in the theory of consumer choice developed by Becker (1965), Lancaster (1966) and Muth (1966). This theory sees households as production/consumption units in which market goods and household resources (mainly time) are combined in a household technology to produce intermediate non-market goods ('Z goods') which are then consumed in combinations that generate maximum utility (or satisfaction or welfare) for the household.

On-farm research seeks ways of increasing farm production, for either the market or home consumption. On small African farms, crop and/or livestock production is organized within the context of the farm household, which is both a production and a consumption unit. The production of non-market goods forms an important part of household activities. In addition, a high proportion of household resources is devoted to non-agricultural, 'household production' activities such as household maintenance and child care.

If farm production is increased through technologies that use more household resources, fewer resources will be available for household production. This implies either that more farm goods will be consumed, or that the proceeds of increased farm production will be used to purchase more market goods. The appropriateness of new technologies depends not only on the extent to which they increase the productivity of household resources used in farming but also on a comparison of current production with potential future production (the investment/security aspect) and on a comparison of the subjective value of the non-market household production goods that have been foregone with the utility and/or price of the substitute goods consumed (the consumption aspect).

Logically, household economics theory and the study of intra-household processes should form an important part of on-farm research, yet this is not the case in practice. On-farm research tends to concentrate on the interactions among different farming activities. Although some attempt is made to account for the opportunity costs of time and money used in non-farm market production, little attention is given to the opportunity costs of resources used in non-farm, non-market production, investment and consumption. Moreover, the relationship between agricultural productivity and household welfare is generally perceived as a one-way process and assumed to be positive. That is, increased agricultural productivity is supposed to lead to increased household welfare. But welfare is a function of the total mix of monetary and non-monetary, tangible and intangible goods. Moreover, perceptions of welfare affect the goals of farm household members and, in turn, their allocation and management of resources. Thus, welfare is not only a function but also a determinant of agricultural productivity (Caldwell 1983). Where household welfare and the household's commitment to farming are affected by non-farm factors, such as the wage employment market, access to consumer goods and household composition, these factors become highly relevant for on-farm research aimed at generating appropriate technology.

On-farm research results are indicating the need to think more in household terms. The new household economics perspective, together with an appreciation of intra-household processes, can contribute to the effectiveness of on-farm research and help move us beyond the notion of a one-way link between farm income and household welfare.

The Consideration of Intra-Household Processes

On-farm research normally focuses sharply on the farm, with minimal consideration given to non-farm household activities and decision-making processes. Research concepts and techniques of analysis have tended to concentrate on how farmers' adoption of new technologies is influenced by natural circumstances, institutional support or cash costs and risks. Farmers' multiple objectives have been less thoroughly treated, partly because there is little theoretical basis for analyzing the multiple market and non-market objectives of a household and partly because many agricultural factors can be handled purely within the context of the farming system. The need to adjust input rates (fertilizers, plant population, etc) to fit local soil conditions or to adapt a new crop to an existing cropping system can be established without reference to non-farm activities and intra-household decision-making processes.

Taking account of farmers' multiple objectives, however, implies extending the area of analysis from the farm to the farm household and from production to consumption. This broadens the focus and complicates the analysis. Nevertheless, experience with on-farm research in Eastern and Southern Africa points towards the need to consider links between the household and the farm more thoroughly in technology generation, and suggests that there may be a case for extending the concept of on-farm research beyond the boundaries of the farm to encompass the larger farm-household unit.

Some On-Farm Research Findings

The importance of the time constraint
According to household economics theory, the time of the household's members is the basic resource of households. The opportunity cost of this resource varies over time and at any one point in time among household members of different genders, ages and skills. An implication of the theory is that time and cash are interchangeable. Time can be 'sold' to generate market or non-market goods, and it can also be 'bought' by spending cash on time-saving technologies or other inputs.

Diagnostic work in on-farm research is indicating that farmers very often compromise on crop and livestock management, not because of lack of knowledge or cash to purchase inputs, nor because inputs are not available, but because of time constraints.

Often, seemingly appropriate production-increasing innovations are not adopted because of their implications in terms of time. Commenting on the results of experimental work on livestock feeding in the Kenya Dryland Farming Research and Development Project, Tessera (1983) concluded that the rate of adoption of innovations was disappointingly slow. He observed that:
• Kenyan farmers tended to value their leisure more than the income they could earn from clearing bush to encourage good forage growth
• Most farmers grazed their crop residues *in situ*, in the knowledge that they were wasting about 40% of production by doing so. They were choosing the least laborious way of doing a job even though they knew that increased labour inputs would give a higher return
• The growing of fodder crops required additional labour and time spent by draught oxen, which the farmer could not provide if he also had to plough, plant and weed for food crop production. Thus, only a handful of farmers could be persuaded to include fodder crops in their cropping system.

Household differentiation
Household economics theory relates differences in behaviour among households to differences in their characteristics and composition and, in particular, to the way these affect the relative time values of household members. On-farm researchers generally recognize that differences in the economic and natural circumstances facing households will affect their ability to adopt new technologies. The identification of different recommendation domains (homogeneous groups of farmers) in on-farm research has tended to be based on external factors such as agro-climatic conditions and access to markets or inputs. However, as research proceeds, the importance of internal household factors in determining appropriate technology is beginning to emerge.

In Table 1, which shows data from Zimbabwe, we see that cattle owners achieved higher crop yields than non-owners. The yield differences are related to management factors. Cattle owners planted and weeded earlier, and a greater proportion of them winter ploughed and applied manure. These management differences are in turn related to internal household factors. As Shumba (1983) states:

> While non-owners and owners obtained the same absolute income from off-farm sources, this represents a much higher proportion of total income for non-owners, who have lower productive capacities in farming because of their smaller labour forces, lack of oxen and greater tendency for the household head to be away. The greater tendency for household heads to be absent in non-owning households is related to the younger age of these households. Job prospects for younger household heads are better than for their older counterparts, and wages provide a relatively low-risk means for young households to generate the necessary funds to hire cattle and purchase fertilizer. The incentive for members of non-owning households to seek wage employment is therefore quite high and, given their already smaller work forces, this further reduces time available for farm activities and contributes to the lower levels of crop management, lower yields and lower farm incomes of non-owners compared with owners.

From a household economics perspective, the influence of the domestic development cycle on the productive capacity of farm households is clear. Ox ownership is a critical factor allowing better crop husbandry, and the distribution of cattle in this society is associated with household maturity. This leads to poorer crop management by the less mature, non-owning households.

Given the relationship between cattle ownership and crop productivity and the decline of cattle in the area owing to drought and to the breakdown of health control, on-farm researchers have looked towards interventions such as improved feeding to increase the size and capacity of the draught cattle pool. However, recognition of the link between ox ownership and the household development cycle poses two questions: (1) would additional cattle be any better distributed between households? And (2) would having cattle enable less mature households with smaller work forces to practise better crop management and would the incentive to seek wage employment be sufficiently reduced to encourage them to do so?

An answer to the distribution question is suggested by the situation in neighbouring Botswana, where cattle numbers have increased at 4.7% per annum over the past decade and the average herd size has increased from 30 to 43 head. Despite this sustained increased in the size of the draught cattle pool, the proportion of households owning cattle has remained unchanged and more than 50% of farmers still do not own their own draught animals.

Women farmers

On-farm researchers in Eastern and Southern Africa have increasingly found themselves dealing with women farmers. At farmers' group meetings women invariably outnumber men. It is said that 50-70% of all farmers in Africa are women.

Table 1 Characteristics of two recommendation domains in Mangwende, Zimbabwe

	Cattle ownership	
	Owners	Non-owners
Resources:		
Family size (persons)	8.4	6.4
Farm workers	3.4	2.8
Size of holding (ha)	3.9	2.9
Area cultivated (ha)	3.6	2.1
% farms with head working away	7	13
% farms with head less than 55 years	17	42
% farms with woman head	12	30
Crop yields (t/ha):		
Maize	3.2	2.1
Groundnut	0.7	0.5
Sunflower	0.2	0.04
Income sources (Z$/year):		
Maize sales	347	168
Vegetable sales	140	84
Groundnut sales	40	26
Off-farm income	159	149
Total income	752	449

Because women everywhere are responsible for household production activities (household maintenance, child care, etc), it follows that much of the agricultural work in Africa competes with household production activities for the allocation of women's time.

On-farm researchers and farm management economists are accustomed to assessing potential interventions in terms of the labour demands of competing farm activities, and to accounting for alternative market-oriented activities by imputing an opportunity cost of time. But the demands of household production are seldom considered.

Rural household studies are beginning to highlight the large amounts of time allocated to non-farm, non-market household activities, especially by women. Often the costs of not performing some of these essential or socially necessary tasks (such as fetching water or working in a neighbour's field) would be very high and would significantly reduce the real benefits of technologies that took up the time that should have been allocated to them.

Factors affecting who does what within farm households and the number of hands available for farming clearly have significant implications for the appropriateness of new farm technology. Tessera's observations, cited above, to the effect that farmers value leisure more than gains from bush clearing, and choose the least laborious way of feeding crop residues, sacrificing higher feed production, are made in a farming systems approach that lacks a household economics perspective.

Towards a Household Economics Perspective in On-Farm Research

The application of a household economics perspective can contribute to the effectiveness of on-farm research in three areas:
• Understanding farmers' objectives and strategies
• Defining recommendation domains
• Evaluating new technologies.

Understanding farmers' objectives and strategies

On-farm research looks at technology development from the farmer's point of view. As Norman et al. (1982) suggest, understanding farmers' objectives and values is crucial to this: 'The goals and motivations of farmers, which will affect the degree and type of effort they will be willing to devote to improving the productivity of their farming systems, are essential inputs to the process of identifying or designing potentially appropriate improved technologies.'

While on-farm research recognizes that farmers have multiple objectives, these objectives are generally considered in terms of the farming system. Multiple and intercropping strategies are manifestations of farmers' multiple objectives as regards cash, preferred staple foods, food security and maximization of returns to farm resources. Non-farm and non-market objectives have been given less, if any, attention. As Behnke and Kerven (1983) state, this concentration on the farming system may have two undesirable results:

First it may encourage researchers to think of those who farm as primarily or solely farmers, and thereby underestimate the role of non-agricultural activities in the larger household economy. Secondly, an exclusive concentration on farming may ill equip FSR to address one of the major issues in agricultural development in Africa: the withdrawal of labour from agriculture due to rural-urban migration.

In Eastern and Southern Africa farming is seldom the only source of income for rural households and in many cases it is not even the major one. Wage employment, beer brewing, handicrafts, trading and teaching are common additional sources.

While on-farm researchers are concerned with measuring and increasing farm income, farmers are concerned with stabilizing and increasing their entire welfare, much of which may come from non-farm production. Thus, in order to understand farmers' goals and objectives, on-farm researchers need to adopt a household economics perspective and to see how diverse production activities are combined to maximize household utility.

Wage employment is an important risk-reducing strategy. Over the past 2 drought years in Southern Africa, households with a wage-earning member have suffered much less than those without this source of income. Clearly, where the chances of earning off-farm income are good, any farm-based risk avoidance strategy, such as planting an extra area of cassava or using tied-ridging, must be compared with the returns and security obtained through wage employment. Norman (1983) notes that in the case of Botswana it may be necessary to accept that farmers will be reluctant to invest much money or time in crop production because this is a riskier venture than livestock production or off-farm activities. This insight has important implications for technology generation in Botswana.

Defining recommendation domains

The concept of the recommendation domain has become central to on-farm research methodology. A recommendation domain is a homogeneous group of farmers who share the same problems and possess similar resources for solving those problems. The group is expected to adopt (or not adopt) the same recommendation, given equal access to information about it. In much of Southern Africa, different recommendation domains occur not only because of differences in farmer resources, cropping opportunities, market access and inherent land fertility but also because, at any one time, farm households have different opportunities for non-farm wage employment or other income-earning activities. Often it is the nature of these non-farm opportunities and the extent to which farm households exploit them that most strongly influence farming practices and the aims and objectives of farm production.

It is commonly observed that, within homogeneous agroclimatic locations with similar market opportunities, neighbouring farmers with similar incomes and/or resource levels farm in very different ways. Households that are less able to exploit non-farm opportunities look on farming more in terms of production and income and tend to give more time and attention to farming activities than their wage-oriented neighbours, who farm for social and security reasons and tend to manage their farms less thoroughly. The cultivation practices of these two types of farmer differ, as do relevant interventions and recommendations.

A recommendation domain exercise was recently carried out in Swaziland, with the expectation that different farming systems would be observed in the very different ecological conditions of the high veld, middle veld and low veld zones of the country (Watson 1983). However, it was found that variations in cropping systems within the zones were much greater than the variations between the zones. The within-zone variation stemmed from differences in internal household circumstances. Table 2 gives a breakdown of household types, relating the differences beteween them to the cropping practices typical of each and to the interventions that might be suitable for each.

The farm household types have been broken down on the basis of off-farm income/resource endowments and labour committed to farming. These factors are, as we have seen, not independent. Three categories are distinguished. Some households find that they are able to exploit off-farm earning opportunities but that, in order to do so, they compromise on time devoted to farming. These fall into Category 1 in the table. Other households have relatively little potential for exploiting off-farm income opportunities but possess reasonable labour and resources for farming. This is Category 2 in the table, which often consists of older households or women-headed households. However, there is a third group of households (Category 3) that are able both to exploit off-farm income opportunities and to commit time and attention to farming. Generally, these are households whose head is not engaged in off-farm employment.

Group 1 households may have the cash and incentive to buy inputs but will tend not to manage them very intensively. Group 3 households, on the other hand, can contemplate more expensive inputs and have the resources to manage them reasonably well. Thus, fertilizer top dressing may be a relevant intervention for both groups, but the conditions under which it is tested should differ. To reflect real life conditions, trials with Group 1 households should be conducted with poor seedbed preparation, late planting and little weeding. The results are likely to be very different to those of trials conducted with Group 3 households, which practise good land preparation, early planting and adequate weed control. The value of yield increases is also likely to be different. For Group 1, who are deficit producers, the value will be the cost of equivalent food purchases. For Group 3, who tend to be surplus producers, it will be the market price of maize.

Another example of the different values of interventions is seen in the introduction of an early maturing short-season maize variety. For Group 3 farmers, this opens the door for double cropping, in which case the benefits attached should take the value of the second crop into account. For households in Groups 1 and 4, however, where circumstances dictate late planting, the advantage of a short-season variety will be that it can better exploit the limited growing period. It should therefore be valued in terms of its production compared with current varieties when planted late. Once again, the composition of the household affects the relevance of improved technology.

This has implications for the definition of farming units. Little thought has so far been given to the question of how the family farm unit is defined and whether it is managed within a nuclear family or through an extended family. There may well be a case for on-farm researchers to pay more attention to this issue in future.

Evaluating new technologies

Researchers now recognize that yield increasing technologies are not the only ones that can benefit small-scale farmers. Technologies that make more efficient use of time or cash are often equally acceptable.

Table 2 Household types, cropping systems and technology generation in Swaziland

Farm household type	Distinguishing features	Cropping practices	
		Fixed non-experimental variables	Potential interventions
1. Cash/resource rich but labour poor	(a) 4 adult equivalents in family farm work force (b) Access to significant non-farm income (c) May or may not own oxen	(a) Only 1 ploughing, late planting, 1 weeding, use of planter (b) High levels of input use, e.g. fertilizers and top dressing, hybrid maize, but no tractors	(a) Top dressing (b) Botswana plough/planter (c) Botswana improved planter (d) Winter ploughing (tractor) (e) Short-season varieties (f) Herbicides
2. Cash/resource poor but labour rich	(a) 4+ adult equivalents in family farm work force (b) Poor access to non-farm income (c) Own oxen	(a) 2 x ploughing, early planting, 2 x weeding (b) Lower levels of input use, e.g. no top dressing, less hybrid maize, no tractors	(a) Winter ploughing (b) 2 x ploughing (c) Better weeding (d) Double cropping (e) Intensive sweet potato production (f) Cutworm banding and scouting (g) Early planting (h) Fodder conservation (i) Tied-ridging
3. Cash/resource rich and labour rich	(a) 4+ adult equivalents in family farm work force (b) Access to significant non-farm income	(a) Winter or 2 x ploughing, early planting, 2+ weedings (b) High level of input use, e.g. fertilizers (top dressing), hybrid seed, tractors	(a) Top dressing (b) Tied- ridging (c) Winter ploughing (tractor) (d) Early planting (hybrids) (e) Double cropping
4. Cash/resource poor and labour poor	(a) 4 adult equivalents in family farm work force (b) Poor access to non-farm income (c) Few if any cattle	(a) 1x ploughing, late planting, 1 x weeding, hand planting in furrow (b) Low levels of input use, local or open pollinated varieties, no tractors	(a) Minimum tillage (b) Tyne plough, e.g. Zimbabwe (c) Short-season varieties (open pollinated)

Technologies which save labour are particularly attractive to small family farm units. The rapid uptake by small-scale farmers around the world of improved implements, herbicides and mechanization, as well as farmers' own labour-saving strategies, bear witness to this.

From a household economics perspective, utility is maximized by producing the desired set of goods at the lowest cost in terms of the ultimate resource—the time of household members. Given the many demands for family labour in farm and non-farm activities, market and non-market production, and work and leisure, household economics sees family labour as being at a premium, with the major objective being to employ it as efficiently as possible. This implies that households seek to maximize the subjective return to the labour of their members, and that what tasks are performed and by whom depends on the opportunity cost of members' time.

The opportunity cost of labour often forms an important component in the evaluation of farm technologies by on-farm researchers. However, these costs are generally assessed in terms of alternative farm activities or of the wages that can be earned off the farm. (The cost of women's time during parts of the season when there is little crop work is generally assumed to be close to zero.)

Commenting on the unresponsiveness of farmers to advice on bush clearing in western Kenya, which experimental results had shown to be productive, Tessema (1983) says: 'Many were unwilling to carry out the work because they say it is a hard and difficult task even though it does not conflict with other operations, as it can be done in the dry season when there is little other activity.' Even when there are few tasks on the farm, the demands on family labour are many. It is therefore wrong to assume that that the opportunity cost to family labour is negligible at such times.

Taking a household economics perspective will help researchers to avoid falling into Tessema's trap, and will provide a basis for making some assessment of what value to place on family labour used outside farming and wage employment. The question researchers need to ask is: what other tasks are being performed by the relevant household members at the time? Answering this question will probably be easier than going on to the next stage and estimating the subjective value of a unit of the member's time spent in the proposed new activity. What value do you put on an hour spent looking after children or collecting firewood or drinking beer with friends? The important point, though, is that the answer is certainly not 'zero' just because the activity does not relate to farming.

Even where positive opportunity costs are assumed, the farm-based and household economics approaches to evaluating technologies can give markedly different results. For example, Table 3 presents a typical partial budget analysis in which the opportunity costs of labour are included and a reasonable return on capital is obtained when extra management time and fertilizer are applied.

Moving from the traditional to the new technology gives an increased net benefit (gross benefit less total variable costs) of 298 cedes. This additional net benefit is achieved at a cost of 642 cedes (1252–610), which implies a return to capital of 46% (298/642x100). On the basis of this conventional analysis it is probably worthwhile moving to the new technology.

Table 3 Farm-based partial budget analysis of benefits of moving from traditional to new technology

	Returns per hectare analysis	
	Traditional	New technology
Yield (kg/ha)	1300	2400
Adjusted yield (–15%)	1100	2040
Gross benefit at 1 cedes/kg	1100	2040
Cost of fertilizer	-	192
Labour input (person-days)	61	106
Cost at 10 cedes/day	610	1060
Total variable costs	610	1252
Net benefit per hectare	490	788

Source: Bruce et al. (1980)

Compare this approach with the following analysis of the same data based on the household economics theory that farm households seek to minimize the costs of producing goods for their own consumption in order to maximize returns to family labour. Table 4 presents the analysis of the data in Table 3 based on a comparison of the costs of producing each unit of the crop, rather than on the returns to capital invested per hectare.

With the new technology, each ton of crop can be produced with 3 fewer person-days of labour input, giving a saving of 30 cedes per ton. However, since the new technology requires an extra cash outlay of 94 cedes, it is 64 cedes more costly than the traditional technology per unit of produce. On a per-ton basis then, the traditional technology, which requires more labour and less cash, is the lower cost alternative (at the given opportunity cost of labour time).

For subsistence producers, the cost of production analysis is probably more relevant than the returns per hectare analysis.

More important than the different answers given by each analysis are the different implications of changes in the value of time of household members. In the farm-based approach, the new technology becomes less attractive as the opportunity costs of time increase, since it uses more labour per unit of the enterprise, reducing net returns per hectare. In the household economics approach, the new technology becomes more attractive as the opportunity costs of time increase because it uses less time to produce each unit of the consumption good.

Table 4 Household time efficiency analysis of the benefits of moving from traditional to new technology

	Costs per ton analysis	
	Traditional	New technology
Time costs/ton		
Person-days required [1]	55	52
Time costs at 10 cedes/day	550	520
Cash costs/ton		
Fertilizer costs [2]	-	94
Total costs/ton	550	614

1. Person-days per ha/adjusted yield per ha
2. Fertilizer cost per ha/adjusted yield per ha

It seems that, where labour hiring is not prevalent and scarce family labour time must be used in a subsistence crop activity, increasing the values of members' time (or household welfare) is likely to encourage the use of a cash-expensive technology that reduces the labour required per unit of production, rather than to discourage it, as the farm-based analysis implies. Thus an understanding of household circumstances, aims and objectives is crucial to the evaluation and design of appropriate technology for small-scale farmers.

References

Becker, G.S. 1965. A theory of the allocation of time. *Economic Journal* 75: 493-517.

Behnke, R. and C. Kerven. 1983. FSR and the attempt to understand the goals and motivations of farmers. *Culture and Agriculture* 19: 9-16.

Bruce, K., D. Byerlee and G. E. Edmeades. 1980. Maize in the Mampong-Sekudmasi area of Ghana. CIMMYT working paper, Mexico City.

Caldwell, J.S. 1983. An overview of farming systems research and development: Origins, applications and issues. In: C. B. Flora (ed.), Proceedings of Kansas State University's Farming

Systems Research Symposium, Farming Systems in the Field. Kansas State University, Manhattan, Kansas.

Collinson, M.P. 1981. A low-cost approach to understanding small farmers. *Agricultural Administration* 8: 433-50.

Hildebrand, P.E. 1981. Combining disciplines in rapid appraisal: The sondeo. *Agricultural Administration* 8: 423-432.

Lancaster, K. 1966. Change and innovation in the technology of consumption. *American Economics Review Supplement,* May: 14-23.

Low, A.R.C. 1982a. A comparative advaantage theory of the subsistence farm household: Applications to Swazi farming. *The South African Journal of Economics* 50: 136-157.

Low, A.R.C. 1982b. Farm-household theory and rural development in Swaziland. Development Study No. 23, Department of Agricultural Economics and Management, University of Reading.

Low, A.R.C. 1982c. Agricultural development in Southern Africa: A household economics perspective. Ph.D. dissertation, Department of Agricultural Economics and Management, University of Reading.

Muth, R.F. 1966. Household production and consumer demand functions. *Econometrica* 34: 699-708.

Norman, D.W. 1983. Helping resource-poor farmers: The Agricultural Technology Improvement Project, Botswana. Mimeo, Department of Agricultural Research, Sebele.

Norman, D.W. 1983. Institutionalizing the farming systems approach to research. Mimeo, IITA Conference, Ibadan.

Norman, D.W., E.B. Simmons and H.M. Hays. 1982. *Farming systems in the Nigerian savanna: Research and strategies for development.* Boulder, Westview Press.

Shumba, E. 1983. The crop-livestock interrelationship in farmer adaptation to problems of reduced cattle numbers and lack of dry-season feed in communal areas of Zimbabwe. CIMMYT Technical Networkshop, Ezualwini, Swaziland. CIMMYT, Mexico City.

Tessema, S. 1983. Animal feeding in small farm systems. CIMMYT Technical Networkshop, Ezualwini, Swaziland. CIMMYT, Mexico City.

De Vletter, F. 1981. Report of a sample survey. USAID, Mbabwane, Swaziland.

Wallace, T. 1981. The challenge of food: Nigeria's approach to agriculture, 1975-1980. *Canadian Journal of African Studies* 15 (2): 239-258.

Watson, V. 1983. Farming systems on Swazi Nation land: Results of extension field officer survey, September-November. Mimeo, Cropping Systems Research and Extension Training Project, Malkerns, Swaziland.

Source

First published in 1986 in Understanding Africa's Rural Households and Farming Systems, edited by Joyce L. Moock and published by Westview Press, Boulder, Colorado. Reprinted by kind permission of the author and J.L. Moock.

Address

Allan Low, Development Project Planning Centre, University of Bradford, Richmond Road, Bradford BD7 1DP, Yorkshire, United Kingdom.

PART THREE

Aspects of Economic Assessment

Mrs Balomtesi Ngongorego assessing crop development and seed quality in a local sorghum variety in her field at Sekgweng, Palapye District, Botswana. Are farmers' criteria adequately reflected in the economic assessment of new technology and farming systems? *Photo: Kees Manintveld*

Soil Mining: An Unseen Contributor to Farm Income in Southern Mali

Floris van der Pol

Introduction: Farming and Soil Mining

This paper focuses on soil depletion. West African farmers are exhausting their soils in order to survive. Lack of fertilizer application has traditionally been compensated for by long fallow periods. With growing population pressure and expanding farm size, this recovery period is being lost. Little by little, sustainable farming is giving way to soil mining—the removal each year of more nutrients than are put back in.

Soil mining may occur either in traditional cereal-based cropping systems, or in association with newly introduced cash crops. In the literature, for example, mining with traditional crops is described by Broekhuyse (1983), Dupriez and Thevenen (1977), and Pieri (1989). Not only is insufficient fertilizer applied, but also nutrient losses due to erosion, leaching and volatilization are generally higher in cultivated than in non-cultivated fields.

The tool used in this study to quantify declining soil fertility is the nutrient balance. Maintenance of soil fertility is determined by the degree to which nutrient 'exports' (uptake by crops plus losses) are balanced by 'imports' (supplied, for example, by fertilizer application and weathering). If the balance is negative, nutrients are being mined from the soil. This paper calculates a regional nutrient balance for southern Mali, as well as specific balances for different cropping systems.

Establishing the value of nutrient exports is essential to the realistic economic analysis of cropping systems. If farming is to be sustainable, the nutrients extracted must be replaced. The value of exported nutrients should therefore be included when calculating the production costs of a given commodity. The nutrient balance is an indicator of the sustainability of current agricultural practices.

This study concerns cropping systems in southern Mali, which lies in the West African Sudanian zone. Traditionally, sorghum and millet have been the main cereal crops. Cotton was introduced here 40 years ago and is still the most important cash crop. In the 1970s, fertilizer application per hectare increased. But in 1982, as a result of structural adjustment, fertilizer subsidies were abolished. Berckmoes et al. (1988) have calculated that rising fertilizer prices made it more profitable for farmers to expand the area under cultivation than to improve the productivity of their existing fields, at least in the short term.

Methodology

The methodology presented here has been designed to quantify soil mining in both physical and economic terms. Five steps are required:
1. Identify and quantify the processes related to the input and output of chemical elements to and from the cultivated area
2. Determine what proportion of this flow of elements is available for use by plants
3. Calculate nutrient balances for the area under study, combining the information from steps 1 and 2 with agricultural statistics on crop yields and the use of fertilizers and manure
4. Estimate the value of the balance for each chemical element, based on current fertilizer prices. The sum of these values establishes a market value for the nutrient deficit
5. Compare any deficit with farmer income: this allows income sustainability to be assessed.

Steps 1, 2 and 3 concern the chemistry and physics of nutrient depletion, while steps 4 and 5 deal with economic aspects.

Soil nutrient pools
Following an approach described by Pieri (1989) and Frissel (1978), the chemical elements in the soil are classified as present in one of three pools:
• Pool A: minerals available to plants
• Pool B: elements present in soil organic matter
• Pool C: mineral reserves in the soil.

The flow of elements in and out of the system, and between these pools, is shown in Figure 1. Not all the chemical elements in the soil are available to plants. Those in pool A can be used directly, and, because we are interested in nutrient availability over the long term, those present in organic matter (pool B) can be considered together with those in pool A. To a great extent these two pools determine the fertility of the soil. Since it is the overall balance that is of interest, the internal exchanges (fluxes) between the available pool and the organic pool are not described. These fluxes occur in a yearly cycle: mineralization (breakdown into mineral constituents) of organic matter, during the early rainy season; production of organic matter that will be returned to the soil in the form of plant roots and litter later during the same season; and immobilization of nutrients in organic matter at the end of the season. This cycle is important for annual crop growth, but does not describe the long-term trend in soil fertility. In the long term, over periods of 10 to 20 years, the two pools are more or less in equilibrium: the depletion of available nutrients is buffered by the mineralization of organic matter, and vice versa.

Elements in pool C, the mineral reserve, cannot be counted as available nutrients. Those that become available, due to weathering for example, are treated simply as inputs to pool A. They are assumed to become available at a constant rate. Irreversible fixation, mainly of phosphorus and potassium, is theoretically possible and would be a source of inputs to this pool.

Figure 1 Soil nutrient pools and flows

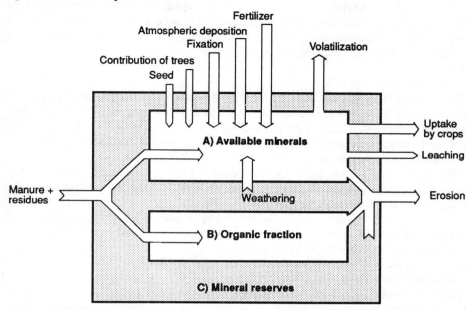

Source: Frissel (1978); Pieri (1989)

In the current approach the following processes will be taken into account as affecting the nutrient balance:

• Export of nutrients:
    export of elements taken up by crops
    losses due to leaching
    losses due to erosion
    losses due to volatilization/denitrification
    irreversible fixation of phosphorus and potassium.

• Import of nutrients:
    fertilizer application
    organic manuring
    return of crop residues
    biological nitrogen fixation (with legume crops)
    asymbiotic nitrogen fixation
    recycling of leached nutrients and biological fixation by trees
    deposition of nutrients from the atmosphere through rain and dust
    dissolution of soil minerals
    elements present in seeds.

For a given element, the difference between the amount exported and the amount imported equals the nutrient balance in the soil. Of course, this balance varies from year to year, according to factors such as the amount of rainfall received, which affects exports through leaching and crop harvests, or the cash income of the farmer, which affects the amount of inputs purchased and applied.

Economic evaluation

The elements in pools A and B can be considered to have an economic value equal to that of an equivalent amount of fertilizer. Thus, in valuing each element, we must take into account its net nutrient balance per hectare and its market price as fertilizer per kilogramme. The value of the overall nutrient deficit or surplus can then be calculated by adding the values for the specific elements.

The value of the nutrient deficit for a given area will be an absolute. To assess how easy or difficult it will be to correct a deficit, this absolute value must be compared to the income farmers obtain from agricultural activities.

Finally, to assess the sustainability of farming in a broader sense, we define the farmer income sustainability quotient as the proportion of farmer income that would remain if the farmer had to meet all environmental costs.

Optimistic and pessimistic views

Three nutrient balances have been calculated (Table 1). The first is the most probable value, based on our knowledge of the soils and rainfall in the various countries of West Africa, and how these compare to southern Mali. This balance in our opinion best reflects the current nutrient balance of the region. The second balance, called the 'optimistic' balance, has been calculated by combining low estimates of nutrient exports with high estimates of imports. The third balance, the 'pessimistic' one, combines high values for exports with low values for imports. These two values, the data for which were selected from the literature on West Africa and from production statistics for southern Mali, indicate the range within which the real value is expected (with 95% probability) to fall.

It must be emphasized that the term 'most probable value' does not mean this value is highly likely to be accurate. Instead it is the best we were able to come up with, given available information. The conclusions of this study must remain tentative, because our knowledge of the processes involved in the import and export of nutrients is still rudimentary. The estimates used are based on the best available data—but they remain estimates. Indeed, the optimistic and pessimistic estimates differ by amounts of the same order of magnitude as the most probable value.

Losses due to erosion are an important source of uncertainty for all elements. Uncertainty regarding the inputs from atmospheric deposition (rain and dust) and from the weathering of soil minerals is also high. For nitrogen, gaseous losses and uptake by the various crops are not known accurately, while for potassium the proportion of crop residues returned to the soil is a source of uncertainty.

Nutrient Balances

Balances have been calculated for the five chemical elements N, P, K, Ca and Mg for the main crops grown in southern Mali. The results are presented in Table 1 and Figure 2. Figure 2 provides a breakdown for the various processes that influence the nutrient balance of the three main elements, N, P and K. The upper hemisphere of each pie chart shows imports; the lower hemisphere shows exports. Note also the deficit between imports and exports; this shows the extent of nutrient depletion.

The table indicates that N and K are the most deficient elements, with negative balances of –25 and –20 kg/ha respectively. Losses are substantial (25 and 17 kg/ha), amounting respectively to 47% and 36% of total nutrient outflow. These losses are mainly due to erosion and volatilization, which account for 17% and 22% of total nitrogen exports respectively. Leaching losses are relatively low, but highly available soluble components are lost. Atmospheric deposition and weathering of minerals in the soil are still important inputs, estimated to contribute as much nitrogen, phosphorus and potassium as organic and mineral fertilizer applications combined.

Table 1 Nutrient balances per hectare calculated for southern Mali, 1988-89

	Balance (kg/ha)				
	N	P	K	Ca	Mg
Probable value	–25	0	–20	+3	–5
Optimistic value	–14	+2	–10	+12	0
Pessimistic value	–40	–2	–33	–8	–10

For N, the most probable value in Table 1 suggests that about 25 kg/ha are removed from the soil each year. Even if we take the optimistic view, the balance for the region is negative. The high nitrogen deficit shown in Figure 2 is caused mainly by the uptake by traditional cereal crops, millet and sorghum. However, the deficits for cotton and maize showed that N fertilizer application for these crops was also far from sufficient. Under present levels of exploitation, even the N balance for fallow land (mostly short-term fallow) was also slightly negative.

For P, the situation is less dramatic than for N. The balance for the region is roughly in equilibrium. Fertilizer applications to cotton compensate for the uptake by cereals, which commonly receive no fertilizer inputs.

For K, the balance resembles that of N. Even in the most optimistic view, it is negative. About 20 kg K/ha is extracted yearly from the soil. As in the case of N, most exports occur in the form of uptake by the unfertilized cereal crops millet and sorghum, but the fertilizer applied to maize and cotton also contains insufficient K.

Figure 2 Breakdown of nutrient balances

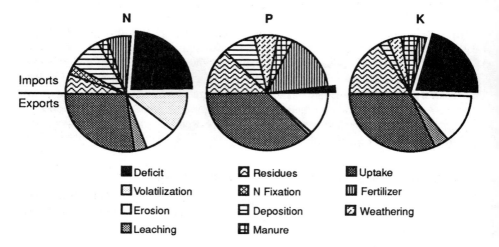

These data suggest that, on average, using present farming systems, soils in southern Mali can be cultivated for about 30 years before their productive capacities break down. However, there will be substantial variations. Nitrogen is liable to be the element most quickly exhausted, because the soil's organic matter is the only reserve that can be used to make up the deficit. A clear consequence of soil mining appears to be a gradual decrease in the organic matter content of the soil, with the accompanying chemical and physical problems this brings.

Caveat
Most of the nutrient balances calculated in this study appear negative, indicating that nutrients are being depleted from the soil. However, this does not automatically mean that additional fertilizer applications should be recommended. Firstly, fertilizer influences the processes on which the nutrient balance depends. For example, applying more fertilizer increases yields; as a result, crops extract still more nutrients. Higher doses may also increase the losses caused by leaching and volatilization. Again, the extra vegetation that results may reduce the losses caused by erosion and leaching. Secondly, recommending higher doses could be technically wrong, as well as economically impractical. Double

doses of fertilizer for local millet or sorghum varieties, for example, often lead only to increased losses. Thus nutrient balances cannot be translated directly into practical solutions to the many problems associated with sustaining the region's agricultural productivity. They may nevertheless constitute an important diagnostic tool, clarifying the consequences of farming for soils.

Impact of technical options
To what extent can these nutrient deficits be overcome through technological interventions? For the reasons outlined above, only a rough indication can be given. Moreover, we should note that:
• The nitrogen deficit of 25 kg N/ha is high, compared to the average amount of N fertilizer used in the region, which is only 10 kg/ha (7 and 3 kg N/ha of mineral fertilizer and organic manure respectively)
• The potassium deficit of 20 kg K/ha is also very large, average doses being 2 kg and 3 kg/ha for mineral fertilizer and manure respectively.

Figure 3 illustrates the positive effects on N and K deficits that might be expected from four types of intervention: reducing erosion losses by half; increasing the return of crop residues by half; doubling the application of organic manure; and doubling the application of mineral fertilizer.

Although the interventions chosen are fairly drastic, no single intervention alone bridges the nutrient deficit to any substantial degree. Even the combination of all four would not be enough.

Economic Evaluation

Sustainability of agriculture as a whole
Table 2 shows the value of nutrient deficits in CFA francs, calculated using 1989 prices for nutrients purchased as mineral fertilizer. The value of the average deficit is alarmingly high: FCFA 15 175/ha (US$ 59/ha), or about 40% of the income of an average farmer.

This suggests that, given the productive capacity of the soil, only about 60% of a farmer's income is sustainable (sustainability quotient 0.6). For the rest, he or she is in essence taking out a loan against future productive capacity.

Part of the solution is to increase farmers' applications of fertilizer and manure. Average investment in fertilizer at present is low (FCFA 4500/ha, or US$ 17.5/ha). In an area where fallow-based systems are being replaced by permanent cultivation, increased efforts are needed to maintain soil fertility.

Reducing the nutrient losses caused by erosion, leaching and volatilization/denitrification would also help. The value of these losses is also high: FCFA 17 900 (US$ 70)/ha, or 50% of farmer income. Clearly, any decrease in these losses would contribute significantly to improved sustainability.

Figure 3 Effects of different interventions on nitrogen and potassium deficits

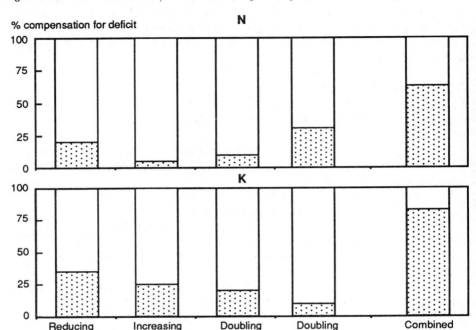

Sustainability of specific cropping systems

Table 2 also describes the sustainability of various cropping systems, which can be compared with the average situation for the region as a whole, described above. The values for the current cotton-maize-sorghum system are shown. These can be compared with the values obtained for the same system using the amounts of fertilizer recommended by the extension service, and with the values for a groundnut-millet-millet system, also using recommended amounts of fertilizer. Data for an unfertilized millet-fallow system are also given (4 years millet + 4 years fallow).

In absolute terms, the deficits are about the same for all systems. However, some systems offer higher returns than others, and thus more scope for investment in soil fertility. This makes their potential sustainability greater.

For the recommended cotton-maize-sorghum system, the value of the deficit is nearly FCFA 3000/ha, mainly due to the cost of lime (needed to neutralize the acidification caused by urea and ammonium). Farmer income under this system is about FCFA 61 000 /ha, giving a sustainability quotient of 0.95. This figure is in line with that

Table 2 Sustainability characteristics of four crop rotations in Southern Mali

	CMDT [1] average	Cotton-maize sorghum		Groundnut-millet-millet	Millet-fallow
		Actual	Recommended		
Balance in kg/ha					
N	–25	–27	–2	–35	–35
P	0	0	7	1	–1
K	–20	–18	1	–28	–23
Lime	–12	–35	–72	–4	0
Balance in FCFA/ha					
N	–7875	–8600	–662	–10868	–10899
P	0	100	1675	300	–250
K	–6500	–5753	325	–9100	–7410
Lime	–720	–2082	–4320	–240	0
NDMV [2]	15095	16334	2982	19908	18559
Gross margin agricultural activities	34200	60162	60977	32625	18750
Nutrient depletion ratio	44	27	5	61	99
Sustainability qotient	0.56	0.73	0.95	0.39	0.01
Investment in fertilizer	4483	11844	21550	5708	0
% of gross income	11	16	25	15	0
Other investment	1461	3307	3307	0	0
Market value of losses	17899	18963	18963	18648	9831

Note: Costs in FCFA; all data calculated per hectare
1. Compagnie Malienne de Développement du Coton
2. Nutrient deficit market value

obtained in long-term fertilizer trials at the N'Tarla experimental station. Compared with the other systems, investment in fertilizer is high, amounting to 25% of gross income. This system is potentially sustainable, but this does not mean that improvements in soil fertility can be expected. Only a small percentage of farmers will actually be able to apply the doses recommended, especially with respect to manure. If all farmers were to apply the recommended dose of manure, three times the current cattle population of the area would be required simply to fertilize the cotton crop! In any case, increased use of inputs is not likely, because the gross margin of the system using recommended doses is not much higher than that of the current system.

For the recommended groundnut-millet system, the cost of depleted nutrients is nearly FCFA 20 000/ha. Farmer income under this system is just under FCFA 33 000/ha, producing a sustainability quotient of only 0.39. It is not clear to what extent earnings from groundnut or millet could offset the costs of replacing lost nutrients. The sustainability quotient of the millet-fallow system is even less favourable. The system relies almost totally on soil mining, having a quotient of about 0.01.

In comparison with nutrient losses, the average annual investment in mineral fertilizers (FCFA 4500 or US$ 17.5/ha) is low: a mere 11% of gross income from agricultural activities.

Conclusions

These results give no grounds for optimism. Increased investment in maintaining soil fertility is desperately needed.

The value of nutrients lost due to erosion, leaching and volatilization appear about as high as the value of nutrients present in crops. Significant gains could be made by applying erosion control measures and by introducing cropping systems with a more closed vegetative cover (van der Pol 1985; Budelman and Huisman 1990).

A second important approach would be to develop ways of applying fertilizer and manure that are better adapted to the conditions actually found in farmers' fields. In other words, location-specific fertilizer recommendations should be developed. However, if these are to prove effective, farmers' managerial capacities also need to be improved. Farmers must be able to adapt the amount and timing of their fertilizer applications to specific circumstances, especially weather conditions.

References

Berckmoes, W., E. Jager and Y. Kone. 1988. L'intensification agricole au Mali-sud: Souhait ou réalité? University of Arkansas, Fayetteville, FSRE Symposium. DRSPR, Sikasso, Mali/KIT, Amsterdam, The Netherlands.

Broekhuyse, J.T.H., 1983. Les transformations du pays Mossi. Amsterdam: KIT, internal report.

Budelman, A. and A. Huisman. 1991. Towards a systems perspective. In: *Making haste slowly*. Royal Tropical Institute, Amsterdam.

Dupriez, H. and P. Thevenin. 1977. Amélioration de la productivité cotonière et développement intégré en zone sud du Chad: Evaluation ex-post pour le compte du FED.

Frissel, M.J. 1978. *Cycling of mineral nutrients in agricultural ecosystems*. London, Elsevier.

Pieri, C. 1989. Fertilité des terres savanes: Bilan de trente ans de recherche et de développement agricoles au sud du Sahara. Ministère de la Coopération and CIRAD-IRAT, Paris, France.

Pol, F., van der. 1985. Rapid production increase and sustainability: Proceedings of the Conference of Ministers on the Realization of Africa's Potential for Food Production. CTA, Ede-Wageningen, The Netherlands.

Source

First published 1992 as *Bulletin* 325 of the Royal Tropical Institute, Amsterdam. Reprinted by kind permission of the author and publisher.

Address

Floris Van der Pol, Agricultural Division, Royal Tropical Institute, Mauritskade 63, 1092 AD Amsterdam, The Netherlands.

Labour Costs: A Critical Element in Soil Conservation

Michael Stocking and Nick Abel

Introduction

Labour is an inextricable part of soil conservation. Yet, in the design of soil conservation schemes, work and manpower requirements are often a forgotten factor. If they are included at all, their cost is usually wrongly estimated. For example, in the digging of a Fanya juu terrace, the prime requirement is labour—lots of it. This labour has a value, not least in other opportunities foregone in order to shovel soil. Certain groups in society—and not necessarily those whose labour is most cheaply provided—supply the labour: womens' groups, small farm households. They suffer the cost of its provision.

New thinking is in vogue in soil conservation (Moldenhauer and Hudson 1988), stressing the perspectives and needs of the land user. Nevertheless, the emphasis is still very much on 'the effective delivery of soil conservation techniques' (Sheng and Meiman 1988, p.29). We are still not focusing on what the farm family can do realistically and rationally with available resources. The majority of land users in Africa and the rest of the developing world are resource-poor farmers. These, almost by definition, possess little or no capital. Virtually the only factor they can apply to soil conservation is their labour. But are they willing to do so?

Various attitudes are adopted with regard to labour. The whole approach to soil conservation on small farms in Kenya is predicated on the ready availability of labour and the willingness of land users to employ labour-intensive methods (Wenner 1980). A typical technical attitude to labour is expressed by Sheng (1986a, p.19): 'terracing by manual labour is ... (the) kind of labour-intensive programme which will be good for most of the developing countries. This type of technology ... uses more labour and relatively less capital to alleviate the unemployment problem on one hand and protect the soil resources... on the other.' In other words, minimal value is ascribed to labour, and its greater use is counted as a benefit, not a cost.

Another typical technical attitude is that soil conservation is an activity for the dry season, when there is a lull in agricultural activities and slack demand for labour. However, as a detailed analysis for Embu-Meru in Kenya shows, this lull is only partial (Barrett 1985). Many other off-farm activities take place in the dry season, especially since transport is much easier then. Promoting soil conservation as a beneficial activity that uses labour surpluses in the dry season can therefore be mistaken.

Land users themselves clearly have a different attitude to the provision of their labour. In the Khatmandu Valley of Nepal farmers have been reported to have a wide fund of knowledge on soil erosion control techniques. Many farmers distinguish between ideal measures and feasible measures. Decisions as to techniques and the intensity of land use are not based on the maximization of total production but on the marginal returns to household labour.

In line with the concern that inadequate consideration of labour is a common cause of failure in soil conservation schemes, this paper looks firstly at how such labour might be appraised. The focus is on 'peasant economics', where the family is the main source of labour and various subjective criteria peculiar to individual households will influence its supply and demand. Secondly, we present evidence of how labour has been valued in a sample of projects. We conclude with recommendations to make the design and appraisal of soil conservation schemes more rigorous.

Economic and Financial Perspectives

Two valuation perspectives need to be considered in relation to soil conservation work: the economic and the financial. The economic perspective concerns changes in the economy as a whole resulting either from the implementation of soil conservation, or from land degradation in the case of non-implementation. Economic prices then reflect society's willingness to pay to protect its soil resources. They frequently differ from market prices because of market distortions (for example, a minimal wage policy; a fertilizer subsidy), or the absence of any market in the case of externalities (for example, the siltation of a reservoir by upstream land users).

The financial perspective deals with changes in the income and expenditure of a household, group or region due to the implementation of soil conservation works. For example, one would monitor whether a household could afford to divert labour to soil conservation from other activities, such as charcoal production or toddy-tapping. Financial prices are market prices, and reflect the costs to the budgets of a peasant household or other group.

Further problems of particular relevance to financially insecure households, and hence to soil conservation, relate to the timing of benefits versus that of costs. Poor households cannot usually afford to wait for the delayed benefits of conservation, even when these outweigh present costs.

This paper will address the financial (private) perspective. But it should be remembered that in a wider discussion one should compare the economic (social) and financial perspectives, which are likely to be different. It may, for example, be economically viable for the government to promote soil conservation, but irrational for the individual to take it up (or vice versa).

Financial Costing of Labour

A peasant household, having access to land and using family labour, produces most of its food and other needs, but also has some market involvement. The more that profit-maximizing is an household aim, the more amenable the household is to financial analysis through cost-benefit analysis.

Adopting soil conservation requires additional labour. Should the cost of this be included in financial analysis? The answer depends on the circumstances:
• If soil conservation takes up leisure time and no other activity is reduced, its opportunity cost is zero. Communal digging and weeding parties are essentially a social occasion. Financially, the labour is 'free'
• If another enterprise is curtailed in order to practise soil conservation, the cost is the income to labour which would have accrued from that enterprise. For example, if the construction and maintenance of tied-ridges prevents the production of cotton, then the cost of tied-ridging is the income that the cotton harvest would have generated, less the cost of non-labour inputs
• If off-farm work is abandoned, then similarly the cost is the earnings foregone
• If workers would have been otherwise employed, then the cost is their wage.

Thus the financial costs and benefits of labour vary enormously according to the circumstances. For the small-farm household engaging in soil conservation activities, the following issues are especially relevant and need to be considered in financial valuation:

Cooperative labour
Significant advantages and cost savings can be gained if small quantities of leisure are combined into useful units of labour. Cooperative labour allows:
• Better planning, since achievements become more predictable. Output from the strong and weak, the healthy and ill, cancel out to give a predictable quantity and quality of labour—an important consideration in watershed conservation planning
• A 'complementation effect', whereby each individual adds his work to the whole work, while only the whole work is useful to each individual. An individual may be able to dig 10 m of cut-off drain, but only if 20 individuals cooperate digging 10 m each will the drain perform its design function
• Combination of labour. Heavy tasks, such as construction of stone terraces or rooting out tree stumps, are impossible for individuals working alone
• Concentration of labour on a single task which must be finished within a critical period—for example, constructing a dam before it rains
• Pooling of technical knowledge and experience. Each person's knowledge complements that of others, so that the group is in a stronger position to evaluate outside advice and make better decisions, for example on the alignment of contours or the reallocation of land

• Encouragement. Many people working together provide a greater incentive for effort than the lone individual.

These advantages of cooperation in agriculture apply with particular force to conservation works, which often require large amounts of labour for construction and continuing cooperation between neighbours for their efficient functioning and maintenance. Potential returns to labour in communal or cooperative ventures can be large, and are probably always greater than in comparable individual enterprises.

Social differentiation

This affects the opportunity cost of labour. Wealthy producers have different labour allocation strategies to those of the poor. In Botswana, Flint (1986) noted that poverty encourages the pursuit of off-farm opportunities such as pottery, beer making and casual labour. One consequence of not being able to brew beer was that women could not then host work parties, and could not undertake operations such as soil conservation which are better done with cooperative labour. Labour constraints can, therefore, have considerable knock-on effects, increasing social differentiation and making soil conservation more problematical.

Differentiation also occurs within the household. The productivity of labour, and hence its value, varies according to age, gender and education (Low 1986). Young males, particularly the educated, can get relatively well paid work off farm. They migrate and remit cash. Older men return to the farm to enjoy the fruits of their earlier remittances. Women tend to remain on the farm because of child rearing and their comparative disadvantage in the labour market. The function of the farm in these circumstances is not income generation or food production, but provision of a rent-free place to live with free fuel and communal pastures on which to keep the cattle in which remittances are invested (Abel et al. 1987). In these circumstances farm improvement, including soil conservation, is of minimal importance, competing for labour with the domestic commitments of women and the higher formal wages of men. Hence, the opportunity cost of labour for conservation is high.

Seasonal variation

Labour bottlenecks can raise the opportunity cost of labour for soil conservation. Failure to plant or to weed on time may jeopardize the whole season's production, and these tasks may therefore take precedence over soil conservation works. Labour bottlenecks are especially critical in several techniques of soil conservation. For example, tied-ridges need to be reconstructed annually at the time of land preparation and sowing.

The allocation of tasks within the household can accentuate seasonal variation if, for example, only women do weeding and maintenance activities during the growing season. It is often the case that intensive home gardens are managed by women, and the more erodible, extensive areas are farmed by men.

Although it may appear that the costing of labour inputs to soil conservation on small farms is extremely complex and varied, we suggest that the problem is amenable to analysis. Financial costings can be calculated by carefully classifying households, and selecting the relevant criteria for each category.

Costing of Labour in Soil Conservation

Labour requirements for soil conservation
Table 1 lists the person-days per hectare required for various soil conservation works. Labour requirements are highly variable, and depend on the method, details of construction, slope and environment.

Unfortunately, information on purely biological methods such as grass strips, agroforestry and intercropping is lacking, but it may safely be assumed that these are the least demanding. Live barriers in El-Salvador take about 40 person-days, and grass strips probably about the same. Conservation systems which only require shaping of the soil surface during normal tillage need up to about 120 person-days/ha. Tied-ridging, which is being promoted in East and Central Africa, needs about 100 person-days/ha, and this will be a regular annual requirement since the ridges need to be reconstructed every planting season (which perhaps accounts for the poor adoption of this system). The highest requirements are for terraces, especially the irrigated, stone-faced structures found in South-East Asia. It is no coincidence that these same areas (for example, Java) have very high population densities and hence relatively low opportunity costs for labour. Even in areas of high population, however, it remains to be calculated whether this enormous demand for labour can be supported, given the low output from degraded lands.

Very few studies report on the labour required for the maintenance of structures and waterways, but the figure for Jamaican bench terraces, at about 40 person-days/ha, provides some guidance.

Price tags on labour
Bojö (1986; 1989) reviewed 20 economic studies of soil conservation, including the way in which they deal with the costing of labour. He identifies the shadow pricing of labour as a major issue, and shows that most studies find that the social profitability (i.e. the value to the whole national economy) of engaging in soil conservation is higher than the private (financial) profitability. The reason is that the economic opportunity cost of labour is nearly always set much lower than the market wage. But almost without exception, research and investigation into the perceived value of labour at household level is lacking. There remains a large field of research here which needs to be undertaken before the viability of specific techniques of soil conservation on small farms can be accurately assessed.

Table 1 Labour requirements (person-days) for soil conservation

Country	Conservation type	Slope (%)	Labour	Source
Thailand[1]	Bench terraces (4m wide)		500	Sheng 1986b
	Hillside ditches	≤40	100	
	Orchard terraces (1.75m wide)		112	
	Individual hand-dug basins (200/ha)		12	
	Contour dykes		100	
	Grassed waterway	≤20	18[2]	
Peru	Terraces with grass-planted side slopes (Abancay):			Alfaro-Moreno 1988
	• terraces		336[2]	
	• contour furrows		110[2]	
	• infiltration ditch		205[2]	
	Terraces with stone side slopes (Cuzco):			
	• terraces		1181	
	• contour furrows		328	
	• infiltration ditch		57	
India (Northeast)	Establishment of terrace cultivation		696[3]	Mishra and Ramakrishnan 1981
Indonesia (Java)	Bench terraces	< 50	750-1800[4]	Barbier 1988
Vietnam	Full agroforestry and soil conservation system:			Field notes
	• tree planting		1500[2]	
	• annual maintenance		55[2]	

Note: All figures are annual requirements. Labour for initial construction, except where indicated
1. Theoretical calculations for typical conservation systems in the north of the country
2. Maintenance measures over and above first year of establishment
3. Based on quoted labour wage and 75% of work done by women
4. Labour dependent on slope. Costed at 1979 prices at US$ 420-2060/ha plus $560-2075/ha for planting materials tools and fertilizers

Table 1 Continued

Country	Conservation type	Slope (%)	Labour	Source
Kenya[5] (high-potential area)	Fanya Juu terrace	5 10 35	136 250 281	Wenner 1980
Kenya (Embu-Meru)	Fanya Juu terrace	5	150	Barrett 1985
El Salvador (Acelhuate River catchment)	Hillside ditches, vegetation, protected main drains	20 30 40	84 114 143	Wall 1981
	Rock wall barriers with drains	20 30 40	253 279 310	
	Bench terracing with masonry-protected main drains	20 30 40	238 266 283	
	Live barriers	20 40	40 43	
Honduras	Biological (with intermediate technology): • maize/cassava/beans intercrop • maize/cassava and terrace		148[6] 207[6]	Rodriguez 1980
Jamaica	Bench terraces (for 1 farm, 0.8 acre)	13	496 42[7]	Sheng 1986b

Note: All figures are annual requirements. Labour for initial construction, except where indicated
5. Estimates based on quoted labour costs, to which should be added the cost of cut-off drains (approx. 60 person-days/ha based on a figure of 200 m of drain needed per hectare)
6. Additional labour over maize monocrop
7. *See* note 2, opposite

Conclusions and Recommendations

The availability of labour is a principal constraining factor in the acceptance or rejection of soil conservation. Labour-intensive techniques are only readily taken up and maintained on prosperous farms with a regular income from cash crops. Elsewhere, soil conservation structures are fewer and in poorer repair, even though farmer response is positive as to their value. Tjernström (1989) provides profiles of small farm households practising different technical standards of soil conservation in Kitiu District, Kenya:

• 'Proper' soil conservation: actively engaged, full-time, working married couple, with both husband and wife having had some agricultural training
• 'Acceptable' soil conservation: farm families in which generally the female members of varying age do most of the agricultural work
• 'Poor' soil conservation: typically, a female farmer living alone with children; if there is a husband living elsewhere, he provides minimal remittances; there are insufficient resources to exchange labour with friends and relatives; there is great dependence on informal-sector activities such as basket-making.

While not the sole factor, the availability of labour is the major differentiating criterion between 'proper' and 'poor' soil conservation. Differentiation becomes greater the more labour-intensive the conservation techniques are. As we have seen, there is enormous variability in labour requirements for conservation and this leaves open the possibility of choosing techniques to match the household rather than just the environment. Tjernström also shows that the returns to investment in soil conservation, both privately and socially, can be very good, but because of labour constraints these returns are only available to specific types of farm household, generally the wealthy.

A major priority in evaluating soil conservation programmes must be to predict the applicability of specific techniques for different groups in society. We recommend that:
• Assessments of labour requirements are routinely made for all small-scale, labour-intensive systems of soil conservation
• At the very least, analyses of returns to labour are carried out; that is, the additional output from household labour invested in soil conservation should be calculated
• Cost-benefit analyses of soil conservation should include in their decision criteria estimates of the returns to all three factors in soil conservation—land, labour and capital—so that these can be compared in their contribution to the benefits. The overall benefits should be calculated from both economic (social) and financial (private) perspectives. Only in this way can the true cost of labour be assessed and incorporated into the planning of acceptable and successful soil conservation schemes.

References

Abel, N.O.J., M.E.S. Flint, N.D. Hunter, D. Chandler and G. Maka, 1987. Cattle-keeping, ecological change and communal management in Ngwaketse, Vol.2: Main Report. Overseas Development Group, University of East Anglia; Integrated Farming Pilot Project, Ministry of Agriculture, Gaborone; International Livestock Centre for Africa, Addis Ababa.

Alfaro Moreno, J.C. 1988. Farmer income and soil conservation in the Peruvian Andes. Paper presented at the Fifth International Soil Conservation Conference, Bangkok.

Barbier, E. 1988. The economics of farm-level adoption of soil conservation measures in the uplands of Java. Environment Department Working Paper No.11, Policy Planning and Research Staff, World Bank, Washington D.C.

Barrett, A.T. 1985. Appraisal of the proposed dryland farming project for Embu and Meru Districts of Kenya. Overseas Development Administration, Land Resources Development Centre, Tolworth, U.K.

Bojö, J. 1986. A review of cost-benefit studies of soil and water conservation projects. Report No.3, SADCC Soil and Water Conservation and Land Utilization Programme, Maseru, Lesotho.

Bojö, J. 1989. Cost-benefit analysis of soil and water conservation projects. A review of 20 empirical studies. Paper presented at the Sixth International Conference on Soil Conservation, Addis Ababa.

Flint, M.E.S. 1986. Crop and livestock production in the Pelotshetla Lands Area. Main report of the 1982/1983 IFAP Farm Management Survey, Integrated Farming Pilot Project. Ministry of Agriculture, Gaborone.

Low, A. 1986. *Agricultural development in Southern Africa: Farm household theory and the food crisis.* James Currey, London.

Mishra, B.K. and Ramakrishnan, P.S. 1981. The economic yield and energy efficiency of hill agro-ecosystems at higher elevations of Meghalaya in north-eastern India. *Acta Ecologica* 2(4): 369-389.

Moldenhauer, W.C. and N. W. Hudson (eds). 1988. Conservation farming on steep lands. Soil and Water Conservation Society, Ankeny, Iowa.

Rodriguez, E. 1980. Manual de cultivos multiples en obras de conservacion de suelos. Working Document No.4, Ordenacion Integrada de Cuencas Hidrograficas Proyecto PNUD/FAO/HON/77/006, Tegulcigalpa, Honduras.

Sheng, T.C. 1986a. Bench terracing. In: Watershed conservation: A collection of papers for developing countries. Chinese Soil and Water Conservation Society, Taipei, Taiwan.

Sheng, T.C. 1986b. The need for soil conservation structures for steep cultivated slopes in the humid tropics. In: Watershed conservation: A collection of papers for developing countries. Chinese Soil and Water Conservation Society, Taipei, Taiwan.

Sheng, T.C. and Meiman, J.R. 1988. Planning and implementing soil conservation projects. In: W.C. Moldenhauer and N.W. Hudson (eds.), Conservation farming on steep lands. Soil and Water Conservation Society, Ankeny, Iowa.

Tjernström, R. 1989. Report on technical and socio-economic evaluation of soil conservation by The Ministry of Agriculture and Livestock Development. In: D. B. Thomas et al. (eds), Soil conservation in Kenya. Department of Agricultural Engineering, University of Nairobi, and Swedish International Development Authority. Nairobi.

Wall, J.R.D. (ed.) 1981. A management plan for the Acelhuate River catchment, El Salvador: Soil conservation, river stabilisation and water pollution control. Land Resource Study 30, Land Resources Development Centre, Tolworth.

Wenner, C-G. 1980. Soil conservation in Kenya, especially in small-scale farming in high-potential areas using labour-intensive methods. Ministry of Agriculture, Nairobi.

Source
Paper presented at the Sixth International Soil Conservation Conference, Addis Ababa, Ethiopia, November 1989. Reprinted by kind permission of the authors.

Addresses
Michael Stocking: School of Development Studies University of East Anglia, Norwich NR4 7TJ, United Kingdom.

Nick Abel: Department of Applied Science, University of Canberra, P.O. Box 1, Belconnen ACT 2616, Australia.

Sustainability Issues with Intercrops

Charles A. Francis

Introduction

Sustaining the yields of intercrops and the income derived from them is the key challenge faced by farmers and, increasingly, by researchers. Much of our past investment in research has been dedicated to improving the productivity of monoculture systems, on the assumption that such systems achieve the highest yields and the most efficient use of resources. Most new technology has been developed and tested in monoculture systems. Yet increasing numbers of scientists are questioning whether this is the only possible route to increased and more sustainable food production. A recent publication, *Enhancing Agriculture in Africa* (Office of Technology Assessment 1988), notes that agricultural systems in Africa that were once sustainable are now breaking down, no longer meeting the rising demand for food and income. The report suggests that high priority be given to ensuring:

- Environmental, economic, social and institutional sustainability
- The targeting of aid to benefit resource-poor producers
- The participation of female as well as male farmers in the planning and implementation of projects; and
- Sound natural resource management, to benefit future generations.

How does intercropping help to meet these objectives? And how do its effects differ from those of monoculture? Before these questions can be discussed, it is essential to define 'sustainability'. This is difficult because of our lack of consensus on the time-frame to be used, because of the unpredictability of the future availability and cost of resources, and of how technology will be used and by whom in agriculture. More simply put, we would need to agree on a set of conditions—the costs of fossil fuels, acceptable limits on environmental disturbance, health and safety for human beings and other species—to be maintained over a defined period of time.

Harwood (1989) suggests an 'umbrella' definition of sustainable agriculture as 'an agriculture that can evolve indefinitely toward greater human utility, greater efficiency of resource use and a balance with the environment that is favourable both to humans and to most other species'. Although this is a useful definition within which to work, it is necessary to be more explicit about which practices and systems fall under this umbrella.

In a practical, research-based extension program in Nebraska, we have used an operational definition of sustainable agriculture as 'a management strategy which helps the producer to choose hybrids and varieties, a soil fertility package, a pest management approach, a tillage system, and a crop rotation to reduce costs of purchased inputs, minimize the impact of the system on the immediate and the off-farm environment, and provide a sustained level of production and profit from farming' (Francis et al. 1987). In this definition there is a need to adapt the terminology used to the production system or research programme concerned, so once again the definition is not perfect, but at least it provides us with a practical starting point.

Biological Sustainability

Conventional ecological wisdom suggests that natural ecosystems are relatively stable because of their genetic and biological diversity. Some authors (for example, Goodman 1975; Loomis 1984) question this relationship, failing to find clear evidence that diversity always makes a system more stable. The left hand side of Figure 1 shows that a range of diversity occurs in natural ecosystems (Francis 1986). These are all climax vegetation patterns, representing an evolution to some degree of stability or sustainability under specific climatic conditions.

A parallel range of diversity (and, we assume, stability) in cropping systems is shown on the right hand side of Figure 1. The most diverse systems are those employing dozens of species in shifting cultivation or the mixtures of 10-15 crops typical of the tropical forest zone of West Africa. The three-crop combinations found in many farming systems in Africa represent an intermediate degree of diversity. The least genetically diverse systems are monoculture maize or wheat in temperate regions. The susceptibility of such monocultures to disease is illustrated by the Irish potato famine and by the attack of Southern corn leaf blight in the USA (Adams et al. 1971). Having identified this range of genetic diversity in cropping systems, what can we conclude about their stability or sustainability?

Results that demonstrate stability statistically are scarce. Experiments in Colombia with maize and beans in 20 environments (Francis et al. 1978) and in India with sorghum and pigeonpea in 94 environments (Rao and Willey 1980) suggest that intercropped cereal/grain legume crops are more stable than monoculture. Table 1 shows both higher yields and lower coefficients of variation from the intercrops than from the sole crops (Smith and Francis 1986). Data from many of the same sorghum/pigeonpea trials are shown graphically in Figure 2 (from Mead 1986). All points above the line with slope 1.00 demonstrate superior yields obtained by the intercrop system. Relative yield totals for the intercrop were determined by assuming a price ratio of 1.8 to 1 for pigeonpea to sorghum—the ratio obtaining in India at the time of the experiments. From these scarce data, we can tentatively conclude that intercrops are more stable in terms of yield and income, and thus potentially more sustainable in a biological sense, than their contrasting sole crop alternatives.

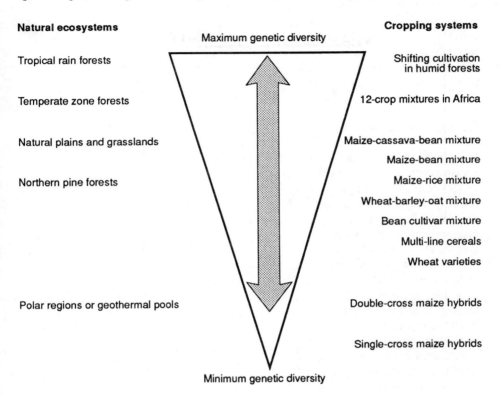

Figure 1 Spectrum of genetic diversity in natural ecosystems and cropping systems

Economic Sustainability

The economic stability or sustainability of cropping systems is even more difficult to predict or analyze than biological sustainability. In addition to the variable and unpredictable climate, factors such as input costs, prices received at harvest, interest rates, and numerous other 'externalities' to the farm become involved. Effects of the interactions of three factors (maize yields, bean yields, and the price ratio of beans to maize) are shown in Figure 3. Three monocrop bean yield levels (4, 3 and 1.2 t/ha) and three intercrop bean yield levels (2, 1.2 and 0.4 t/ha) represent maximum experimental yields, average experimental yields and average on-farm yields respectively. Maize yields were the same in monoculture and when intercropped with beans in these trials. Bean/maize price ratios from 1 to 8 were plotted, representing the range occurring in Latin America at the time of the trials. Net income was highest for monocropped beans at all price ratios above 3, assuming maximum experimental yields; if average experimental yields were assumed,

Figure 2 Bivariate plot of returns to sorghum/pigeonpea intercrop and to monocropped sorghum (51 experiments)

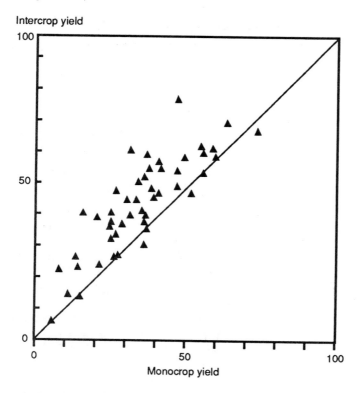

Source: S.P. Singh, All-India Coordinated Sorghum Improvement Project (unpublished data)

it was highest at all ratios above 4. However, when average on-farm yields were assumed, the advantage of the intercrop extended up to a price ratio of more than 7; this indicated a rational economic basis for resource-poor farmers to continue with the intercrop system.

Further evidence of why farmers use intercrop systems is shown in the economic summary in Table 1, with the data from both Colombia and India. With intercropped maize and beans, the probability of income greater than 0 is 0.92, while that of income above 10 000 CP/ha is 0.73. These figures are higher than the corresponding probabilities with either monocrop. Intercropped sorghum/pigeonpea had probabilities of 1.00 and 0.65 of producing income greater than 250 Rs/ha and 3250 Rs/ha respectively, both levels being higher than those achieved from monocrops of the component species. Mead (1986) illustrated the economic risk of monocropped sorghum versus intercropped

Table 1 Yield stability of intercrops

Cropping pattern	Yield		Total income		Probability of an income > Y/ha	
	kg/ha	CV	CP/ha	CV	Y>0 CP	Y> 10 000 CP
Maize and climbing bean:[1]						
Maize monoculture	4 986	23.6	1 944	242.5	0.65	0.04
Bean monoculture	2 941	29.4	16 061	88.2	0.80	0.55
Intercrop	6 114	22.9	16 521	60.0	0.92	0.73
			Rs/ha	CV	Y> 250 RS	Y> 3 250 RS
Sorghum and pigeonpea:[2]						
Sorghum monoculture	3 208	47.0	3 208	-	0.95	0. 40
Pigeonpea monoculture	1 446	42.7	2 892	-	0.91	0.28
Intercrop	3 856	39.0	4 473	-	1.00	0.65

Note: CV = Co-efficient of variation; Y = Variable yield/ha; Rs = Indian Rupees; CP = Colombian Pesos
1. Analysis of the results of 20 trials in Colombia, 1975-78 (Francis and Sanders 1978)
2. Analysis of the results of 94 trials in India, 1972-78 (Rao and Willey, 1980)

sorghum and pigeonpea (Figure 4). For example, if there is a 0.5 probability of the return to sorghum being less than a specified level ('d'), the corresponding probability of the return to the intercrop being still lower is less than 0.25. More quantitative evaluation of the risk incurred with different types of technological intervention, both in monocrop and in intercrop systems, is needed urgently.

Research Agenda for Sustainable Intercropping Systems

The farming systems research approach described by Gilbert et al. (1980) has been widely implemented in one form or another during the past decade. This approach represents an attempt to resolve some of the problems associated with research recommendations that were listed by Collinson (1982), who maintained that current research results are often not applicable because:

• A prescriptive tradition of improved management practices passed from researcher to extension specialist to farmer often ignores the real constraints and farm-to-farm variation that characterizes resource-poor farmers

• The isolation of researchers on experiment stations away from their farmer clients makes it difficult for them to understand the real circumstances under which their results will be applied

• The almost total reliance by researchers on biological/grain yield per unit area rather than on the economic and other criteria used by farmers to evaluate technology makes it difficult for the two to communicate with each other about 'improved' systems and practices.

Success in the application of farming systems research methodology has been highly variable, often due to the discipline-specific approaches that team members continue to

Figure 3 Net income from three cropping systems at different field bean/maize price ratios and different levels of bean yield

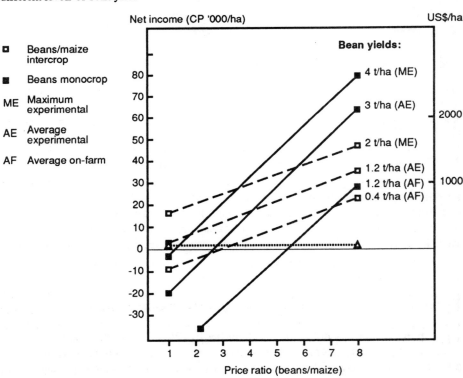

Source: Francis and Sanders (1978). Reprinted by kind permission of the authors

Figure 4 Relative risk[1] graph for monocrop sorghum versus intercrop sorghum and pigeonpea

Intercrop risk

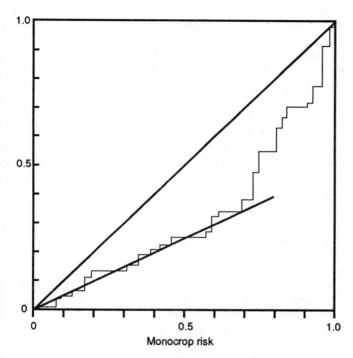

Monocrop risk

1. Risk that the returns to an intercrop yield will be less than d, plotted against the risk that returns to an intercrop yield will be still lower
Source: Mead (1986)

bring to farming systems projects. It has been difficult for scientists trained in specific subjects to develop a concept of how their specialities fit into the team's multidisciplinary work. Yet the complex nature of farming systems is now better appreciated, and there is greater awareness of the problems of trying to introduce single components of technology without first considering their impact on the system as a whole. There is also growing concern about the nutritional, social and political implications of the decisions made—whether by farmers or by policymakers—in relation to cropping systems.

These changing perceptions have had an impact on the research agenda. Better communication between research-station personnel and those in the field has increased our understanding of the systems being used and of why farmers insist on preserving the diversity of their crops and other sources of income. This has broadened the perspective of the research community and accelerated the search for appropriate technologies for resource-poor farmers (Francis 1985). The number of journal publications on intercropping has increased rapidly during the past decade. The interest shown by technical people at workshops and symposia has been even more spectacular, as indicated by the number of special meetings with a focus on intercropping organized by national programmes and the international centres.

Some of the areas relevant to sustainable agriculture in which more research is needed have been listed by Miller (1988), as an outcome of a planning workshop in Raleigh, North Carolina. Since many of them are relevant to intercropping, the list has been edited for presentation here:

- Alternative nutrient sources and nutrient cycling
    information base on legumes and organic wastes
    nutrient cycling processes and efficiencies
    role of the rhizosphere and its associated organisms
- Cropping systems research
    information base on rotations and practices
    tests of cover crops, tillage, and chemical inputs
    intercropping alternatives
- Alternative weed control strategies
    cultural factor effect on competition and populations
    weed ecology and biology
    biological control of weeds
- Alternative disease and nematode management strategies
    effects of cultural practices on micro-organism balance
    methods for encouraging indigenous antagonists and biocontrol
    improved genetic resistance/tolerance to pathogens
- Alternative insect management strategies
    ecology of cropping systems as they influence insects
    methods for the cultural and biological control of insects
    improved genetic resistance/tolerance to insects
    understanding regional insect pest dynamics.

Future strategies for research on intercropping need to take into account the information already available, both from research stations and from farmers.

There is a large body of knowledge on the biological principles of crop growth and productivity and the interaction of crops with the environment. Even though much of this knowledge has been derived from monoculture systems, it is still applicable to some degree to intercropping systems. Our challenge is to find out what principles are relevant and how they can be applied efficiently. There is an even greater need to continue our emphasis on interdisciplinary research and on the links between researchers, extensionists and farmers, so as to develop methods and systems that will help improve the productivity of intercropping systems.

References

Adams, M.W., A.H. Ellingboe and E.C. Rossman. 1971. Biological uniformity and disease epidemics. *Bioscience* 21:10671070.

Collinson, M.P. 1982. The use of farming systems research for understanding small farmers and improving relevancy in adaptive experimentation. In: C.L. Keswani and B.J. Ndunguru (eds), Intercropping: Proceedings of the Second Symposium on Intercropping in Semi-Arid Areas, Morogoro, Tanzania. Ottawa: International Development Research Centre.

Francis, C.A. 1985. Rationality of new technology for small farmers in the tropics. *Agriculture and Human Values* 2 (2): 54-59.

Francis, C.A. 1986. Variety development for multiple cropping systems. *CRC Critical Reviews in Plant Sciences* 3 (2): 133-168.

Francis, C.A. and J.H. Sanders. 1978. Economic analysis of bean and maize systems: Monoculture versus associated cropping. *Field Crops Research* 1:319-335.

Gilbert, E.H., D.W. Norman and F.E. Winch. 1980. Farming systems research: A critical appraisal. Michigan State University Rural Development Paper No. 6. East Lansing.

Goodman, D. 1975. The theory of diversity-stability relationships in ecology. *Quarterly Review of Biology* 50: 237- 266.

Harwood, R.R. 1989. History of sustainable agriculture: US and international perspective. In: C.A. Edwards, R. Lal, P. Madden, R.H. Miller and G. House (eds), *Sustainable agricultural systems*. Soil and Water Conservation Society.

Loomis, R.S. 1984. Traditional agriculture in America. *Annual Review of Ecological Systems* 15: 449-478.

Lynam, J.K., J.H. Sanders and S.C. Mason. 1986. Economics and risk in multiple cropping. In: C.A. Francis (ed.), *Multiple cropping systems*. New York: Macmillan.

Mead, R. 1986. Statistical methods for multiple cropping. In: C.A. Francis (ed.), Multiple cropping systems. New York: Macmillan.

Miller, R.M. 1988. Planning conference on research and extension needs for alternative agriculture. Draft report of the workshop, 24-26 August 1987, Raleigh, North Carolina. North Carolina State University.

Office of Technology Assessment. 1988. Enhancing agriculture in Africa: A role for US development assistance. US Congress Summary Paper OTA-F-357.

Rao, M.R. and R.W. Willey. 1980. Evaluation of yield stability in intercropping studies on sorghum and pigeon pea. *Experimental Agriculture* 16: 105-116.

Smith, M.E. and C.A. Francis. 1986. Breeding for multiple cropping systems. In: C.A. Francis (ed.), *Multiple cropping systems*. New York: Macmillan.

Source

First published 1990 in Research Methods for Cereal/Legume Intercropping, Proceedings of a Workshop on Research Methods for Cereal/Legume Intercropping in Eastern and Southern Africa, edited by S.R. Wardington, A. F. E. Palmer and O.T. Edje. Network Report No. 17, published by CIMMYT, Mexico City. Reprinted by kind permission of the publisher.

Address

Charles Francis, Department of Agronomy, University of Nebraska, Lincoln NE, 68583-0910, USA.

Crop Yields and the Small-scale Family Farm Economy: An Example from the Central Andes

Pierre Morlon

Introduction

Accurate, detailed knowledge of the yields obtained by small-scale farmers and an understanding of the relationship between these yields and natural environmental conditions, the technology and practices used, and the small-scale family farm economy, are needed to better identify the objectives of agronomic research and extension work.

In the Andes of Peru and Bolivia, observations and measurements in the field show that yields are sometimes far higher than those recorded in official statistics or noted in surveys (Hibon 1981; Horton 1984; Morlon 1990). They reflect the extreme variability, for all crops, between:

• Years
• Categories of producers
• Individual producers within categories
• Different plots cultivated by the same family.

The latter source of variation may be explained in large part by the fact that plots in different agro-ecological zones may be cultivated by the same family (Mayer 1985), some intensively, with chemical fertilizers, pesticides and modern plant varieties, and others in the traditional way, with few purchased inputs.

The variability of yields within categories of producers means that recommendations targeted to groups of producers based on average results have little meaning.

When low yields are observed, these should not be seen in isolation, but rather as the lower extreme of a very wide range. All too often in the past, the wrong conclusions have been drawn when low yields have been considered at face value. It is not enough to know what the yields are—the figures must also be explained.

The need to assess yields accurately raises several methodological and conceptual issues (Morlon 1988, 1990a):

• Interviews versus direct measurements in the field
• The frequency with which sampling is carried out
• How to evaluate yields in intercropping situations
• How to evaluate the byproducts of crop production (straw for animal feed may be just as important to the farmer as the grain on which the external technician habitually focuses his attention)

- Choice of productivity criteria in the light of the factor perceived as a constraint: returns per hectare, labour productivity (Bourliaud et al. 1988); return to the amount of seed used; irrigation water efficiency, etc.

Yields as a Consequence of Small-scale Farming Strategies

Marketing: A production constraint
It has often been observed that small-scale farmers limit their output for market, either because of the low prices received from greedy middlemen in obsolete marketing systems (Sabogal Wiesse 1966), or because demand is low. Big business and agro-industry prefer to buy bulk, uniform cargos of imported foodstuffs, often at artificially low, subsidized prices, rather than to collect the many small and diverse surpluses, which are never subsidized, produced by the small-scale farmer.

Subsistence production thus emerges not as a hangover from the past, but as a response to very real, continuing problems.

Combined with the natural risks of a poor harvest, marketing problems induce farmers to minimize the purchase of inputs, since they cannot be sure of recovering even the cost of these through the sale of the surpluses obtained, let alone of making a profit. This often occurs with crops that are normally consumed on the farm in any case, when the ratio between market prices and production costs is unfavourable, and in the agro-ecological zones where production is most risky. On the other hand, producers at the very bottom of the economic pile and in the most precarious circumstances have been known to adopt unhesitatingly new, more productive techniques when these are adapted to their situation and are perceived to give more reliable returns than the family's other economic activities. This explains why the same farmers apply traditional practices without purchased inputs for plots in one zone, while turning to modern technologies using a high level of inputs for crops grown in other zones.

Competition for labour
Returns per unit area depend on the choice of priorities decided by the farm family—primarily its choice between agricultural and non-agricultural activities.

For example, in 1978-79 we studied the activities of farm families in the Peruvian *altiplano* (Montoya et al. 1986). Two families appeared similar in terms of size, economic circumstances and land ownership (just over 0.5 ha each). Yet, in the fields of the first family, potato yields that year were between 15 and 40 t/ha, whereas the second family harvested an average of only 5.5 t, with a maximum of 9 t. The difference could not be explained by natural environmental factors. It turned out that the head of the first family had decided *not* to migrate temporarily that year, in order to devote labour to the crops and so ensure a good harvest. In contrast, the second family had concentrated on off-farm activities, and had either carried out certain cultural operations (such as weeding) too late or else not performed them at all. Some of the differences in labour allocations to the crop component of the system may have been due to the ownership of livestock, which also provides a cash income.

Variability

Brunschwig (1988 and personal communication) found that farmers in the Laraos 'community' growing maize on irrigated terraces at between 3200 and 3400 metres altitude obtained a yield of 5100 kg/ha, this being the average obtained with traditional varieties and without the use of purchased chemical inputs for all fields of the five families studied during a year in which the weather was good. However, this average masked extremes ranging from 1600 to 12 000 kg/ha (Figure 1). A yield of 12 000 kg/ha is doubtless exceptional—but we should be interested in these exceptions precisely because they illustrate the considerable potential of small-scale farming in this zone and provide a surprising answer to the question: 'What yields can be obtained from traditional farming?' This question should be replaced by another: 'Why are these high yields not obtained everywhere?'

Climatic factors inevitably cause marked variations between years and, in the same year, between fields. In response, farmers have traditionally adopted two main complementary strategies:

- Reduce the level of risk by:
    Developing the environment through irrigation, terraces, ridged fields (these technologies reduce variability but do not get rid of it altogether)
    Tilling and working the soil in ways that reduce or prevent soil water loss (depending on the type of soil, topography, and rainfall (Lescano 1979; Bourliaud et al. 1988)
    Adapting the plant cover to prevailing microclimatic characteristics (frosts in particular)
- Spread risk:
    Through time, by:
        Staggering sowing dates
        Dehydrating tubers (so that the results of good years can be carried over to bad ones)
    Through space by:
        Exploiting the maximum number of ecological niches (Murra 1975)
        Cropping a large number of dispersed plots (Martinez 1981; Morlon et al. 1982).

The result of this risk spreading strategy is to multiply the combinations of components found in the farming system—sites cultivated (soil, climate, topography), multiplied by ways of working the soil, multiplied by species and varieties grown, multiplied by sowing dates, and so on—such that at least some of these combinations will be productive, whatever the conditions that may arise during the cropping season. This accounts for the variability in yields from different fields cultivated by the same family. The unpredictability of the climate means that the farmer cannot foresee which combinations will prove best, and in fact each year only a small proportion of them produce high yields (except in very favourable environments such as the *campiñas*, which are irrigated fields protected by hedges and woods in valley bottoms at about 3000 m). Returns from the other plots can be very low, and thus the average also appears low.

In conclusion, looking at averages only is of no use for improving production and the lot of the small-scale farmer. To work more effectively, we must begin by studying the yields obtained from many fields, and analysing the factors which intervened in each case. Nor let us forget that although crop yields affect the producers' standard of living, the overall economy of the small-scale farm family is one of the principal determinants of these yields. That is to say, factors such as the family's leisure, the processing of food, social obligations, and off-farm income earning opportunities may be just as important as agronomic and farm management factors.

Figure 1 Yield variations between different irrigated maize fields of five peasant farmers at Laraos, in the same year

Yields (t/ha)

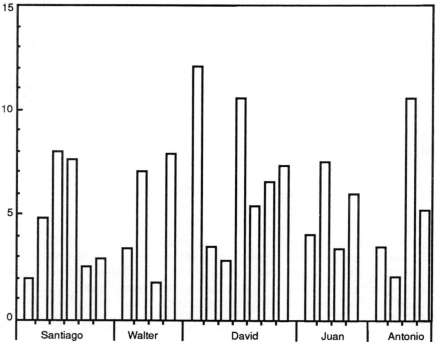

Source: Brunschwig, personal communication

100

References

Bourliaud, J., R. Reau, P. Morlon and D. Herve. 1988. Chakitakila: Estrategias de barbecho e intensificación de la agricultura andina. ORSTOM-PISA, Lima.

Brunschwig, G. 1986. Sistemas de producción en laderas de altura. Bull. IFEA 15 (1-2): 27-52.

Hibon, A. 1981. Transfert de technologie et agriculture paysanne en zone andine: Le cas de la culture du maïs dans les systèmes de production du Cusco (Pérou). Thèse Dr. Ing., INP-ENSA-CNRS, Toulouse.

Horton, D. 1984. Social scientists in agricultural research: Lessons from the Mantaro Valley Project, Peru. IDRC, Ottawa.

Lescano, J. L. 1979. Technología agrícola tradicional en el Altiplano Peruano. 1er Seminario Nacional sobre Technologías Adeuadas. Ayacucho.

Martinez, G. 1981. Espacio Lupaqa: Algunas hipótesis de trabajo. 2da Jornada del Museo Nacional de Historia, Lima: 263-280.

Mayer, E. 1985. Production zones. In: S. Masuda, L. Shimada and C. Morris (eds), *Andean ecology and civilization: An interdisciplinary perspective on Andean ecological complementarity.* Wenner-Gren Foundation for Anthropological Research, Symposium No. 91. University of Tokyo Press.

Montoya, B., P. Morlon and S. Channer. 1986. Los sistemas agropastoriles andinos: Un estudio de casos de cinco familias del Altiplano Peruano. In: Proceedings of the Fifth International Congress on Andean Agriculture, Puño.

Morlon, P. 1988. Qué sabemos de los rendimentos de los cultivos de los campesinos en el Peru? Como interpretarlos? Paper presented at the Sixth International Congress on Andean Crops, Quito.

Morlon, P. 1990. Que sait-on des rendements obtenus par les paysans dans les Andes Centrales? Comment les interpréter? In: J. Bourliaud, J-F Dobremez and P. Vigny (eds), *Sociétés rurales des Andes et de l'Himalaya.* Editions Versants, Grenoble.

Morlon, P., B. Orlov and A. Hibon. 1982. Tecnologîas agrícolas tradicionales en los Andes Centrales: Perspectivas para el desarrollo. UNESCO/UNDP/COFUDE, Lima.

Murra, J.V. 1975. El 'control vertical' de un máximo de pisos ecológicos en las economías de las sociedades Andinas. In: *Formaciones económicas y políticas del mundo Andino.* Instituto de Estudios Peruanos, Lima.

Sabogal Wiesse, J. 1966. El maíz en Chacán. First draft. UNA, La Molina, Lima.

Source

First published 1990 in *Sociétés Rurales des Andes et de l'Himalaya,* edited by J. Bourliaud, J-F. Dobremez and F. Vigny. Published by Editions Versants, Grenoble, France. Reprinted by kind permission of the publisher and the author.

Address

Pierre Morlon, Institut National de la Recherche Agronomique, 26 bd du Docteur Petitjean, 21100 Dijon, France.

Farmers' Assessment of Ecological Cropping Techniques

Anne Floquet

Introduction

How do farmers cope with problems of land scarcity and degradation? Working in the *terres de barre* (acid soils) area of southern Benin, our research team explored why farmers chose their current farming practices and economic activities and what factors limited their choices. We spoke with farmers who had tried but given up using fertilizers to restore soil nutrients. We brought farmer groups to researchers' field trials on planted fallow and to farmers' field trials where green manure, planted fallow and alley cropping were being tested. The sample of farmers was stratified so that their assessment of the techniques, which differ in resource requirements, could be related to their economic situation.

Terres de Barre

Crop yields on *terres de barre* depend mainly on the organic matter content of the soil. As long as a dense bush fallow can grow before the land is cropped again, fertility can be restored. When land becomes scarce (more than 150 people/km²), the fallow period shortens, the composition of the vegetation degenerates and the soil becomes acidic and poor in N, K, P and S. Maize, the main crop grown, then has only shallow roots and is more sensitive to dry spells. Yields fall until, eventually, maize can no longer be grown and is replaced by groundnut, cowpea and cassava.

In response to land scarcity, the farmers have tried different strategies, such as:
• Cultivating all available (even marginal) land and integrating oil palms into the rotation
• Including cassava as an intermediate fallow, growing more legumes in rotation with maize, ridging, and incorporating crop residues into the soil
• Intensive compound farming using household waste, in some densely populated areas with very impoverished soils
• Part-time farming purely for home consumption, and other activities, such as seasonal migration, off-farm work and processing, to earn cash
• Collecting and selling tree products from fallow land
• Resettling on unused land in the north of the country.

The degradation of the resource base is occurring against a highly unfavourable economic background of general recession, characterized by a tight local market due to rising unemployment and low salaries and by a deteriorating standard of living in rural areas. This affects nutrition, health and education and, thus, the productivity of labour.

Various research institutes have long been working in the *terres de barre*, studying fertilizer use, green manure, improving fallow with fast-growing trees, and alley cropping. However, thus far, few farmers have integrated these innovations into their cropping systems.

The Innovations Sudied

Fertilizers

Fertilizers have long been advocated, but farmers adopt them only in cotton-growing areas. This has both agronomic and economic reasons.

The extra yield gained from applying fertilizer to local varieties is not high enough to justify the costs. Improved varieties (IITA composites), which would benefit more from fertilizer, are not acceptable to farmers, as they do not store well and have a long cycle (120 days). Farmers have been replacing their 120-day varieties by 105- or even 90-day varieties because the risk of flowering during a dry spell has become too high.

On degraded land, applying fertilizer without sufficient organic matter only accelerates soil impoverishment. On newly cleared land, where the crop can still benefit from the ashes of the burnt vegetation, the extra yield obtained by using fertilizers is also very low. The extension services have not yet adjusted their recommendations to the fertility status of the soil, and few experiments have been conducted on the synergy between organic and non-organic fertilizer.

Some farmers tested fertilizers on maize and obtained good results for a few seasons, but many were eventually discouraged by cash losses. As the climate is very variable, there is a high risk of not having enough extra yield to pay for the fertilizer. Moreover, because of illness or other unpredictable events, some farmers are not sure whether they will be able to do the work associated with fertilizer application on time. The probability of such events, and of subsequent yield losses, is particularly high in the case of farmers with small families and of women farmers with insufficient income to hire labourers.

Where cash income is low and unpredictable, it is difficult to save money to invest in farming. Farmers regard cash as the most limiting factor preventing increased production. If they make an investment, it must be profitable. Assessment of profitability differs from farmer to farmer, depending on their objectives.

Those farmers who are sure of having a marketable surplus and can invest money in hiring labour or renting more land compare the cash returns of these with other activities, especially distilling palm wine. Returns to investment in distillation can be more than 100%. A development project in a neighbouring province chose this as a threshold to evaluate the profitability of fertilizer use by farmers. In on-farm trials it was found that this threshold was reached by fewer than 50% of farmers.

Farmers who are not sure whether they will have enough maize for family needs will try to secure this first. They are willing to strive for additional yields, but only with minimal additional costs. In cases where family labour cannot be mobilized, these extra costs include labourers' wages. Comparison of costs revealed that extending the normal cropping period (3-4 years) by applying fertilizer is not as profitable as renting and clearing fallow land, unless the farmer can be sure of getting an average yield higher than 975 kg/ha (using family labour) or 1000 kg/ha (using paid labour) by purchasing and applying fertilizer. For as long as fallow land is available to rent or borrow, farmers will not invest in fertilizers (*see* Table 1).

Table 1 Minimizing the extra costs of a maize surplus: A comparison between lengthening the cropping period with fertilizer and clearing new rented land

	Clearing new land (fallow)	Applying fertilizer
Farmers with family labour:		
Additional costs	Rent: 45 000	Fertilizer: 15 000/year Seed: 3 300/year
Total over 3 years	45 000	54 900
Additional yields	Year 1: 1000 kg + wood Year 2: 800 kg Year 3: 600 kg	
Results:	Additional costs/kg of maize: 18.75	Average yield to be obtained for addditional costs to be less than 18.75: >975 kg/ha
Farmers employing labourers:		
Additional costs	Rent: 45 000 Hoeing: 15 000 /year Sowing: 3 000 /year Weeding: 9 000 /year	Hoeing: 15 000 /year Sowing: 3 000 /year Seed: 3 300 /year Fertilizer: 15 000 /year First weeding: 9 000 /year Second weeding: 7 500 /year
Total over 3 years	126 000	158 400
Additional yields	As above	
Results	Additional costs/kg of maize: 52.5	Average yield to be obtained for additional costs to be less than 52.5/kg: >1005 kg/ha

Note: all prices in FCFA

Green manure

Farmers have not adopted green manure to improve soil fertility, despite the fact that there seems to be little economic disincentive. Green manure does not require extra labour, since a shrub like *Cajanus cajan* or a herbaceous vine like *Mucuna utilis* can be planted in association or in relay with the main crop in the first rainy season. The plants form a pure stand in the second rainy season and the subsequent dry season (Figure 1). No work need be done in the second rainy season, and clearing for cultivation at the beginning of the next cycle is easy, the soil being weed-free. Thus, over 2 years, the labour balance is positive. So, the next obvious question is: what are the agronomic benefits of green manuring..

Results of green manuring trials are contradictory. In 6-year researcher-managed trials on *terres de barre* in Togo, the sacrifice of one maize harvest a year because green manure

Figure 1 Rotation patterns with green manure

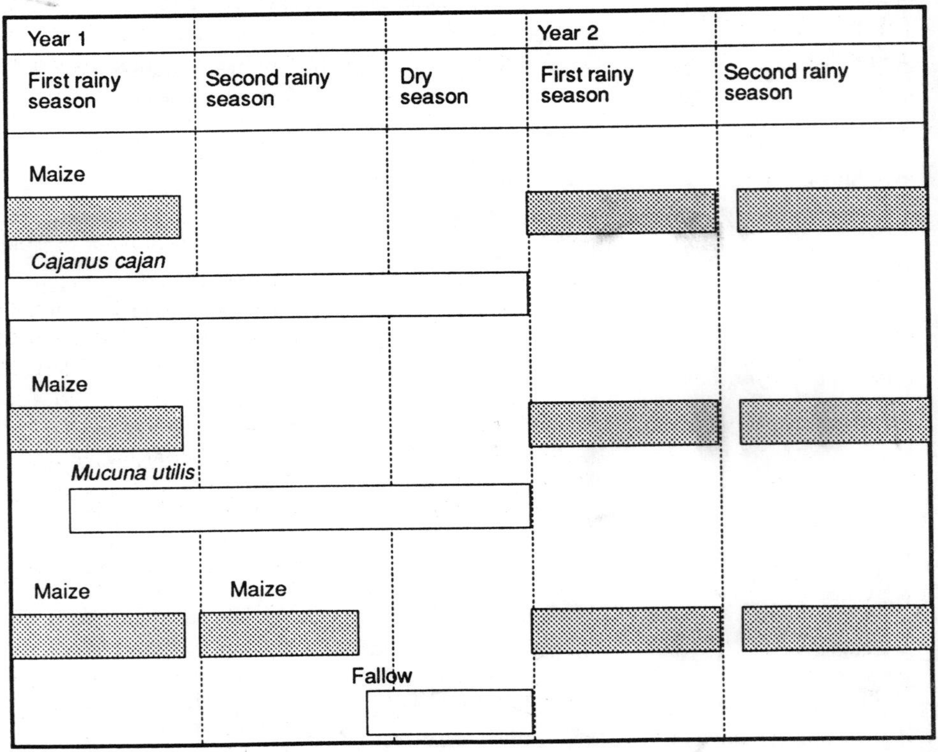

Year 1			Year 2	
First rainy season	Second rainy season	Dry season	First rainy season	Second rainy season
Maize				
Cajanus cajan				
Maize				
Mucuna utilis				
Maize	Maize			
	Fallow			

Note: Fallow = bush regrowth between second-season weeding and hoeing during the first season of the following year

(*Crotalaria juncea*) was planted in the second season was offset by a better yield in the subsequent maize crop. The rotation system produced as much maize as maize-maize double monocropping. These plots had fertilizer applications, however. In on-farm trials on non-degraded land, with a rotation of maize + *Cajanus/cajan* maize/maize (as in Figure 1), the additional maize yield in year 2 did not compensate for the maize harvest foregone in year 1. In similar trials conducted by farmers on degraded land, the maize yields were equal in both alternatives.

A rough comparison between incorporating green manure and incorporating crop biomass (cassava, maize, groundnut) as mulch indicated that *Cajanus cajan* provides more biomass than do food grain crops at sites where it grows well, but that it requires fairly fertile soils. Nevertheless, on farmers' fields where the natural fallow was vigorous, the biomass of bush regrowth during the second rainy season and the following dry season, added to the biomass of the crop residues, appeared to be just as great as the biomass produced by planted *Cajanus*. On degraded *terres de barre*, *Cajanus* does not grow well and probably does not produce as much biomass as cassava.

Some farmers are adopting *Mucuna utilis* to control the weed *Imperata*. If this weed invades a field, they must either invest much labour to reclaim it or else abandon it altogether. Farmers are prepared to spend time establishing a green manure crop if it helps control this weed.

Fallows

Researchers regard fallow merely as a way of enhancing soil fertility; farmers also see it as a way of generating cash. Marketable products can be collected from fallows. Especially in peri-urban areas, firewood is in high demand.

Natural fallow was—and, in some areas, still is—the most efficient way to 'wake up' the soil (the local expression for land regeneration). The optimal length of fallow is about 7-9 years, but when the cropping period is still short enough (5-7 years) to allow the roots of fallow shrubs to survive, a fallow period of 3-4 years is sufficient to produce firewood and ensure acceptable yields after clearing.

Planted fallows, using fast-growing species such as *Cassia siamea* and *Acacia auriculiformis*, produce firewood and stakes within 2-3 years. They appear more productive than natural fallow, although the relevant measurements have not yet been made.

An interesting variation is the indigenous palm agroforestry system. As land becomes scarce, palms are integrated into the seasonal cropping system. They are planted together with maize, which ensures their protection from weeds during the first years. Later, they grow with the bush regrowth, which is sometimes cleared yearly. As soon as the trees mature, they are sold and/or felled for wine extraction and distillation. Palm trees have a good market value and are the farmer's best form of saving. Some palm systems also restore soil fertility. For these reasons, farmers with access to enough land almost always plant palms on it.

The profitability of fallowing must be assessed in terms of the cash income and capital accumulation it permits. For farmers who can save and invest in productive activities, the returns are higher in agroforestry than in seasonal cropping, especially if labour is employed.

For farmers with little land and insufficient maize production to secure family needs, any reduction in cropped area to allow for planted fallow must be offset by higher subsequent maize yields. Frequently, this happens only after 2-4 years, and these farmers cannot wait that long. One partial solution is to mulch the cropped area with litter taken from the growing planted fallow.

Farmers who have more land and a secure food supply but not enough income for investment seek to maximize their income. These farmers compare what they can gain from different systems: planted or natural fallow, or seasonal crop rotation. Near towns, where firewood commands a high price, the income from agroforestry is sometimes higher than from seasonal cropping, especially for farmers who hire labourers, since the agroforestry system requires less labour. Nevertheless, the two incomes differ in 'quality'. In the agroforestry system, farmers obtain a fairly high income all at once. They must choose the period of harvest to coincide with large expenditures. In seasonal cropping, the income is more evenly distributed over the years and, if the market is poor, the crops can be consumed. Thus, although an agroforestry system may earn a higher total income than a food cropping system, it is usually established on only part of the farm. On degraded land in overcropped areas, the agroforestry system appears more profitable than natural fallow, especially in view of its favourable effects on the soil.

Not all farmers are free to choose how to use the land. Less than half the arable land in the *terres de barre* is cultivated by its owners; most is rented or borrowed. Women do not inherit land and cannot buy large plots. Tree planting symbolizes ownership. Where there is enough land, farmers rent fallow and use it for 3-4 years. If the owner needs money urgently, tenants rent fields 'in advance' when the fallow is still young, and wait several years before clearing. Measures which restore the soil and produce wood more quickly than natural fallow are advantageous to both parties.

In another form of tenancy the tenant plants palms for the field's owner in return for the right to grow annual crops for as long as the palms are sensitive to weeds. This *taungya* system could be extended to other trees, provided these too were profitable to the owner.

Here again, the non-adoption of planted fallow seems to be due neither to economic nor to tenurial factors but rather to the lack of proven agronomic benefits. Data on the effects of planted fallow on the productivity and sustainability of cropping are scarce, and the fallow species being researched are exotics. Little has been done with local species, not even those valued by farmers for their capacity to restore soil fertility.

Alley cropping

This is an elegant system in which fallowing shrubs are integrated within cropped fields to reduce leaching and runoff losses and to produce and recycle biomass. However, the agronomic results of alley cropping with *Leucaena leucocephala* and *Gliricidia sepium* on *terres de barre* have been disappointing.

Competition between crops and shrubs can be so great that less maize is produced in the alley system than in open fields. Competition for water is acute in the second rainy season, such that any delay in pruning the shrubs causes high crop losses. To improve the water balance, trials have been conducted with shrub species with a slower growth rate and litter which decays more slowly. Researchers are also trying to reduce the crop/shrub interface by using wider alleys and double rows of shrubs.

But the fact remains: alley cropping is time-consuming. To be adopted by small-scale part-time farmers who cultivate for subsistence and earn a cash income from off-farm activities, alley cropping must produce an additional yield which pays more for the additional labour than do off-farm activities. Similarly, farmers who invest savings in hiring labour for alley cropping expect a cash return at least as high as their alternative investment possibilities. The higher the labour costs, the lower the probability of getting this return.

Farmers with large families may be interested in adopting alley cropping to 'employ' their dependents, if the system brings them more maize to consume or sell. These farmers also run less risk of not being able to prune the shrubs on time. They can earn cash by selling *acadjas* (branches planted in water to attract fish). For these farmers, the system can be profitable, especially if modified to reduce crop-shrub competition. Good farmers might be better able to optimize the management of alley cropping than researchers, who tend to stick to a trial plan. But, even then, this system will probably interest only a small group of farmers.

Conclusions

Tables 2 and 3 present the improved practices studied in terms of their use of resources and the degree to which they meet the multiple objectives of different types of farmer.

Individual practices
The major criteria on which the farmers in southern Benin based their decisions were food supply, cash income and return on investment. For farmers without a secure food supply, a land-consuming innovation such as green manuring or planted fallow can be used to increase maize yields only on a relatively small area. In the case of labour-consuming practices such as alley cropping, if the extra labour required obliges the farmer to reduce off-farm activities, this work has to be remunerated as well as the given up activities if the technology is to be adopted. For farmers with secure food supply but insufficient income for investment, an innovation must raise income either after paying for inputs and wages or on a relatively small cropped area.

Table 2 Evaluation of practices according to resources consumed

Resources: Practices:	Land	Labour	Cash
Fertilizer application	Saving	Neutral	Consuming
Green manure	Consuming	Neutral	Saving (for farmers employing labourers) or neutral
Planted fallow (instead of seasonal cropping)	Consuming	Saving	Saving (for farmers employing labourers) or neutral
Planted fallow (instead of natural fallow)	Neutral (or saving, if shorter fallow)	Consuming (little)	Consuming (little, for farmers employing labourers), or neutral
Alley cropping	Saving, if productively managed	Consuming (much)	Consuming (much, for farmers having to employ labourers or give up other activities)

Each practice may become profitable for some category of farmer: nutrient-restoring fertilizers as soon as fallow land becomes scarce, if the risk of losses is reduced (appropriate varieties, better water balance with mulching, etc); green manuring and planted fallow to replace degraded natural fallow for small-scale and medium-sized farmers, there being no risk of cash losses as in the case of fertilizers. Cash-saving practices are likely to be profitable to large-scale farmers, as cash returns will be improved.

Combining practices
However, none of these practices, on its own, can fulfil all the objectives of farmers. Practices should therefore be combined. Assessment has to take the specific situation of each farmer into account.

Researchers should check whether the practices they propose fulfil certain minimum criteria. Farmer testing of innovations is meaningful only when the problem they are meant to solve actually arises. As long as land is still available, farmers will look for natural fallow to clear rather than investing labour and cash in intensifying land use. But if a problem is critical, for example the invasion of *Imperata*, an innovation such as *Mucuna utilis* will spread very quickly among farmers as soon as they see that it works.

Above all, new practices must perform well in agronomic terms. Species for green manure and improved fallow should be screened for different locations, and the productivity

110

and stability of the new system must be compared with that of the existing system(s). Too little research has been done in such a way as to allow comparison of the results from different locations. Nor can the results achieved on station be compared with those on farmers' fields. Detailed research tends to be conducted on specific topics before the appropriateness of the new system as a whole has been assessed. Client-oriented assessments have to be done by researchers before truly sustainable farming practices will spread amongst resource-poor farmers.

Table 3 Evaluation of practices in terms of degree to which farmers' objectives are met

Types of farmer	Farmers saving and investing cash in agriculture	Farmers securing food supply but having low cash income	Farmers with insecure food supply
Objectives	Maximizing cash returns	Maximizing cash income, minimizing cash losses	Maximizing food supply, minimizing cash losses
Fertilizer application	Cash returns >100% unlikely in 50% of cases, if applied alone	Cash losses very probable	Cash losses very probable
Green manure	Cash returns higher than for seasonal crop rotations very likely	Total income higher than for seasonal crop rotation likely	Total maize production higher than for seasonal crop rotation possible
Planted fallow (instead of seasonal crops)	Cash returns higher than for seasonal crop rotation, secure forms of saving	Returns to planted trees higher than to seasonal crops likely, secure forms of saving	Total maize production lower than for a seasonal crop rotation, but secure forms of saving compensate
Planted fallow (instead of natural fallow)	Cash returns higher than for natural degenerated fallow	Returns to planted trees higher than for natural fallow likely if family labour available	Higher maize production likely
Alley cropping	Cash returns higher than for other activities very unlikely	Returns higher than for other activities likely if no labourers employed	Maize production higher, but farmers may have to give up off-farm jobs

Source

First published in the *ILEIA Newsletter* 1 and 2, 1991, under the title 'Farmers assessment of techniques.'

Address

Anne Floquet, Uhlbacherstrasse 97, D-7000 Stuttgart 61, Germany.

PART FOUR

Comparing Farming Systems

The sophisticated Bontoc rice terraces were made with stones from the river, using only simple tools. A variety of traditional practices, including the use of a compost containing pig manure, enable this traditional low-external-input system to achieve yields equal to those of the Green Revolution. *Photo:* Hilario Padilla

Low-input Cropping for Acid Soils of the Humid Tropics

Pedro A. Sanchez and José R. Benites

Introduction

Stable alternatives to shifting cultivation are needed for humid tropical locations where increasing demographic pressure no longer permits traditional slash-and-burn agriculture. In previous articles we have given an overall appraisal of soils of the tropics (Sanchez and Buol 1975) and described fertilizer-based continuous cultivation technology as one soil management option (Sanchez et al. 1982). Subsequent research in the Amazon of Peru and Brazil has shown promise for an array of management options for humid tropical landscapes dominated by acid soils. Some of these options, shown in Figure 1, are applicable to specific combinations of topography, soil type, and level of economic development (Sanchez and Benites 1986). Acid soils, classified mainly as Ultisols and Oxisols, cover approximately two-thirds of the world's humid tropics (Sanchez 1976). Differing management options have been developed for high base status, non-acid Alfisols and Andisols of the tropics where the subsoil is rich in bases that can be recycled (Kang et al. 1981; Alvim 1982). In both acid and non-acid soils, evidence shows that the continuous production of food crops is possible in the humid tropics with the judicious use of lime, fertilizers, crop rotations and soil conservation practices (Kang et al. 1981; Sanchez et al. 1982; Lopes et al. 1987; Lal 1987). But it is unlikely that the majority of shifting cultivators in the humid tropics can readily switch to continuous production systems. Intermediate systems of low-cost and low-input technologies may be more useful as a first step towards more permanent land use.

Low- Versus High-input Approaches

Agronomists disagree about the use of the terms 'high-input' or 'intensive' systems, on the one hand, and 'low-input', 'minimum-input', 'zero-input', 'alternative agriculture', or 'resource-limited' systems on the other. For soil management purposes, high-input systems have been defined as those that aim to eliminate soil constraints to crop growth by appropriate levels of liming, fertilizer application, irrigation, or other purchased inputs (Sanchez and Salinas 1981). A high percentage of the world's food supplies are produced according to this approach, both in the developed world and in the more fertile lands of

Figure 1 Some soil management options for humid tropical landscapes dominated by Oxisols and Ultisols

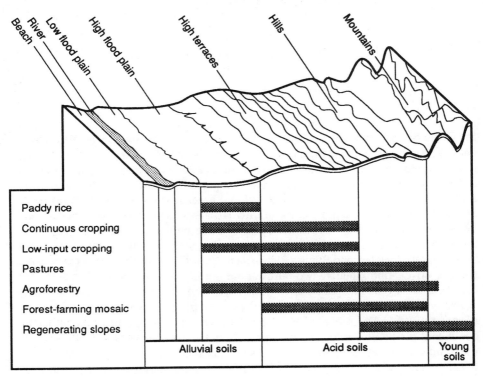

Source: North Carolina State University (1985). Reproduced by kind permission of the Management Entity, School of Agriculture and Life Sciences, North Carolina State University

the developing world. Conversely, low-input systems for acid soils are defined as the cultivation of plant species adapted to the main soil constraints, minimizing but not eliminating purchased inputs, and maximizing nutrient recycling. Low-input systems differ from zero-input systems, the latter being typified by the effective nutrient cycling that exists between native forests and acid tropical soils (Nye and Greenland 1960). Such systems operate as long as there is zero output, which is what happens in undisturbed natural systems. When farmers remove nutrients in their crop harvests, they deplete available nutrient stocks and induce nutrient deficiencies in subsequent crops. In naturally fertile soils this process may take years, but in acid Oxisols and Ultisols it takes months (Sanchez et al. 1983). Nutrients removed at harvest must be replenished if production is to be sustained. Nutrients can be replenished by biological nitrogen fixation, liming, fertilizer application, and organic inputs such as mulches or manures brought from outside the field. With the exception of biological nitrogen fixation, these means involve direct cash or labour inputs, such as the purchase of fertilizers and their application, or the gathering, transport and application of organic inputs. The low-input approach aims at minimizing but not necessarily eliminating the need for inorganic and organic inputs from outside the field.

Perspectives of Farmers

In 1982 a group of Peruvian and North Carolina State University scientists interviewed shifting cultivators around Yurimaguas, Peru, a humid tropical area with a mean annual temperature of 26°C, annual rainfall of 2100 mm without a pronounced dry season, an elevation of 182 m, predominantly acid soils, tropical rain forest vegetation, and a shifting cultivation system in disequilibrium because of rapid population growth (Tyler et al. 1978; Rhoades and Bidegaray 1984). When asked what their most important agricultural wish was, the farmers' most common reply was 'to grow a second crop of upland rice before abandoning the land'. Rice (*Oryza sativa*) is the main cash crop of the region. After only one harvest the land either reverts to forest fallow or is planted to cassava (*Manihot esculenta*) or plantain (*Musa paradisiaca*) and eventually fallowed. When asked what they perceived as the major impediment to growing a second rice crop, farmers answered 'weed control'. One farmer also indicated that a tropical kudzu (*Pueraria phaseoloides*) fallow could be an alternative to the secondary forest fallow. Armed with these perceptions, and with experience on how to grow crops continuously with appropriate fertilizers, scientists from the national Tropical Soils Research Program began to design a low-input cropping system.

Selecting Acid-tolerant Germplasm

The first step in the research programme was to identify sufficiently acid-tolerant species and varieties that would produce acceptable yields without liming. Field research was conducted at the Yurimaguas Experiment Station. The soils used were fine-loamy, siliceous, isohyperthermic Typic Paleudults. They were well drained, acid (pH values between 4.0 and 4.5, topsoil aluminum saturation ranging from 50 to 80%), and low in inherent fertility (Tyler et al. 1978). Germplasm believed to have high yield potential under humid tropical conditions was collected from different countries and then tested in limed and non-limed plots at aluminum saturation levels of 20 and 80% respectively (Piha and Nicholaides 1983; Nicholaides and Piha 1987). Cultivars were considered highly tolerant if their yields in acid soils were 85% or more of those obtained in the limed plots. In addition, the absolute yields had to be agronomically attractive. The overall results indicate a high degree of acid tolerance in upland rice and cowpea (*Vigna unguiculata*), an absence of acid tolerance in the maize (*Zea mays*), soya bean (*Glycine max*), and winged bean (*Psophocarpus tetraglobulus*) germplasm tested, and evidence of moderate tolerance in groundnut (*Arachis hypogaea*) and sweet potatoes (*Ipomoea batatas*). We selected an upland rice-cowpea rotation, using germplasm from the International Institute of Tropical Agriculture (IITA) in Nigeria, as the basis for the low-input cropping system. The acid tolerance of the selected cultivars, Africano Desconocido rice and Vita 7 cowpea, has been confirmed in a wide variety of trials on farmers' fields in the Peruvian Amazon.

The First Cropping Cycle

One hectare of 10-year-old secondary forest fallow on an Ultisol with a topsoil clay content of 28% was slashed on 15 July 1982, allowed to dry, and burned in the traditional manner on 20 August 1982. Previous studies demonstrated that traditional slash-and-burn is the best land clearing method (Seubert et al. 1977; Alegre et al. 1986; Alegre and Cassel 1986). The entire hectare was planted to the Carolino upland rice variety and grown by traditional shifting cultivation. After the first harvest, the field was split in half, and a low-input trial was initiated with the Africano Desconocido rice variety. Half the field was not fertilized, whereas the other half received an application of 30 kg of nitrogen, 22 kg of phosphorus and 48 kg of potassium per hectare when Africano rice was grown. After the burning, a total of seven crops, five of rice and two of cowpea, were harvested over a period of approximately 34 months. No tillage or lime was used, and all crop residues were evenly distributed to the field. Commercially available herbicides (Mt Pleasant 1987) and manual labor were used to control weeds. The chronology of the system is shown in Table 1. The seven crops occupied the land for 76% of the time. The average time interval between crops was 39 days, reflecting the field-size plots, farmer timing, and labour availability. The experimental design was considered to be completely randomized; ten crop yield and soil sample replicates were taken per treatment.

Yields of the seven successive crops harvested over 3 years are also shown in Table 1. A total of 11.5 t/ha of rice and 2.3 t/ha of cowpea grain was produced without any fertilizer or lime additions on this soil, which had a pH of 4.5. The only purchased chemical inputs were locally available contact herbicides and insecticides. Similar results were obtained in six other replicated trials at the Yurimaguas Station. Such results contrast sharply with our experience with intensive cropping systems, in which crop yields approached zero if the soil was not limed or fertilized within 1 year (Sanchez et al. 1982). The use of aluminum-tolerant cultivars, maximum residue return and zero tillage are believed to be responsible for this difference.

Essentially, no responses to the fertilizer applications to the Africano rice crops were observed in the yields of the first six crops (Table 1). Both upland rice and cowpea yields

Table 1 Productivity of seven successive crops grown in a low-input cropping system over 34 months following cutting and burning of a secondary forest at Yurimaguas, Peru

| Crop sequence | Chronology | | Grain yield (t/ha) | |
	Planting date	Harvest date	Non-fertilized system	Fertilized system
Rice cv Carolino	1//9/82	17/1/83	2.4	2.4
Rice cv Africano	11/2/83	11/6/83	3.0	3.1
Cowpea cv Vita 7	7/9/83	11/11/83	1.1	1.2
Rice cv Africano	15/12/83	23/4/84	2.8	3.2
Cowpea cv Vita	9/5/84	23/7/84	1.2	0.9
Rice cv Africano	5/9/84	2/1/85	1.8	2.0
Rice cv Afrciano	26/2/85	30/6/85	1.5	2.5
Total			13.8	15.3

Note: Fertilizer was applied only to the four Africano rice crops

were high in comparison with the regional average of about 1 t/ha for upland rice and 0.3 t/ha for cowpea. A sharp response to fertilizer was observed in the seventh crop, rice.

Soil properties
Topsoil chemical properties indicated favorable changes from 3 to 11 months after burning in response to the nutrient value of the ash, particularly in increasing base status (Table 2). From 11 to 35 months little change in topsoil pH, organic matter and exchangeable bases took place. There was a slight decrease in soil organic matter content, in contrast to the 25% decrease observed in similar soils under high-input systems at the same location (Sanchez et al. 1982). Residue return and absence of tillage are probably responsible for this less drastic decline.

By the 35th month there were significant decreases in available phosphorus and potassium, which reached values below their critical levels for the site, 12 mg /dm^3 for phosphorus and 0.15 cmol/dm^3 for potassium (Table 2). Nutrient additions in the fertilized plots, however, were apparently sufficient to offset this decrease. We assume, therefore, that the supply of nutrients for this system could be sustained by modest fertilizer applications.

Nutrient removal and cycling
The calculated nutrient accumulation by the seven crops (Table 3) is based on nutrient composition of Africano rice and Vita 7 cowpea grain, stover and roots obtained in

Table 2 Topsoil (0-15 cm) fertility dynamics over the first 35 months of the low-input cropping system on an Ultisol at Yarimaguas, Peru

Months after burning	3	11		35		LSD
Fertilizer applied?	No	No	Yes	No	Yes	
pH (H$_2$O)	4.4	4.6	4.7	4.6	4.6	0.1
Exchangeable (cmol/dm^3):						
Al	1.10	1.46	1.14	1.65	1.23	0.25
Ca	0.30	0.92	0.97	1.00	1.16	0.17
Mg	0.09	0.28	0.27	0.23	0.20	0.04
K	0.13	0.19	0.19	0.10	0.16	0.03
EEC (cm/dm^3)	1.62	2.85	2.58	2.99	2.76	0.20
Al saturation (%)	68	51	45	53	44	7
Available P (Olsen) (mg/dm^3)	20	13	18	5	16	2
Organic matter (%)	2.12	2.06	2.07	1.92	1.77	0.15

Notes: Mean of 50 samples per treatment. The co-efficients of variation (CV) were as follows: pH, 6%; Al, 46%; Ca, 46%; Mg, 41%; K, 43%; ECEC, 9%; Al saturation, 37%; available P, 39%; and organic matter, 20%. Comparisons for least significant differences (LSDs) and CV do not include sampling at 3 months after clearing. The LSDs are for comparing two sampling dates within a treatment at $P = 0.05$. ECEC = effective cation exchange capacity

neighboring experiments (Gichuru 1986; Scholes and Salazar 1987). Even though only the rice grain and cowpea pods were exported from the field, these harvested products represented considerable nutrient removals over the 3-year period. The amounts of nutrients accumulated by the crops but returned to the soil as above- or below-ground organic inputs were larger than the amounts removed, except in the case of phosphorus. Crop residues plus root turnover returned to the soil accounted for 62% of the dry matter, 54% of the nitrogen, 70% of the magnesium, 89% of the potassium, 95% of the calcium, but only 38% of the phosphorus accumulated by crops. If we assume there was 200% fine root decomposition (Scholes and Salazar 1987), root turnover accounted for a relatively minor proportion of the nutrients amounts recycled. The actual amounts returned, therefore, are equivalent to an annual fertilizer application rate of 98 kg/ha of nitrogen, 7 kg/ha of phosphorus, 199 kg/ha of potassium, 33 kg/ha of calcium and 13 kg/ha of magnesium respectively. However, a proportion of the nitrogen returned as above-ground residue may be lost before it enters the soil, by denitrification on the mulch-soil surface interface. Biological nitrogen fixation by cowpea may counteract such losses, but neither process was measured. Other nutrient inputs are likely to be transferred entirely to the soil. Phosphorus, therefore, appears to be the critical nutrient, since about two-thirds of the crop uptake was removed in the harvested products, giving this element the lowest recycling percentage and the lowest absolute amounts returned to the soil among the five nutrients evaluated.

Weed pressure

In our view, increasing difficulty of weed control was the single most important factor contributing to the instability of this low-input system during its third year. The initial weed population was mainly broad-leaved, which is typical of shifting cultivation fields in the area. With time, the weed population gradually shifted to more aggressive grasses not subject to economically sound control by commercially available herbicides (Alegre et al. 1986). Of particular importance was the spread of *Rottboelia exaltata*, a non-rhizomatous grass, particularly during rice growth. Cowpea was more competitive with weeds than upland rice because it covered the soil surface more thoroughly.

Studies on weed control in low-input systems at Yurimaguas indicate that the absence of tillage and burning promotes weed build-up (Alegre and Cassel 1986). Rice straw mulch may reduce weed growth in cowpea, but cowpea residues do not have the same effect on rice, perhaps because of the rapid decomposition rate of cowpea residues. Mt Pleasant (1987) concluded that six crops is a realistic estimate of the duration of the upland rice-cowpea low-input system in terms of economically sound weed control in Yurimaguas.

Economics

Table 4 summarizes the costs and returns for the first seven crops in the plots without fertilizer. Labour inputs for the first crop include land clearing; thus labour for the

Table 3 Total dry matter and nutrient accumulation by five rice and two cowpea crops harvested over 35 months without fertilizer applications

Plant parts	Dry matter [1] (t/ha)	N	P	K	Ca	Mg
				(kg/ha)		
Grain and pods	14.2	250	34	73	5	18
Straw or stover	18.1	232	15	565	80	35
Roots	5.2	6.3	6	44	18	5
Total	37.5	545	55	682	103	58

1. Based on mean grain to straw ratios of 0.84 for rice and 0.52 for cowpea; mean cowpea pod weight of 0.032 t/ha per crop, and fine root biomass of 0.65 and 0.97 t/ha per crop for rice and cowpea in the top 30 cm of soil

subsequent crops averages half that required for the first crop. Returning and redistributing crop residues required an average of 10 person-days/ha, or approximately US$ 20/ha per crop. Another major labour input was for bird-scaring, for which boys were hired near harvest time. The next major cost items were interest on crop loans from the agrarian bank and government fees for receiving and processing rice at the mills. Shifting cultivators routinely obtain bank loans that are used primarily as an advance on their labour. Interest charges fluctuating from 40 to 101% on an annual basis in local currency reflect the high inflation rate in Peru, which averaged 125% annually during the study period. Even in US dollar terms the indirect cost of purchased chemical inputs (herbicides and insecticides)

Table 4 Labour inputs, production costs and returns to the low-input system without ferilizer applcations

Labour, costs and returns	Crop sequence						
	Rice	Rice	Cowpea	Rice	Cowpea	Rice	Rice
Labour (person-days/ha)	172	79	99	79	99	79	79
Costs (US$/ha):							
Labour	380	140	113	134	167	130	95
Herbicides	21	21	25	26	25	24	25
Insecticides	0	11	14	14	13	0	0
Seed	19	17	75	18	51	16	17
Bags	16	18	8	20	7	18	50
Thresher rent	0	34	0	38	0	34	80
Transport to market	12	12	14	14	14	12	14
Loan interest and fees	135	80	86	105	108	111	225
Total costs	583	333	335	369	385	345	506
Returns:							
Grain produced (t/ha)	2.44	2.99	1.10	2.77	1.19	1.84	1.52
Price (US$/t)	321	281	1420	305	1127	265	274
Gross revenue (US$/ha)	783	840	1562	845	1341	488	416
Net return (US$/ha)	200	507	1227	476	956	143	−90
Net return/cost (%)	34	152	366	129	248	41	−18

and other items (seed, bags and thresher rent) comprised 8 and 19% of the total production costs respectively. Since most shifting cultivators have no title to the land they used, no land costs were included in this estimate.

The low-input system without fertilizer applications was highly profitable, averaging net returns of US$ 1144/ha per year, or a 121% return on total costs (Table 5). The low-input system with fertilizers was also quite profitable, averaging an annual net return of US$ 1125/ha and a 100% return on total costs. Fertilizers accounted for 9% of total costs, and incurred additional labour, interest, thresher use and transport costs. With or without fertilizers, the low-input system was more profitable than traditional shifting cultivation.

Continuing the Low-input System

Traditional shifting cultivation involves a secondary forest fallow period of 4 to 20 years, supposedly to replenish soil nutrient availability and control weeds, although the processes involved are not well understood (Gichuru 1986). Farmer experience around Yurimaguas indicates that a minimum desired age of fallow is about 12 years, but population pressures reduce this period to an average of 4 years (Rhoades and Bidegaray 1984). Slashing and burning young forest fallows results in faster grass weed invasion than would occur in older fallows because the weed seed pool declines with age (Szott and Palm 1986). Considering the diminishing likelihood of long secondary fallow periods in humid tropical areas in developing countries, the need for an improved fallow is apparent. Following a farmer's suggestion, Bandy and Sanchez (1981) studied the use of tropical kudzu (*Pueraria phaseoloides*) as a managed fallow.

Kudzu was seeded in the low-input experiment on 28 August 1985, after harvesting the seventh rice crop, which was heavily infested with *Rottboellia exaltata* and other weeds. No fertilizers were added to the kudzu plots, but the tall *Rottboellia* plants were weeded once by hand. Kudzu was slow to establish, but within 3 months it had developed a complete ground cover and provided a layer of surface litter. The kudzu was slashed with machetes on 13 September 1986; after 10 days of dry weather, it was burned off in a total time of 4 minutes for the 1250 m² plots. Ash sampled 1 day after burning contained considerable amounts of nutrients, which were incorporated into the soil by the first rains.

Africano rice was planted 3 days after the burning of the kudzu and harvested on 22 January 1987. Like the previous rice crops, it received 30 kg/ha of nitrogen, 22 kg/ha of phosphorus and 49 kg/ha of potassium. Grain yields were the highest obtained to date at this site (3.9 t/ha). These yields were partly due to favorable rainfall, as evidenced by similar rice yields obtained in other experiments at the same time, but they were also a result of the absence of significant weed pressure. The 1-year kudzu fallow suppressed weed growth far more effectively than the herbicide combinations attempted to date. A subsequent crop of upland rice was grown without any fertilizer application, and it averaged 1.9 t/ha, an adequate yield given the time of planting.

Table 5 Cumulative production costs and returns to seven crops over 3 years in the low-input system with and without fertilizer application and under shifting cultivation

| Costs and returns | Low-input system | | | | Shifting cultivation | |
| | Non-fertilized | | Fertilized | | | |
	US$/ha	%	US$/ha	%	US$/ha	%
Costs:						
Labour inputs	1159	41	1185	36	380	65
Chemical inputs:						
Fertilizers	0	0	292	9	0	0
Herbicides	167	6	167	5	21	4
Insecticides	39	2	27	1	0	0
Other inputs:						
Seed	213	7	213	6	19	3
Bags	137	5	140	4	16	3
Thresher use	186	7	189	5	0	0
Transport to market	92	2	96	3	12	2
Loan interest and fees	850	30	1017	31	135	23
Total costs	2843	100	3326	100	583	100
Returns:						
Gross revenue	6275		6688		783	
Net returns	3432		3362		200	
Net return/cost		121		101		30

Changes in topsoil chemical properties in the kudzu fallow plots at the end of the first cropping cycle, after 1 year of kudzu fallow (1 day before burning), and after the first harvest of the second cropping cycle are shown in Table 6. The effect of the kudzu fallow on topsoil chemical properties includes a significant decrease in exchangeable calcium and potassium, presumably owing to plant uptake, with no changes in acidity, aluminum saturation, or available phosphorus. Topsoil properties at 54 months after initial burning—that is, after seven crop harvests followed by 1 year of kudzu fallow and one crop harvest—were as good as or better than they were at 3 months after burning the original forest (Table 2). Topsoil organic matter contents increased, probably as a result of the kudzu fallow litter inputs. The second cropping cycle is being continued in order to determine how long these effects will last; however, in this cycle no additional fertilizer is being applied, and weed control will be only at the traditional level.

Ecological Implications

The low-input system has several potentially positive environmental impacts. It provides a low-cost alternative to shifting cultivation in highly acid soils. To produce the grain yields reported in Table 1, a shifting cultivator would need to clear about 14 ha in 3 years, in comparison to clearing 1 ha once only for the low-input system. Furthermore, the system works well using secondary forest fallows instead of primary forest (although it should also work well starting from primary forest).

Erosion hazards are largely eliminated by the absence of tillage and the presence of a plant canopy on the soil surface, be it slash-and-burn debris, crop canopies, crop residue

Table 6 Changes in selected topsoil (0-15 cm) chemical properties after 1 year of kudzu fallow and harvest of subsequent crop

Plot status	End of first cropping cycle (seven crops)	After 1 year of kudzu fallow (before burning)	At first harvest of second cropping cycle	LSD (P = 0.05)
Months after burning	35	52	54	
pH (H_2O)	4.5	4.5	4.8	0.2
Exchangeable (cmol/dm^3):				
Al	1.9	1.8	1.6	0.3
Ca	0.98	0.60	1.05	0.25
Mg	0.10	0.09	0.18	0.05
K	0.26	0.13	0.23	0.05
Al saturation (%)	50	68	52	11
Available P (Olsen) (mg/dm^3)	4	7	14	6
Organic matter (%)	1.92		2.44	NS

Note: Plots did not receive fertilizers during the first cropping cycle. The CVs were as follows: pH, 4%; Al, 25%; Mg, 32%; K, 9%; Al saturation, 21%; available P, 48%; organic matter, 15%

mulch or a managed fallow. Nutrient recycling is maximized, but nutrients exported as grain must be replenished by outside inputs in soils low in nutrient reserves. Perhaps just as importantly, the low-input system does not lead the farmer into a corner; instead, it provides a wide range of options after the first cropping cycle is complete.

Limitations of the Study

We have demonstrated the agronomic and economic feasibility of this transition technology at Yurimaguas. Its basic components (slash-and-burn clearing, acid-tolerant cultivars, zero tillage, maximum residue return, minimum fertilizer application, and weed eradication by managed fallows) may be applicable in much of the humid tropics, but the choice of crop species and varieties, managed fallows, and duration of the system are probably site-specific. When the system was replicated at a sandier site in Yurimaguas, the number of crops obtained was reduced from seven to five.

Low-input cropping is viable when initial conditions are favorable in terms of nutrient inputs from ash and low weed pressure, as in the 10-year-old secondary forest used in these experiments. This system is unlikely to perform as well in nutritionally depleted, compacted, or weedy soils that are a product of mismanagement. The duration of the cropping period is probably a function of initial soil conditions and of processes related to fertility depletion and weed populations. A network of validation trials throughout the humid tropics, with the use of locally adapted cultivars, would help further ascertain the applicability of this transition technology between shifting and continuous cultivation.

References

Alegre, J.C. and D.K. Cassel. 1986. *Soil Sci.* 142, 289.

Alegre, J.C., D.K. Cassel and D.E. Bandy. 1986. *Soil Sci. Soc. Am. J.* 50, 1379.

Alvim, P.T. 1982. In: S.B. Hecht (ed.), Amazonia: Agriculture and land use research. CIAT, Cali Colombia.

Bandy, D.E. and P.A. Sanchez. 1981. *Agron. Abstr.*, 40.

Gichuru, M.P. 1986. Thesis. North Carolina State University.

Kang, B.T., G.F. Wilson and L. Sipkens. 1981. *Plant Soil* 63, 165.

Lal, R. 1987. *Tropical ecology and physical edaphology*. Wiley, New York.

Lopes, A.S., T.J. Smyth and N. Curi. 1987. International Board for Soils Research and Management (IBSRAM) Proceedings, Vol. 2. IBSRAM, Bangkok.

Mt. Pleasant, J. 1987. Thesis, North Carolina State University.

Nicholaides, J.J. and M.I. Piha. 1987. In: Sorghum for acid soils. CIAT, Cali, Colombia.

North Carolina State University. 1985. *Topsoils: The first three years*. Raleigh.

Nye, P.H. and D.J. Greenland. 1960. *Tech. Commun. Commonw. Bur. Soils*, No. 51.

Piha, M.I. and J.J. Nicholaides. 1983. In: J.J. Nicholaides, W. Couto and M.K. Wade (eds), Agronomic-economic research on soils of the tropics 1980-81. Annual Report, North Carolina State University, Raleigh.

Rhoades, R.E. and P. Bidegaray. 1984. Agrarian ecology in the Peruvian jungle, Yurimaguas. CIP, Lima, Peru.

Sanchez, P. A. and J.R. Benites. 1983. Opciones tecnológicas para el manejo racional de suelos en la selva Peruana. Estación Experimental de Yurimaguas, Instituto Nacional de Investigación y Promociön Agraria (INIPA), Yurimaguas, Peru. In: Proceedings, 1st Symposium on the Humid Tropics. Empresa Brasileira de Pesquisa Agropecuária (EMBRAPA), Belém, Brazil.

Sanchez, P. A. and S.W. Buol. 1975. *Science* 188, 598.

Sanchez, P. A., D.E. Bandy, J.H. Villachica and J.J. Nicholaides. 1982. *Science* 216, 821.

Sanchez, P.A. 1976. *Properties and management of soils in the tropics.* Wiley, New York.

Sanchez, P.A. and J.G. Salinas. 1981. *Adv. Agron.* 34, 279.

Sanchez, P.A., J.H. Villachica and D.E. Bandy. 1983. *Soil Sci. Soc. Am. J.* 47, 1171.

Scholes, R.J. and A. Salazar. 1987. In: TropSoils/NCSU Technical Report for 1986-87. North Carolina State University, Raleigh.

Seubert, C.E., P.A. Sanchez and C. Valverde. 1977. *Trop. Agric. (Trinidad)* 54, 307.

Szott, L.T. and C.A. Palm. 1986. In: Proceedings of the First Symposium on the Humid Tropics, vol. 1 (EMBRAPA, Belém, Brazil)

Tyler, E.J., S.W. Buol and P.A. Sanchez. 1978. *Soil Sci. Soc. Am. J.* 42, 771.

Source
First published in *Science*, Volume 238, pp. 1521-1527, December 1987. Reprinted by kind permission of the author and the publisher. Copyright 1987 by the AAAS.

Addresses
Pedro Sanchez: ICRAF, P.O. Box 30677, Nairobi, Kenya
José Benites: FAO Soils Department, Via delle Terme di Caracalla, Rome 00100.

Indigenous Soil Management in the Latin American Tropics: Neglected Knowledge of Native People

Susanna B. Hecht

Introduction

During the past 20 years, more than 20 million ha of lowland forests have been converted to other land uses in the Amazon basin (Moran 1982). Most of this land eventually ends up as cattle pastures, which rapidly become degraded and unproductive. As soil nutrients become exhausted and the labour required for weeding becomes more arduous, farmers and ranchers abandon old areas and clear new ones, thereby creating an ever-expanding front of forest removal and land degradation.

In contrast, an emerging body of work in Amazonia suggests that native populations have developed complex systems of resource management that are ecologically sustainable, yield well, and generate levels of income that exceed the regional average.

This paper deals with soil management issues in small farm development. It discusses the indigenous and modern approaches to soil management in Amazonian research and development. It then describes the practices of a native group in the Brazilian Amazon, the Kayapo Indians. The Kayapo system is compared with the dominant modern agricultural systems prevailing in Amazonia—colonist agriculture and livestock production. Data on the Kayapo system were derived from yield measurements of crops in the field, household harvests, and informant estimates. Because Kayapo planting and harvesting are continuous and our field presence was not, the numbers cited are probably underestimates. Colonist production data were derived from field interviews, and estimates from the local Conceicao de Araguaia office, as well as generalized estimates on colonist agricultural productivity found in government and academic literature. Data on livestock production were derived from field research. Field work on colonist and livestock systems was undertaken 25 km from Redencao in the direction of Gorotire.

From Transnational to Tribal Paradigms

Amazonian soils are for the most part extremely poor, and soil constraints are severe for many crops grown under current cropping systems. Over 90% of Amazonian soils are deficient in phosphorus and nitrogen; about 75% are deficient in potassium and have serious problems of aluminum toxicity òr low levels of calcium and magnesium. Only about 4% exhibit no major agricultural constraints. The problems inherent in conventional crop-soil management in areas with such poor soils have given tropical zones a reputation for 'fragility'. This perception ignores the resilience of many tropical forest formations, and overlooks the fact that indigenous Amazonian populations have developed complex systems of agriculture and intensive soil management practices that have overcome these difficulties.

The dramatic nature of soil degradation following forest conversion is recognized in much regional research on tropical agronomy. Several researchers have argued that soil constraints can be overcome by the application of fertilizers and other modern inputs. In fact, one of the main justifications of conventional soils research in humid tropical lowland areas is the idea that if the production of annual crops could be stabilized through the use of modern inputs, then the migration and deforestation associated with crop failures could be diminished. Hence the overwhelming preponderance of fertilizer and varietal trials at tropical agricultural research stations.

The Yurimaguas model

The most famous Amazonian example of this approach is that developed by Sanchez's group in Yurimaguas (*see* p.117, this volume, as well as Sanchez and Benites 1987; Sanchez et al. 1982; Sanchez 1985). Following the US Land Grant College model of agronomic research and development, the soil and crop management strategies used by this group focus on target crops or soil problems, with minimal reference to the knowledge and practices of local people. This kind of approach has generated useful information on crop-soil dynamics for specific tropical zones, but as a strategy it concentrates primarily on what scientists have been able to learn on research stations through the application of western scientific techniques to rather narrowly defined pedological/agronomic problems. The response of such groups to soil management problems has emphasized agronomic techniques rooted in temperate zone models of agricultural intensification consisting principally of fertilizer applications. In this approach, a large body of local knowledge about soil potential and management is ignored, and the social and economic contexts in which most farmers in the humid tropics must operate is often overlooked. There are a number of reasons why an approach based largely on chemical fertilizers, such as the Yurimaguas model, is open to question:

• Agronomic reasons, including soil nutrient imbalances and micronutrient deficiencies that cannot be easily detected by most Amazonian colonists, pest outbreaks that can reduce yields regardless of soil management, erosion problems, and physical changes in soil properties

• Institutional problems, including the unavailability of inputs at the proper time, the high cost of inputs, and their inadequate quality

• Market factors, such as inadequate returns to farmers, high transport costs, and credit that is too expensive.

Broader structural questions that impinge on the use of such technologies include problems of land tenure. Farmers with insecure tenure cannot afford to invest in costly technologies when they may be expelled from their land. Given the very low incomes of most Amazonian inhabitants, usually under US\$ 1000 per annum, fertilizer costs, at US\$ 250 to 300/ha, can take up almost one-third of an average household's income to produce commodities whose prices are often controlled, whose marketing is difficult and costly and whose production in Amazonia is risky. Credit is usually proposed as the solution to this impasse, but only about 4% of Amazonian peasants receive credit at present.

In short, the inherent riskiness of annual crop production, and the high opportunity costs of the labour and cash invested in it, reduce the incentive to use high-input technologies. As a result the Yurimaguas approach has undergone several modifications over the years, increasingly incorporating practices that are less input demanding.

Some analysts are beginning to argue that tropical land use models should be based on management methods developed by local populations, which are presumably more closely integrated with the dynamics of tropical ecological systems and better suited to the needs of local peoples. Researchers increasingly recognize the role of native populations in the development of ecologically sound, productive land uses. However, the amount of research on indigenous soil management techniques remains negligible. How well they perform is a research question that has received little attention in spite of the enormous budgets devoted to tropical pedology and agronomy. One might well ask why research on such a central issue in tropical development has so systematically ignored local knowledge and experience. A bag of fertilizer is not necessarily a 'bad' technology for Amazonian soils, but it is not the only one available. The real question is what is the *range* of technical options for the Amazon? Existing native practices could suggest useful hypotheses for land management that could be tested under experiment station conditions. Indigenous systems could be used as a springboard for integrating the best of both systems. It is a great irony that the Yurimaguas group, responsible for what are perhaps the finest studies of Amazonian agriculture, and the team headed by Denevan and Padoch (1988) have interacted so little.

The Kayapo model

The characteristics of the the Kayapo and Yurimaguas systems are outlined in Table 1. This table shows the rich array of techniques and strategies available for managing soils of relatively low fertility and the points of intersection between the modern and traditional models.

The Kayapo system includes a soil taxonomy, selection for varietal diversity, and complex planting patterns in space and time. Figure 1 shows an idealized version of the cropping pattern, often called concentric ring planting. This pattern involves spatial segregation of some crops, relay planting and other successional management techniques. Soil conserving practices are incorporated within this physical and temporal

Table 1 Agriculture formations of the Kayapo

Village gardens

    1. Household gardens

    2. Swidden plots

    3. Successional plots derived from swidden

    4. Grave sites

    5. Marantacac gardens on hill slopes

Planting associated with movement

    6. Trails between villages and gardens

    7. Trails between villages

    8. Hunting/trekking trails

    9. Planting around old camp sites

Forest planting

    10. Natural ecosystem gaps

    11. Man-made gaps

    12. Plantations in mature forest

    13. Fruit grove in memory of the dead

Cerrado planting

---

structure. These include the use of multiple cropping systems, crop rotation, crops such as sweet potato whose vines cover the ground, concentrated tillage and soil turning in high use areas, direct additions of nutrients in the form of applications of ashes, mulches, residues, dung and enriched soils, transferring forest litter, composting, and controlled periodic in-field burning. The points of similarity between the Yurimaguas and Kayapo systems lie in the use of crop residues, relay planting, nutrient additions and short fallows. However, the 'arsenal' of the Kayapo agricultural system is richer, with the result that the system requires no purchased inputs.

A complex intellectual system underlies the native management of soil resources. The study of this system we may call 'ethnopedology'. Ethnopedology includes the study of native land classification systems, management techniques and their variations, and how the practical and theoretical knowledge is developed, expanded, encoded and reproduced. Land uses reflect some implicit or explicit assessment of the relative capabilities of soils, and the choice of practical techniques ranging from crop selection to soil management to address these capabilities. Folk soil taxonomies are widespread, and generally correlate well with discernible quantitative differences among soil types.

The study of indigenous soil management has many of the advantages of classic soils research: soil properties can be more precisely specified than vegetation processes; edaphic data from one area can illuminate the probabilities of land use outcomes on similar sites more clearly than vegetation data; soil data are particularly powerful tools for evaluating and comparing the impact of land management over time. In addition, insights from tropical land management systems that have survived the test of time can help inform new strategies and formulate testable hypotheses. Given the power of this form of analysis, it is surprising that so little serious attention has been paid to native land management techniques. If Kayapo techniques can sustain or increase productivity over time, they could serve as the foundation for sustainable agricultural systems for the Amazon basin's newer, less experienced small-scale farmers.

In the next section, Kayapo agricultural yields and soil dynamics are compared with the two dominant regional land uses: colonist agriculture and livestock production.

Systems Comparison

The Gorotire Kayapo inhabit an area characterized by a complex geology and geomorphology in southern Para, Brazil. Lying at the interface between the Precambrian

Figure 1 Schematic view of Kayapo concentric ring agriculture

Brazilian shield and more recent metamorphic and sedimentary formations, the area contains several major soil orders, found within short distances. Most Kayapo agriculture is carried out on four main soil types: a high fertility alfisol, a relatively high fertility ultisol, a low fertility ultisol and a low fertility oxisol. Because the four soil orders managed by the Kayapo are similar to more than 80% of Amazonian soils, the principles, techniques and impact of Kayapo management could have wider implications for tropical soil management in the Amazon Basin.

The Kayapo designate 14 types of land use as 'agriculture' (*see* Table 1). These various land uses are complex, and include ceremonial planting, reforestation and trek gardens, as well as swidden plots. The Kayapo practise concentric ring/crop segregation agriculture based on sweet potato, cassava, yams and perennials, periodically intercropped with maize, beans, cucurbits, introduced rice and numerous other minor crops and ritual plants. Kayapo swiddens stay in active root crop production for about 5 years, and continue to contribute these products at reduced levels for as long as 11 years. This exceptionally long production period is a function of eight main factors:

• A mixture of short- and long-cycle cultigens and cultivars
• Sequential harvesting and replanting
• Root crop cultivars well adapted to burning (including fire-tolerant cassava, sweet potato, yams and marantaceaes)
• Systematic, differential, periodic burning within the agricultural field for the entire production sequence
• Mulching
• Nutrient additions
• Agricultural structure
• Manipulated fallows.

The practices of the Kayapo and Yurimaguas production systems are compared in Table 2.

Informants indicate that the concentric zones facilitate the creation or manipulation of in-field micro-variability that fine-tunes soil nutrients to crop demands. Slight lateral changes in the physical and chemical properties of the soils can be strongly reflected in the growth and productivity of most annual and biennial crops. Concentric field architecture permits the controlled use of specific soil nutrient management techniques. For example, the frequent use of in-field burning throughout the agricultural cycle requires that particular crops be separated from others to control nutrient additions and minimize fire damage. Mulch application, specific nutrient additions, soil aerating and other tasks can be more effectively practised when crops are spatially segregated.

Comparing land uses

The dominant modern forms of land use in the Amazon are short-cycle agriculture and livestock production, which are notorious for their unsustainability and low rates of economic return. The features of Kayapo agriculture are outlined and compared with

Table 2 Kayapo and Yurimaguas production systems

	Kayapo	Yurimaguas
Soil classification	Yes	Yes
Clearing	Slash-and-burn	Slash-and-burn
Crop diversity	High	Low
Medium cycle crops (2-4 years)	Yes	No
Tree species	Yes	Rarely
Polyvarietal planting	Yes	No
Plant structure	Concentric ring	Pure stand monocultures
Nutrient inputs	Yes: Ash, mulch, termite nests, litter, palm fronds	Yes: 30 kg N, 22 kg P, 48 kg K
Residue return	Yes: Rice, maize, banana leaves, yam vines, sweet potato, cassava peelings	Yes: Rice and cowpea stover
Cultivation practices:		
Intercropping	Yes	Rarely
Relay planting	Yes	Yes
Mulching	Yes	No
Continuous planting	Yes	No
In-field burning	Yes	No
In-field mulch pits	Yes	No
Weed control:		
Manual	Yes	Yes
Fire	Yes	No
Mulch	Yes	Sometimes
Allelopathy	Possibly	No
Scandent crops	Yes	No
Herbicides	No	Yes
Fallow	5-10 years	Yes: kudzu (1-2 years)

these two other land uses in Table 3. These production systems differ fundamentally in structural terms, including field pattern, crop species diversity, total time in production, use of tree species, harvest patterns, and degree of integration with the larger economy. The table demonstrates a gradient of management intensity, ecological complexity and declining labour allocations per hectare. Because the systems are so different the production comparison focuses on production yields and proteins.

Table 3 Comparison of the structure of Kayapo, colonist agriculture and livestock production systems

	Kayapo	Colonist agriculture	Livestock
Clearing	Slash-and-burn	Slash-and-burn	Slash-and-burn
Clearing size	About 1 ha	2-5 ha	<20 000 ha
Planting patterns			
Crop zonation	Yes	Rarely	No
Continuous cropping	Yes	Sometimes	Yes
Continuous planting	Yes	Rarely	No
Relay cropping	Yes	Yes	No
Monocropping	No [1]	Often	Usually
Intercropping	Yes	Sometimes	No
Polyvarietal crops	Yes	Rarely	No
Tree species	Yes	Rarely	Rarely
No. of cultivated species in field	10-42+	5-10	1-5
Harvest pattern	Continuous	Periodic	Periodic
Practices to maintain soil fertility	Yes [2]	Rarely	Rarely, occasional use of legumes
Main crops	Sweet potato, yam, cassava, maize, musa, beans, squash	Rice, cassava	Panicum, Braciaria
Labour	40 person-days/ha	25 person-days/ha	4.5 person-days/ha

1. Parts of the Kayapo system are monocultured in the concentric field, but the entire field is rarely monocropped
2. Mulching, controlled in-field burning, use of nutrient accumulating species, application of soil fertility inputs, use of crops with scandent habits, complex co-planting arrangements

Table 4 Production (kg and proteins/ha) of Kayapo, colonist agricultural and livestock production systems over time

Production system	5 years	10 years
Kayapo:		
Production of all crops (kg/ha) [1]	61 750	84 050
Protein (kg/ha) [2]	1 248	1 704
Colonist agriculture:		
Production of all crops (kg/ha) [3]	21 800	-
Protein (kg/ha)	602	-
Livestock:		
Production (kg/ha)	350	700
Protein (kg/ha) [2,4]	105 (63)	210 (126)

1. Estimates based on in-field harvest weights, household harvests and informant estimates. The crops included here are sweet potato, yams, cassava, plantains and bananas, maize, beans, squash and groundnut. Many other minor crops, such as *Colocassia* and other tubers, papaya, water melon, pepper, mango and pineapple, are not included in the calculation
2. Protein estimates derived from various sources
3. Based on average yields of rice, maize and cassava in colonist agriculture in Amazonia
4. Assumes that virtually the entire animal, including the hide, is consumed, of which roughly 30% is protein. If the animal is dressed out it weighs about 60% of its live weight. The dressed out protein yield is indicated in parentheses

The edible harvest and protein yields for each land use are outlined in Table 4 for periods of 5 and 10 years. Over 5 years the Kayapo yields are roughly 200% higher than those in colonist systems and 175 times those of livestock systems. Colonist agriculture rarely continues beyond 5 years, hence there can be no comparison between the Kayapo and colonist systems over the 10-year period. However, the comparison between the Kayapo and livestock systems shows that in the latter production is a mere 700 kg of animal per hectare whereas production in the Kayapo system is more than 84 t.

The data follow the same trends when protein production is analysed. Kayapo protein yields from vegetable sources are roughly double those of colonists and more than ten times the protein production for the entire animal. The protein per 100 g of beef is roughly 30 g. If the dressed out animal (that is, one with hide, bones and offal removed, usually about 40% of live animal weight) is used as the basis of the analysis, the pure protein produced over 5 years is a scandalous 63 kg/ha. In 10 years, using these calculations, 1 ha of pasture produces less than a tonne of meat and slightly more than 100 kg of protein, or roughly 5% of the protein generated by the Kayapo system. Incidently, Kayapo gardens in their later phases become a habitat for animals such as agouti, peccaries and deer, and thus producers of animal protein during the fallow period. This protein production is not taken into account in this analysis.

The Kayapo system is based on root crops, especially sweet potato, which are very productive in the tropics and also drought tolerant, continuing production even during the dry season. The sheer volume of production ensures sufficient carbohydrate and, with minor supplements, protein also. While these crops are often reviled for their low protein contents, nutritional studies on adult Yami tribesmen show that their diets were nutritionally adequate when they were given 2.5 kg of sweet potato a day. Several studies in New Guinea show that protein content varies significantly between cultivars, and that the intestinal flora of some groups of New Guinean sweet potato eaters may have been able to fix nitrogen.

Soil effects

The next question is what impact this high production has on soil properties. Soil samples were taken on sites with similar soil characteristics, in this case dystrophic paleudults. Adjacent forest sites were used as 'controls', and samples were collected on areas in the first year of production, the fifth year of production and the tenth year. Sampling areas were roughly 1 ha in size, and the samples were collected randomly. Ten samples were taken per 'treatment'.

Table 5 shows several clear trends. First, pH tends to improve with burning, and this effect persists over time in all three systems, mainly as the result of decomposition of larger tree boles. In the Kayapo case, higher pHs are maintained for a longer period, probably due to the continual in-field burning, the cooking of food within the fields themselves, and the importing of wood for the cooking fires. Nitrogen levels are very low in all three systems, but low nitrogen is less important in Kayapo agriculture because of its emphasis on root crops rather than grains for most of the production cycle. Rice requires about 23 kg of nitrogen to produce a tonne of crop, while cassava and sweet potato remove only 3.7 and 4.3 kg per tonne respectively, and require little nitrogen for good production. Phosphorus levels are low in all the soils, but Kayapo production maintains higher levels of phosphorus over time. Potassium is a very labile element, easily leached in tropical conditions and closely associated with productivity in root crops. The use of mulches with a high potassium content, such as *Maximiliana* leaves and crop residues enriched with cooking ash, compensates for the production losses. This element stays at levels equal to the first year of production because of these practices. Calcium and magnesium levels are also maintained over time.

The Kayapo have developed several soil management techniques that are relevant for small farm development in the humid lowland tropics. Of interest is the sheer diversity of inputs, mulches and cropping patterns used to produce high-yielding sustainable production systems.

Table 5 Changes in soil fertility elements in the Kayapo, colonist and livestock production systems

	Forest	Year 1	Year 5	Year 10
		Kayapo		
pH	4.7	5.4	5.6	5.4
N (%)	0.05	0.07	0.03	0.06
P (ppm)	1.0	5.0	3.0	3.16
K *	0.17	0.37	0.23	0.33
Ca *	0.75	1.55	1.31	1.90
Mg *	0.31	0.89	0.97	1.67
		Colonist agriculture		
pH	4.8	5.4	5.4	-
N (%)	0.12	0.10	0.06	-
P (ppm)	1.2	6.0	1.0	-
K *	0.12	0.32	0.09	-
Ca *	1.90	2.1	1.30	-
Mg *	0.34	0.59	0.42	-
		Livestock		
pH	4.7	5.5	5.2	5.0
N (%)	0.10	0.07	0.06	0.06
P (ppm)	2.0	7.0	2.0	1.0
K *	0.10	0.17	0.10	0.05
Ca *	1.3	1.7	0.92	0.64
Mg *	0.42	0.65	0.60	0.30

* Data derived from soil samples taken at Gorotire (Kayapo), Nixdorf Fazenda located near Rendencao (livestock), and colonist agriculture of squatters on the Nixdorf Ranch. Colonist and livestock agriculture sampled in 1982

A new approach to soil management is needed by those responsible for small farm development. The approach would build on what is already known, testing native knowledge in controlled circumstances. What are the folk soil classifications and soil lore found in the area? How well do these coincide with what 'western knowledge' tells us?

And are there hidden reasons (plant disease control, fertility enhancement, and so on) behind particular practices?

Fire is one of the most powerful tools that tropical farmers have, and yet we know very little about the subtleties of fire management in native agricultural systems. The current attitude to burning in tropical agro-ecosystems borders on a 'Smokey the Bear' fire suppression approach, yet some fire-based technologies may be extremely appropriate in some environments, particularly when associated with fire-tolerant cultivars.

Mulching and alternative input systems are necessary for sustainable tropical systems. Local systems can provide valuable clues as to what species are most likely to be useful, and how, when and in what form they should be used.

Finally, developers should look at the landscapes and agricultural systems around them and ask what it takes to keep each running, and what features of each system could potentially contribute to the others. The Kayapo and other rural populations don't just manage agricultural fields, they manage whole landscapes.

Conclusion

To sum up, Kayapo land management produces more product and protein at lower environmental cost than the colonist agricutural or livestock production systems. Although the labour demands are greater in this system, it ensures subsistence and conserves tropical forest. Tropical soils are difficult but not impossible to manage. The Kayapo have much to teach us about how this can be done. Yet there are no great mysteries to Kayapo agricultural systems—they simply use good agricultural practices.

Colonist migrations and slash-and-burn agriculture are a central feature of the Amazon's 20th century history. The sorry tale of livestock production in the region has been the subject of a spate of recent articles. Hundreds of millions of dollars have been funnelled into surveys and experiments which have not made colonist agriculture more stable, nor livestock more productive. Meanwhile, the budget for exploring sustainable, productive indigenous Amazonian soil management has received virtually no support. Why this critical source of knowledge has been systematically ignored requires explanations-few of which have to do with the welfare of Amazonian populations.

The people who have created sustainable production systems in the rain forest are under extraordinary pressure. Our society pays for libraries, universities and research facilities. It ought to be prepared to pay also to protect the indigenous small-scale producers of the Amazon. No other investment in research and development is likely to bring greater returns.

References
Moran, E. 1982. *Underdeveloping the Amazon.* University of Indiana Press, Bloomington.
Sanchez, P. and J. Benites. 1987. Low-input cropping systems for the tropics. *Science* 238, 1521-1527.

Sanchez, P., D. Bandy, J. Villachica and J. Nicholaides. 1982. Soils of the Amazon and their management for continuous crop production. *Science* 216, 812-827.

Sanchez, P. 1985. Management of acid soils in the tropics. Paper presented at the Acid Soils Network Inaugural Workshop, Brasilia.

Denevan, W. and C. Padoch (eds). 1988. Swidden-fallow agroforestry in the Peruvian Amazon. *Advances in Economic Botany,* New York Botanical Garden.

Acknowledgements

Funds for this project were generously provided by the Wenner-Gren Foundation, Resources for the Future, the US Fullbright, and World Wildlife Fund. The Kayapo field work was carried out with Darrell Posey through the Kayapo Project of the Museu Goeldi and the Federal University of Maranhao. This paper is modified from one presented at the 1988 Fragile Lands Symposium organized by LASA.

Source

First published 1990 in Agro-ecology and Small Farm Development, edited by Miguel A. Altieri and Susanna B. Hecht. CRC Press, Florida, USA. Reprinted by kind permission of the author and the publisher.

Address

Susanna Hecht, Graduate School of Planning, University of California, Los Angeles, USA.

High and Stable Crop Yields: The Bontoc Rice Terraces

Hilario Padilla

Introduction

The famous rice terraces of Northern Luzon in the Philippines are one of the wonders of the world. Many people are astonished to see how the steep rocky mountains have been transformed into rice fields, like stairways to the sky, using only simple tools. The centuries-old terraces are believed to have been carved by 'Indonesians'—people who came from Southern China, sailing to Luzon in dugout boats. These migrants arrived with copper and bronze tools, and the knowledge of how to build rice terraces (Scott 1975).

It is a wonder, too, that one of these terrace systems—Bontoc, at an altitude of over 1500 m—has maintained high yields through time under very difficult conditions. Omengan (1981) reported that the Bontoc rice paddies yield 6.2 t/ha without the use of modern cultivars, chemical fertilizers and pesticides. My own sampling gave an average rice yield of 6.1 t/ha. Both measurements excluded the terrace borders, which produce more tillers, more filled grains and, hence, still higher yields. In comparison, IRRI's long-term experiments with NPK fertilizer applications of 140-30-30 in the dry season yielded 7.3 t/ha (Chang 1975). The Philippine national average yield is about 2.5 t/ha. The Bontoc farmers estimate that 0.25 ha of their paddy will yield as much as 1 ha in lowland Tabuk, a nearby rice-producing area using Green Revolution technology. There is obviously much to learn from the Bontoc farmers.

Unfortunately, their rice-growing system is now beginning to disappear without having been thoroughly investigated and documented. How do the Bontoc maintain their high yields without the use of modern techniques? Does their success have anything to do with their cultural traditions? What makes this traditional system ecologically viable? Why has it not spread to other parts of the Cordillera with almost the same cultural traditions?

The Importance of Tradition

Rice is central to the social, economic and religious life of the Bontoc people. It is the main dish on all festive occasions and is also made into wine, which is highly valued for rituals. Rice production therefore demands the utmost care, and the people live very close to the rice terraces. Rice is much more valued than the other main staple food, sweet potato. To have an abundant supply of rice is a status symbol.

The Bontoc have developed a highly complex sociopolitical system, known as the Ato, which centers on the Council of Elders, who act as priests (*mumba'i*) during rituals. The Ato is the seat of all major decisions in the community. Without the Ato, the age-old rice production technology would have long been abandoned.

Water as a Tool in Terracing

Terraces are built by the men, mainly for soil and water conservation. Areas are chosen where there is ample water, regardless of slope, and a nearby source of construction materials. Slopes prone to landslides are avoided.

Water is an essential tool in construction, which usually takes place at times when water is abundant. When terracing, the Bontoc never lift what water can move. Impounded water is used to transport tonnes of rocks, granules, debris and soil fill. Topsoil is carefully saved as the last filling material. Water is conveyed from its source by gravity flow and is sometimes diverted 1-4 km upstream. This hydraulic technology and the Bontoc's stone-walling skills are incredible feats of engineering. Terrace construction requires high labour inputs and is usually done through mutual assistance (*ob-ob-fo*).

Paddy dikes and walls are religiously maintained. Seepage and weak points are immediately repaired, requiring constant field visits. A unique feature of the Bontoc terraces is their long curved walls of smooth stones (other terraces use angular broken rocks). The river-stone linings are said to conserve heat, and may influence the crop's uptake of nutrients (Omengan 1981) and the activity of soil micro-organisms.

The long perimeters of the terraces are a Bontoc adaptation to increase yield, based on observations that the borders (paddy edges) produce more tillers and filled grains. This may be due to the effect of solar radiation.

Soil Puddling by Foot

The women clear and weed the terrace walls and their immediate surroundings. Farmers are very particular about the cleanliness of terrace dikes and walls, for fear of rat infestation. The weeds are not burned, but dumped in heaps for partial decomposition.

After clearing and weeding, the women puddle the soil with their feet. In some cases, if the terrain permits, animals are used to trample the mud. During puddling the partially decaying weeds cut from the surroundings and the weeds in the pond (especially the floating azollas and blue-green algae) are trodden deep into the mud. The value of azollas had long been recognized in the area, long before scientists started investigating its potential as fertilizer. Nitrogen-fixing algae are thought to be a major source of N in the paddies.

In some parts of the pond where the water is shallow, weed vegetation is mixed with mud and formed into mounds that protrude above the water table. These are used later to grow onions, garlic, legumes and other greens. As the women move forward, working the organic matter into the mud, they also gather fish, especially *yoyo*, an eel-like fish the size of a pencil.

Sowing with Whole Panicles

Two to five traditional varieties, usually long-season ones, are planted in a medium- to large-sized field. Seeding starts with the appearance of the *kiling*, a migratory bird (*Erythruru hyperythra brunneiventris*). Whole, unthreshed rice panicles are laid parallel to each other in the seedbed.

Little is known of the scientific significance of this practice. A new approach to raising the yield potential of rice is to manipulate the weight of single grains. Increasing the number of high-density (HD) grains increases yield, milling recovery and head rice recovery. Varieties differ in the number of HD grains they produce. Within a panicle, certain spikelets invariably develop into HD grains. Most spikelets on the primary branches are HD grains. Leaves near the panicle are more important in grain filling. Removal of the fourth leaf from the top increased grain weight and the number of HD grains (Vergara 1987). It is possible that the Bontoc's careful selection of panicles as seed sources contributes to their high yields.

Seeding is done simultaneously in every community. This is related to a traditional holiday (*tengao*), which is declared before sowing. During this holiday, when it is taboo to go to the fields, seed is selected. Simultaneous sowing helps prevent the subsequent build-up of pests, especially rats (Valentin 1986), and allows the re-utilization of irrigation water and whatever nutrients it carries for other paddies.

Dense Transplanting and Little Weeding

Rice seedlings are transplanted singly and randomly at a spacing which depends on variety, elevation and season. Generally, planting density is high, with a hill spacing of 8-12 cm. Seedlings are already very large when transplanted. The village agricultural priest (Tomona) declares when to transplant. The large seedlings and close spacing could be ways of controlling weeds. Plants are spaced more closely in poorer soils and during the rains, because tillering is slower in these conditions.

In many areas, transplanting is exclusively done by women. They also gather shell and mudfish at this time, and some transfer small mudfish to less well stocked terraces. At this stage of rice growing, the women work in many fields and become familiar with the soil conditions of each plot and the agronomic response of the different varieties grown. After transplanting, no-one enters a field for almost 4 days.

Weeds are not a major problem. Often, only one weeding is enough, and the time spent weeding is also used for collecting snails and weeds as food supplements, as well as for replacing missing hills.

Communally Managed Irrigation

Irrigation water is maintained at 5-10 cm deep throughout the growing period. Farmers are very particular about water depth. After transplanting, a ritual is held to regulate the headwater source gate to avoid excess flow and so reduce the nutrient loss due to water overflow. Irrigation water is usually stopped a week before harvest.

During dry periods, irrigation water is a common source of conflict. The role of the elders in settling such conflict is highly significant in the local management of the communal irrigation systems.

Omengan (1981) studied the nutrient content of water coming in and out of the fields and found that irrigation water contributes to the nutrient content of the paddies. She also found that significant quantities of P and N accumulate within the paddies. She inferred that the compost was the P source and that probably nitrogen fixation from blue-green algae and azolla in the paddy was the N source.

Water quality differs from place to place. The occurrence of the disease *lisao*—the wilting and drying of seedlings 2-3 weeks after transplanting—could be related to water quality, as the disease occurs close to where the irrigation water enters the fields (Valentin 1986).

Few Pests and Diseases

No major pests and diseases occur in the rice terraces, only minor ones like *lisao*, which could be due to a zinc deficiency brought about by continuous flooding. This physiological disorder is manifested by red tops and rotten roots. In some areas, used batteries are ground and applied to the affected fields, as people claim this helps prevent *lisao*. The Bontoc say that draining the fields also helps prevent this disease. This corresponds with experience at IRRI, where paddies were dried up to prevent zinc deficiency resulting from oxidation.

Rats are prevented by keeping the paddies clean. Birds are driven away by scaring and the *felew* ritual. A large worm (*tuwing*) that causes paddy seepage is controlled by scattering sunflower (*Thitania* sp.) and *paswek* (family Sapindaceae) tops all over the paddy field after land preparation, when the field is ready for transplanting.

Another characteristic is the practice of *bangkag* or soil drying to prevent the occurrence of *lisao*, to make the soil easier to manage during land preparation, and to enhance the rooting of seedlings. Moreover, various scientific reports suggest that soil drying could enhance soil fertility by releasing some nutrients fixed in the soil organic complex.

Pig Manure

Besides the weed vegetation used as green manure, the Bontoc incorporate compost, mountain soil gathered from the woods, and *lamud* during land preparation.

Lamud is a weathered soil parent material gathered in the rocky mountains. It is whitish, with streaks of blue, red and yellow. It smells like magnesium. It is dried and applied in the rice fields in small quantities. Jokingly known as 'mountain urea', *lamud* is claimed to significantly increase yield. It is suspected to have liming ability and could be a source of zinc.

The Bontoc way of composting is sophisticated. Compost is produced under the 'management of the pigs' in the village. Unlike other pig enclosures, the pig pen used to make compost has half of its area excavated to about 1-2 feet and all stones removed. In this area the pigs wallow. Decomposable materials such as rice husk, straw panicle, kitchen refuse and grass clippings are dumped in the area as litter. The pigs' excrement falls into the litter and mixes with it as the pigs' snouts work all into the soil. The resulting compost is regularly collected and replaced with fresh litter. During land preparation, this material is incorporated into the rice paddy.

In other parts of the Cordillera, such as Kalinga, the use of pig manure is taboo. This may explain why some parts of Kalinga, where altitudes are similar to those of Bontoc, have lower yields.

A Classical Integrated System

The Bontoc rice terraces provide a classic example of a traditional farming system that is highly productive and whose sustainability is proven. Elsewhere in the region, the cultural rites concerning rice and the terracing systems are quite similar, but the Bontoc have more advanced techniques to enhance soil fertility, make narrower terraces and use rounded river-stones for terrace walling.

They make maximum use of local resources and conserve water and soil. Soil life is maintained through nutrient recycling and the use of biomass from weeds and other crops such as sunflower. The pig, already part of their tradition as a ritual animal, is an important part of the system's nutrient flow pattern, as it consumes crop byproducts such as rice bran, while its dung, together with the bedding material cut from the grasslands, produces excellent compost. The Bontoc composting technique is worth emulating in other parts of the Cordillera, where pigs are free-roaming. However, labour and cultural differences seem to constrain its diffusion. Other groups such as the Kalinga regard the use of manure as taboo.

The sociopolitical structure of the Bontoc and the careful work of their women are very important aspects in the perpetuation of this traditional rice-growing system. However, the increasing influence of modern culture and technology may eventually consign it to oblivion. The attraction of cash income from growing temperate vegetables is a major reason for the conversion of rice terraces into gardens. Some observers regard diversification into vegetable growing as sound, because the farmers then have both rice and cash. But how long can they stand the commercial pressures of vegetable production, with its dependence on external inputs and its unpredictable returns and cash flow?

Still Room for Improvement

Commendable as the Bontoc rice system is, it could be still further improved. For example, the women's task of puddling the soil with their feet is very laborious. Some of the recommendations made by the Agricultural Sector Committee (on which I serve) are:
• Appropriate farm mechanization, for example the introduction of hand-operated puddlers or carabao-drawn ploughs, should be encouraged wherever possible to replace soil puddling with the feet. Weeding tools such as the rotary weeder could also be introduced to free women's time for other tasks and help reduce labour bottlenecks
• Crop rotation with legumes should be encouraged. The planting of 'legume banks' in unused spaces near rice terraces should be promoted as a source of green manure. This could be an alternative source of fertilizer in parts of the Cordillera where there is cultural resistance to using pig manure
• Modern rice-growing technology of the kind being promoted by the government, and particularly the use of modern varieties, should be carefully studied in the light of the Bontoc's cultural traditions. For example, since harvesting is done by panicle, varietal characteristics such as resistance to panicle shattering should be considered
• The Bontoc rice-growing technology, and particularly the nutrient cycling practices, should be promoted in other areas. The building of pig pens to facilitate manure production and collection could be encouraged
• To permit self-sufficiency in rice, the construction of more terraces should be encouraged
• The irrigation system could be improved. The use of concrete channels to convey water from its sources up to 5 km away would greatly reduce current seepage problems.

The Bontoc rice terraces are a national heritage embodying invaluable knowledge which is in danger of being lost under the pressure of modernization. Gaining insights into the wisdom of this traditional system could help us rethink current agricultural policies and learn more about farming practices that can be at once sustainable and highly productive.

References

Chang, S.D. 1975. The utilization and maintenance of the natural fertility of paddy soils. ASPAC Food and Fertilizer Technical Center, Extension Bulletin 71.

Omengan, E.A. 1981. Nitrogen and phosphorus cycles in a Bontoc rice paddy system. MSc thesis, University of the Philippines at Los Baños.

Valentin, P. 1986. Proceedings of the DATC-MRDC Workshop on Rice Production in the Cordillera. *Organic Matters*, April 1986.

Vergara, B.S. 1987. Raising the yield potential of rice. IRRI, Los Baños.

Scott, W.H. 1975. Beyer's migration and Keesing's runaways. In: *History of the Cordillera*. Baguio Printing and Publishing Co., Baguio City.

Source

First published 1991 in the ILEIA Newsletter 1 and 2, under the title 'Assessing low-external-input farming techniques: Report of a workshop'.

Address

Hilario Padilla, AGTALON, Nalsian, Manaoag, Pangasinari 2428, Philippines.

The Sloping Agricultural Land Technology Experience

Jeff Palmer

Introduction

The Sloping Agricultural Land Technology (SALT) model grew out of problems that farmers expressed to the staff of the Mindanao Baptist Rural Life Center (MBRLC), either in formal meetings or during on-farm visits. Low and declining farm yields were the most serious of these problems. Over the 1960s maize production on hillside farms had fallen from 3.5 to 0.5 t/ha per season. Yields of other crops, such as banana, coffee, coconut and fruit trees, had also fallen, by 100-200% over the same period. Farmers also expressed the need for better income distribution throughout the year. There were times during the year when a family had no money or food, since they depended on a monocropping system. Another problem was the lack of ready cash for fertilizers, insecticides and seeds of improved varieties of maize and other crops.

Recognizing these problems, the MBRLC team began, in 1971, to develop a system now known locally as SALT and internationally as alley cropping/farming. After testing different intercropping schemes and studying Leucaena-based farming systems, both in Hawaï and at the Center, the team finalized the prototype for SALT in 1978. During the development stage the team felt that the SALT model should meet the following criteria:
- Adequately control soil erosion
- Help restore soil structure and fertility
- Produce food efficiently
- Be applicable to at least 50% of hillside farms
- Be easily duplicated by upland farmers using local resources and preferably without making loans
- Be culturally acceptable
- Have the small farm family as the focus and food production as the top priority (fruit trees for cash, forest products, and other outputs were seen as second priority)
- Bring acceptable returns in as short a time as possible
- Require minimal labour
- Be economically feasible and environmentally sound.

SALT is a package technology for soil conservation and food production. Field and permanent crops are grown in bands 4 to 6 m wide between contoured rows of nitrogen-fixing tree species. The tree species are densely planted in double rows to form hedgerows. When a hedge is 1.5 to 2.0 m tall it is cut back to a height of 40 cm and the cuttings are placed in the strips between the hedgerows, also called alleys, to serve as organic fertilizer.

Rows of permanent crops, such as coffee, cacao, citrus and banana, are dispersed throughout the plot. The strips not occupied by permanent crops are planted to cereals (such as maize, upland rice, sorghum), or to legumes (such as mung bean, soybean, groundnut), or to other crops (such as sweet potato, melon, pineapple, castor bean). This cyclical cropping system provides the farmer with several harvests throughout the year.

Testing the SALT Model

In 1978, a 1-ha test site was selected at the MBRLC premises to serve as a 'testing ground' for the new technology. As was typical of the surrounding farms, the slope was greater than 15° and had been farmed for at least 5 years. The soils too were similar to those of most farms in the area. The average annual rainfall at the test site was about 2600 mm.

After drawing a diagram of what the SALT system should look like, the Center's team began to establish the project. The staff began at the top of the hill and slowly constructed the contour lines 4 to 6 m apart (depending on the slope), more or less 'feeling their way' from one contour line to another until the hectare was fully contoured. Ipil-ipil (*Leucaena leucocephala*) seeds were planted along the contours. Alternate strips between contour lines were planted to maize, leaving the others uncultivated to help control soil loss until the ipil-ipil trees were large enough to hold the soil. The first crop of maize was harvested later that same year.

The Center had pledged not to promote the system until the basic objectives of controlling soil erosion and restoring soil productivity were met. It was soon realized, however, that waiting for long-term results would delay meeting the farmers' immediate needs for food and cash. The Center therefore decided that if comparison of the performance of the SALT model with that of non-SALT farmers showed a marked difference in yield, and if observations also indicated that other goals were being met, it would proceed in expanding and disseminating the system.

The staff proceeded to compare maize yields of the SALT model with local maize yields. The hours of work required in each system were also compared. The tools and equipment used for the model were similar to those used by local farmers. Soil losses were also monitored. The model was in operation for about 1 year before comparisons were made. Table 1 illustrates the comparisons.

The comparisons showed that the SALT model requires more labour than conventional farming methods in the first year, but that the increase in yields compensates for this. The tools used to cultivate 1 ha of the SALT model were the same as those used by local farmers (carabao, plough, harrow, and long knife for cutting grass). The hoe was later introduced into the SALT system.

Table 1 Initial comparisons between the SALT model and local farmers' system

	SALT	Local farmer
Labour (first year)	100% of work hours	50% of work hours
Maize yields (two crops, 2 years)	2t/ha/crop	0.5t/ha/crop
Tools needed	Same tools used for both systems	
Soil loss	Slight	Severe

1. *Leucaena* cut from hedgerows was used as fertilizer in the SALT model. The local farmer used no fertilizer and no *Leucaena*

The Center's method for monitoring soil loss in the first SALT model was not precise. Stakes were placed at different locations along the contour lines. The staff simply measured the loss on the upper side of the alley and the accumulated soil on the lower side. The latter was then subtracted from the former to determine how much soil was actually being lost from the alley. On the local farmer's land, the staff observed the amount of topsoil that remained. In some cases, coconut trees remaining in the field gave indications as to how much soil had been lost.

By 1980, the team felt that the SALT model could adequately fulfill the objectives listed earlier. After searching the literature and looking at several other projects, the Center came to the conclusion that the system was simple enough for any hillside farmer on Mindanao to follow, was applicable to at least 50% of hillside farmers on Mindanao, had low costs in comparison with making bench terraces or conventional terraces, and was urgently needed to save what little topsoil remained.

The first SALT model later became known as Demonstration SALT. The first few years of work with the model were spent in checking for the adaptability of the crops grown, crop production, and soil erosion control, and did not focus in detail on how much income could be made from the 1-ha plot. In 1982, the Center began to stress income in its Demonstration SALT, planting crops that would yield the highest financial returns. The staff felt that farmers would understand and appreciate economic benefits better than environmental ones.

In 1980, another 0.5-ha experimental plot was established. This was followed in 1984 by Test SALT and Contour Hedgerow Test SALT. In 1987, SALT II and SALT III were developed and implemented at the Center.

Alternatives to *Leucaena*

In the beginning, SALT was a *Leucaena*-based agroforestry system. However, in 1986 this tree species was virtually wiped out by the jumping plant lice epidemic of *Heteropsylla cubana* Crawford. The Center therefore began working with alternative hedgerow species, many of which had already been collected and established in the above-mentioned Contour Hedgerow Test SALT.

About 35 local and foreign potential hedgerow species for SALT have been studied. The criteria used for screening include survival, biomass production, seed production, rate of litter decomposition, nitrogen-fixing capacity, fuel potential, feed potential, drought resistance and resistance to pests and diseases. Using these criteria, five species have so far been identified as good alternatives. They are: *Flemingia macrophylla* (formerly sp. *congesta*), *Desmodium rensonii*, *Gliricidia sepium*, *Leucaena diversifolia* and *Calliandra calothyrsus*.

Maize Production

Most of the Center's crop tests pertained to maize, since this is the chief food and grain crop of the hillside farmers in Mindanao.

In one test, the effects of nitrogen sources on maize production were observed. The test period began in March 1982 and continued until July 1986. Continuous maize was planted, with an average of about three harvests per year for a total of 13 harvests. Five different soil fertility treatments were tested. The results for four of them are shown in Table 2.

Table 2 Effect of nitrogen sources on DMR-2 maize production over 13 harvests

Treatment	Maize yield (t/ha)
No fertilizer, no leucaena	1.2
Leucaena (SALT)	2.5
Commercial only [1]	4.4
Commercial + leucaena	4.2

1. Commercial fertilizer applied = 100 kg/ha N, 50 kg/ha P

The table shows that maize yields increase when either *Leucaena* or commercial fertilizer is put into the system. *Leucaena* doubled the yield over the no fertilizer treatment while commercial fertilizer more than tripled it. The significant result here is the increase in maize yield over a typical subsistence farmer's system (no fertilizer) achieved by the relatively low-input SALT system, from 1.2 t/ha to 2.5 t/ha. If farmers can sustain their yields at this level by using SALT, they could probably afford the use of commercial fertilizers at some later point, thereby improving their returns still further.

Another test compared the responses of a commercial maize variety (DMR-2) and the local variety (Tinigib) to *Leucaena* as a sole fertilizer.

As Table 3 shows, there is little or no difference in yields at low fertilizer applications. This suggests that it may be more economical for small-scale farmers to use local varieties until they can afford commercial fertilizers. This test was also conducted against several other hybrids, and it was also found that, using low inputs, local varieties are usually more profitable.

Table 3 Yields of DMR-2 and Tinigib maize in a SALT experiment with *Leucaena* as the sole fertilizer (six croppings)

Variety	Yields (t/ha)
Tinigib (local variety)	1.99
DMR-2 (composite variety)	2.18
Mean	2.09

Returns from SALT

The Demonstration SALT project was in the beginning both a model and an experiment. It became a substantial income-generating venture for the Center. Table 4 shows gross income, total costs and net income during the 1980s.

The income for 1980 and 1981 was rather low, partly because the Center was not at that time emphasizing this aspect. Although 1983 was a drought year, income was remarkably high: the diversified system represented by SALT had begun to pay off, and the Center was able to harvest at least some crops, while monocropping systems failed. During those early years, minimum amounts of inputs such as fertilizer and insecticides were used.

The average annual income for hilly land farmers in the Center's vicinity is about P 4000 (US$ 200), with most farmers farming more than 1 ha of land. At the current rate of income for 1 ha of SALT, farmers can potentially triple their farm income by adopting the SALT system.

Results of Test SALT

As described earlier, Test SALT is a side-by-side comparison of the SALT system with a non-SALT system, called Farmer's Farm. It was established in 1984. It is a duplicated test with individual plots being 800 m² (40 m x 20 m). The test was undertaken to measure changes in the relative benefits of SALT and the traditional sole-crop system in terms of

Table 4 Costs and returns analysis for the Center's 1-ha Demonstration SALT plot, 1980 to 1990

Year	Gross income	Total costs[1]	Net income	Income/month
		(pesos)		
1980	5 693	1 117	4 575	381[2]
1981	3 055	583	2 472	206[2]
1982	9 007	1 833	7 174	597
1983	6 471	1 228	5 242	436[3]
1984	14 287	1 741	12 545	1 045[4]
1985	15 559	1 858	13 701	1 141
1986	13 294	1 710	11 584	965[5]
1987	17 257	3 062	14 195	1 182[6]
1988	13 869	2 764	11 105	925
1989	18 795	2 814	15 980	1 331
1990	17 310	1 982	15 327	1 277

1. Inputs such as seed, insecticides, fertilizer. No labour included
2. Permanent crops were not yet productive
3. A 6-month drought occurred during this year
4. Permanent crops began producing
5. Psyllid infestation was at its highest level
6. No *Leucaena* available; used commercial fertilizers. *Leucaena* hedgerows were replaced by *Flemingia macrophylla*

soil erosion, crop productivity, soil fertility, net income, and labour. Results are as follows:

Soil erosion
Soil losses in Test SALT were calculated from changes in soil level measured by using a staking method. However, as the test progressed it was observed that the stake method was inadequate to reflect true soil loss. The raw data indicated a rather high erosion rate, especially when compared with figures in the literature. Through verbal and written communications with various other workers, the stake or peg method was confirmed to be unreliable for accurate soil loss measurements.

Since the raw data indicated too high a level of erosion, the question arose as to how to treat the data gathered. It was noticed that the placement of stakes in the SALT system seemed to present the largest problem. Since stakes had been placed just below and above each contour hedgerow, large areas of soil accumulation within the hedgerow were not being measured. Also, there was a 'humping' effect in the middle of the alleys that indicated unrecorded soil deposition.

Therefore, with the aid of a transit, a field survey resembling a grid survey was conducted on the SALT treatments and the unmeasured humps were back-calculated to reflect a more accurate picture of soil loss. A correction factor was calculated and the soil losses were adjusted downwards. The final results are shown in Table 5.

Table 5 Soil losses in Test SALT and Farmer's Farm

Months from start	SALT system [1]	Farmer's system	SALT system [2]	Farmer's system
		Losses (mm)	Cumulative losses (t)	
0	0.0	0.0	0.0	0.0
5	0.5	4.0	6.2	0.25
34	0.8	20.9	10.6	278.0
45	1.2	46.5	15.6	618.1
50	1.6	58.4	21.3	776.2
57	1.7	71.4	22.0	950.1
60	1.7	77.1	23.1	1025.4
68	1.6	82.8	21.4	1101.1
72	1.5	87.4	20.2	1162.4
Annual totals (t/year)				
SALT	3.4			
Farmer's	194.3			

1. Loss calculated with a correction factor
2. Loss measured using a stake

The table indicates that the SALT system is very effective in controlling soil erosion. Whereas the Farmer's Farm experienced soil erosion of 1162.4 t/ha over 6 years, the SALT farm lost only 20.2 t/ha during the same period—almost 58 times less.

The annual rate of soil loss in the Test SALT is 3.4 t/ha/year. This is well within the tolerable limits given in the literature. Most soil scientists place acceptable soil loss limits for the tropics within the 10-12 t/ha/year range. Compared to the rate of loss of 194.3 t/ha/year in the farmer's treatment, SALT is a very effective erosion control system.

Another interesting feature noted while calculating the soil erosion data was the rate of soil movement in the perennial crop alleys as compared to the annual crop alleys. Erosion in the perennial alleys was about 14 times lower. In many cases these alleys showed slight or no erosion at all. In other words, the bulk of the measured erosion in the SALT plots came from the annual strips. The data indicate that perennial cropping is virtually essential in any hillside farming scheme. The perennial alleys can be used as 'belts' to help hold precious topsoil on the hillsides. This finding confirms the validity of the original design of SALT, which calls for perennial crops on every third alley.

A third observation in relation to these data is that while the soil erosion rate is increasing over the years in the farmer's treatment, it appears to be declining on the SALT plots. This may be due to the build-up of crop residues/organic matter in the soil, the increased infiltration rate, and/or the 'terracing' effect that the hedgerows exert on the SALT system. More years of data will confirm whether this is true or not. However, at present it looks as if SALT may become a better soil erosion control system the longer it is used.

Crop productivity
Comparisons of crop productivity between the two systems were restricted to maize yields. The farmer's treatment was planted 100% to maize with an average of two harvests per year from 1985 to 1990. The SALT treatment was planted 80% to maize for the first year, 60% for the second and then 43% in succeeding years. These differing percentages of seasonal crop areas are due to the fact that the permanent crop areas in SALT were used for seasonal production while the permanent plants were small. As the permanent plants grew, they increasingly occupied their allotted space until the area for seasonal crops equalled 43% of the total plot area. This final spacing occurred in 1987. The remaining 57% of land area in SALT (1987-1990) was taken up by perennial crops (30%) and hedgerows (27%). Table 6 shows the maize yields for the two systems from 1985 to 1990.

The first two lines in the table show that the farmer's maize yield (dry shelled weight) is greater than that achieved in the SALT treatment until the fifth year. However, it should be noted again that the area under maize in the SALT system is only 43% of the farmer's area. Thus, by 1989, the SALT plot is producing the same amount of maize as the farmer's treatment, but using less than half the area. It should also be noted that the other 57% of the SALT farm is generating production in permanent crops and leguminous biomass.

In terms of production per unit area, SALT is consistently superior to the farmer's treatment. Even after five cropping seasons (at an average of two maize crops per year), the SALT treatment remains highly productive, whereas the Farmer's Farm is steadily declining. Of the two systems, SALT is clearly the more sustainable.

Net income
Annual net income from the SALT treatment was less than that from the farmer's treatment for the first 2 years of the test (Figure 1). However, the overall trend (1985-90)

Table 6 Maize yield comparisons in a SALT farm versus a Farmer's farm

Treatment	1985	1986	1987	1988	1989	1990
Farmer's yields (t/ha)	4.7	6.3	4.2	3.0	2.6	2.1
SALT actual (t/ha) [1]	3.9	4.1	2.7	2.1	2.6	2.4
SALT per unit (t/ha) [2]	4.9	6.8	6.3	4.9	6.0	5.7

1. These figures represent the amount of maize harvested on a per hectare basis
2. These figures represent the amount of maize per unit area cropped between the hedges

for the farmer treatment decreased, while net income from SALT increased or remained constant. As a result, the ratio between the two increased each year, so that by 1990 the net income from SALT was more than double that from the farmer's treatment. The contribution of perennial crops to income from the SALT treatment increased each year until, in 1990, perennial crops contributed the major portion of income (Figure 2).

Soil physical and chemical properties
There is little to report on changes in soil fertility in the two systems; data are still being gathered. It seems to take more than 5 years to change the physical and chemical properties of the soil. However, there is some evidence of a trend towards increased organic matter, infiltration rate and nutrient uptake efficiency in the SALT treatment. These conclusions are based on visual observation of surface organic residue build-up, increased earthworm activity, and a more 'crumb-like' structure of the soil in the SALT treatment. Also, the good maize production (2-3 t/ha/harvest) suggests more favourable soil properties in the SALT as opposed to the farmer's system.

Labour requirements
One of the surprising results of the Test SALT study was in the area of labour inputs. It had been thought that SALT farming would be more laborious due to the tasks of establishing and maintaining the contour hedgerows. However, from Figure 3 it can be seen that, although the labour requirements in the first year were greater, less labour was needed in the succeeding 4 years. The relatively low labour requirements of the SALT system from 1986 to 1989 can be explained by the smaller area under annual crops and the low intensities of labour use on land under perennial crops and hedgerows. By contrast, in 1990, the labour requirement in the SALT system was once again greater, due to the production of permanent crops (primarily citrus). It should be noted that this extra labour is harvest labour, which is readily accepted by the farmer.

In both treatments, the largest allocation of labour was to the weeding of annual crops. In all, the mean annual labour input for SALT was slightly lower than that for the farmer's treatment over the 6 years.

Figure 1 Annual net income from SALT and farmer's treatments

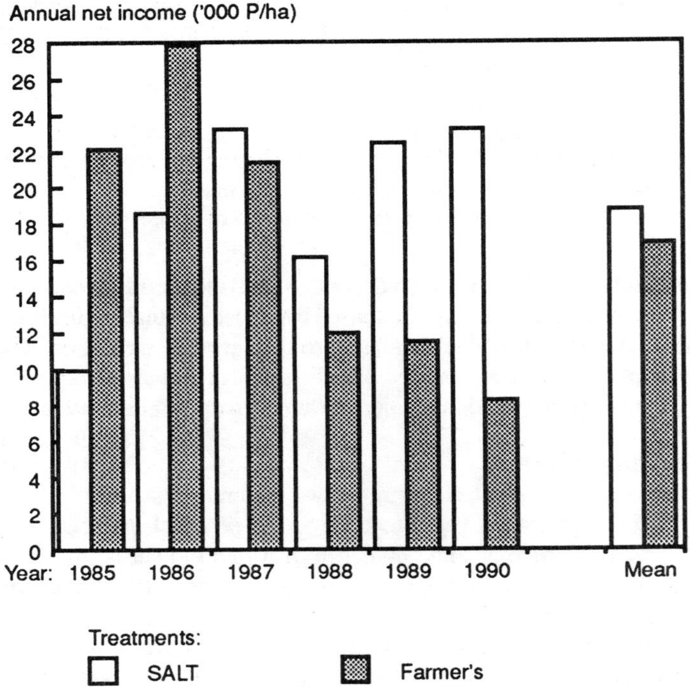

Annual net income ('000 P/ha)

Adoption

Modifications made by users
Filipino farmers are like farmers anywhere else in the world. When offered a new technology, many begin immediately to change or improve on it rather than trying it out as suggested. Technology, after all, is for the farmer and not the other way around. Often, the farmer knows better than the researcher what is best for his or her farm and family.

This is what happened to the SALT system as it started becoming popular among hilly land farmers in the project area. A SALT farm laid out according to the Center's recommendations has about 20% of its area to contour hedgerows, 25% to perennial crops and 55% to annual crops. The project staff, which include extension workers, have observed several variations on this standard recommendation. Among the more notable modified SALT systems that emerged were:

• Row crop system. The farmer plants only maize, beans or other annual crops in the alleys. This system is more economical for the farmer in the short run, but the permanent crops in every third or fourth alley will ultimately pay off in soil saved and even in added income. Some farmers say that since they do not own the land they do not wish to plant permanent crops other than the contour hedgerow materials

• Permanent crop system. The farmer plants all the alleys with bananas, coffee or fruit trees. Center staff like this system, but are waiting for data to show cost and returns. We also recognize that it may not be desirable, in terms of food security, to grow only cash crops and no food crops.

Common problems
Some farmers did not apply the recommended techniques for SALT farming. The result has been substandard or ineffective work in some areas, and problems that would not have occurred had standard SALT guidelines been observed. Among the more common mistakes made are:

• Establishing single-line instead of double-line contour hedgerows. Some farmers feel that double lines of trees take up too much space and so plant only one row in the hedgerow. The Center's experience is that a single row cannot adequately hold the soil.

Figure 2 Breakdown by crop of net income from SALT

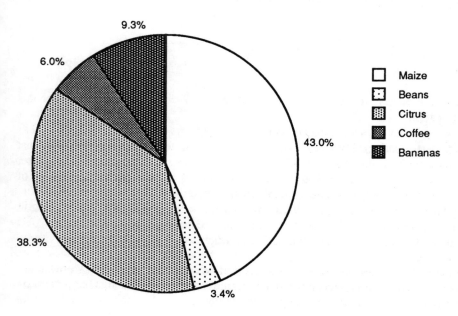

Figure 3 Comparison of labour inputs to SALT and farmer's treatments

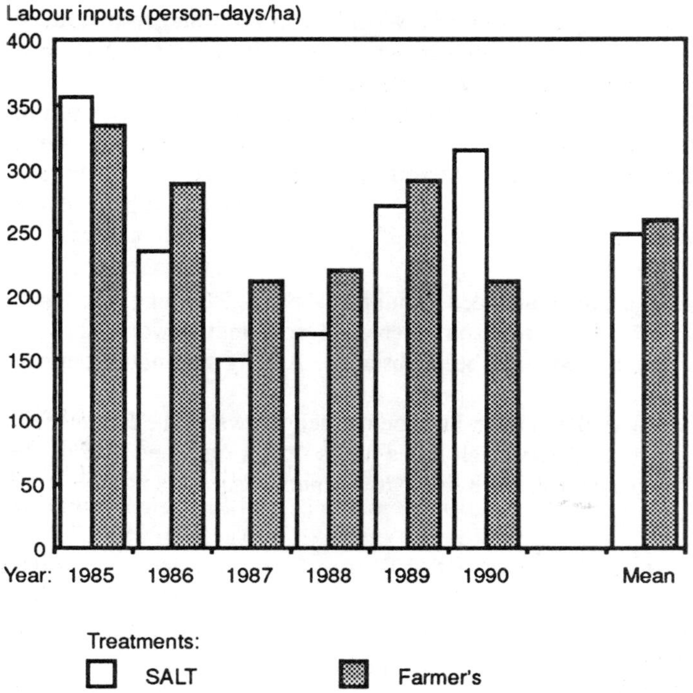

Labour inputs (person-days/ha)

Treatments:
□ SALT   ▨ Farmer's

Also, the biomass production used for fertilizer is reduced by about 50% under this modification
• Spacing hedgerows more than 6 m apart. Some farmers space their hedgerows 10 to 20 m apart, creating wider alleys. To overcome this problem, the extension agent must visit the farmer and re-convince him of the need for closely spaced hedgerows. The closer the hedgerows, the better their soil-holding capabilities and the greater the amount of biomass production per hectare available for use as fertilizer
• Planting hedgerows in straight lines across the hill with uniform alley widths, instead of along contours. This often results in weak and erosion-susceptible alleys
• Not planting the trees densely enough in the hedgerows. Again this defeats the purpose of the system
• Failing to weed and clean the contour hedgerows when the tree seedlings are small
  Several weaknesses observed in SALT farms are not of the farmers' making. Education is sometimes faulty. Sometimes technicians do not fully understand the SALT system

before teaching farmers or laying out demonstration projects. This results in poorly constructed SALT projects and, consequently, unfavourable reaction to the new technology. Also, some farmers expect the SALT system to do miracles—creating little work but high income. In fact the SALT system requires considerable discipline on the part of farmers, although once established it demands little or no further work or development beyond the increased harvesting activities. Other problems beyond the farmers' control are as follows:
- Shortage of tree seeds with which to create dense hedgerows
- Stray animals eating the young trees. One solution to this problem is to have several farmers begin SALT projects in a cluster rather than on isolated sites. Arrangements can then be made to prevent farmers' animals feeding on their neighbour's plants.

Conclusions

The SALT system can reduce soil erosion and restore moderately overexploited hilly lands to a profitable farming system. It can be operated by the typical Mindanao hill farmer. Minimum tillage, the recycling of crop residues, the holding of topsoil by the hedgerows of nitrogen-fixing tree species and perennial crops, and the nutrients furnished by the leaf matter grown in the hedgerows—all account for the success of SALT.

We do not claim that SALT is a perfect farming system. There is not and never will be one system for all farmers. SALT is not a miracle system, nor a panacea for all the ills of rural life in resource-poor farming areas. To establish a single hectare under the SALT system requires much hard work and discipline.

Soil erosion has reached emergency levels in South-East Asia. This is especially true in the Philippines, where it is estimated that over 65% of topsoil has already vanished. What can be done in a few years with careless or uninformed farming methods can take decades to restore. No system can bring depleted, eroded soils back into production in a few short years. The price of soil loss is poverty. Nevertheless, the staff of the Rural Life Center have seen land restored to a reasonable level of productivity by using the SALT system.

Source
Not previously published.

Address
Jeff Palmer, Mindanao Baptist Rural Life Center, P.O. Box 94, Davao City, Philippines.

Benefits of Diversity:
Organic Coffee Growing in Mexico

Boudewijn van Elzakker, Rob Witte and Jan-Diek van Mansvelt

Introduction

Coffee is grown widely throughout the humid regions of the developing world. Much of the world's coffee crop is produced by smallholders, using variable (but usually low) amounts of chemical inputs. With the demand for organic products and the awareness of global development issues increasing rapidly in developed countries, opportunities are arising for a new type of coffee production—one which is both more sensitive to the environment and more equitable to producers.

In this case study, organic coffee growing is compared with traditional coffee growing as practised by indigenous smallholders, and with high-external-input coffee growing as practised on a nearby large estate. The main features of the three systems are compared in Table 1. Two examples of organic coffee growing are described in detail—one is a privately owned estate, the Finca Irlanda Coffee Estate, the other a community venture launched by the Indian population.

The Finca Irlanda Coffee Estate

The oldest and probably the best known organic coffee farm in the world, Finca Irlanda, is situated in the Soconusco area of the state of Chiapas, southern Mexico. The manager is Walter Peters. His brother and co-owner, Ralph Peters, is the trader and contact person.

The farm was bought by the father and an uncle of the present owners in 1928 from an Irishman; hence its name. At that time it was a ranch. It was converted to coffee growing, which was and still is done without using any mineral fertilizers. In 1962, Walter Peters started converting part of the farm to biodynamic agriculture, a form of organic agriculture based on the philosophy known as anthroposophy. Most of the farm is still under organic management only. In this case study only the organic farming activities are described, since it is not possible to explain the features of biodynamic agriculture in brief.

The main crop is Arabica and Robusta coffee. Cardamom and cocoa are also grown, and cattle are kept for beef and dairy production. The purpose of the farm is commercial, but also experimental and educational. Besides farming, Walter Peters is very interested in nature conservation, and is a devoted ornithologist. The total area of the estate is 320 ha, of which 270 ha is cultivated and 50 ha deliberately left under natural vegetation.

Table 1 Main features of three different coffee growing systems found in the Soconusco area of Chiapas State, Mexico

Feature	System		
	Traditional	Organic	Intensive
Layout	Contour lines	Contour lines	Up and down the slope (typically)
Plant density	100 plants/ha	2500-2800 plants/ha	400-500 plants/ha
Coffee varieties	Tall, 2 to 3 varieties	Tall and short, 8 varieties	Low, 4 varieties
Shade trees	Tall and short	Tall and short	No , or sparse, shade, tall trees
Species of shade trees	10-20	Over 40	3, Inga spp.
Amount of shade	Excessive	Regulated	Virtually none
Use of legumes	Trees and shrubs	Trees and shrubs	Little, Inga spp.
Biodiversity	High	High	Very low
Pesticide/herbicide use	Low	Nil	High
Nutrient input	Organic/inorganic, 240 kg/ha of 18-12-06	Composted organic material 6t/ha, and recycled biomass	Inorganic, 1000kg/ha of 18-12-06 and 1000kg/ha of urea
Crop residues	Not used	Maximum use	Not used
Pest control	Natural	Natural, cultural and biological	Insecticides, 1-2 litres/ha of Endosulphan
Use of energy	Closed circles	Closed circles	Open system
Renovation	3% annually	10% annually	25% annually
Yields (kg/ha dried beans)	460-552	828-920	1150-1380

The Soconusco area

The climate of the the Soconusco area is humid, with 85% of the rain falling in summer. Annual rainfall averages 4500 mm. Average temperature is 20-21°C. The topography is mountainous, with slopes averaging 35-40%. Altitude ranges from 800 to 1200 m. The soil is volcanic and granite in origin, and the texture is sandy to loamy. The original vegetation was a 30 to 40 m high tropical evergreen rainforest in which the following species dominated: *Terminalia amazonica, Sterculia mexicana, Virola guatamalensis, Micropholis mexicana* and *Sloana ampla.*

There are several constraints associated with climate and soil. Torrential rain may occur from May to October, often with 150 mm falling in 2 hours. Occasionally, 1000 mm may fall in just 7 days. These rains cause considerable runoff and landslides, and contribute to the leaching of nutrients and high soil acidity. The topography is conducive to erosion when the soil is not carefully protected by shade trees and a mulch layer. It also prohibits mechanization, resulting in high labour costs. The high acidity of the soil (4.3-5.6) causes pronounced fixation of phosphates.

Soil fertility

The first objective of the soil fertility strategy is to improve the recycling of nutrients on the estate. This is done through:
• Utilization of all the residues generated in the estate, such as coffee berry pulp, cocoa husks, manure, urine and kitchen wastes
• Incorporation of biomass produced by deep rooting trees (fallen leaves, pruned branches). The majority of this material remains in the field as a mulch layer, while a smaller part is used for making compost. The trees bring up nutrients which were leached out to depths below the rooting depth of the coffee. Shade trees which have to be cut because they have grown too big and threaten the aeration of the plantation are used as a source of energy for drying the coffee. Ash, as well as the *pergamino* (shell) of the coffee, is recycled through the compost
• The planting of shade trees, especially leguminous species. These are planted in three levels, *Crotalaria* and *Tephrosia* spp. as low shade, *Inga, Leucaena* and *Cassia* spp. as medium shade, and *Acacia, Schizolobium* and *Gliricidia* as high shade.

The second objective is to supply the crops with organic fertilizer through the application of compost. Composting is preferred as it allows the inclusion of up to ten different ingredients (*see* Table 2) into a fertilizer which does not only contain nutrients but is also an important soil conditioner, enriching both soil life and soil organic matter.

Approximately 750 t of compost are made on the farm each year. The compost is applied at a rate of 6 t/ha. To alleviate soil acidity, a program of liming was started, applying 1 t/ha of dolomite lime annually. This is applied both by broadcasting and through the compost.

Renovation

The majority of the coffee was planted at the beginning of this century. Many plants have thus been in production for more than 75 years. Planting density was 1600 plants/ha, using tall varieties. Because of the increase in labour costs the old plantations need to be renovated to increase production to a level of 920-1150 kg/ha. This is possible by

Table 2 The main ingredients of compost on Finca Irlanda

Ingredients	%
Coffee pulp	40
Cattle manure [1]	20
Loppings and weeds	10
Sugar cane bagasse and palm residues [2]	10
Bone, horn and hoof meal [2]	5
Dolomite [2]	5
Milled granite [2]	5
Wood ash	4
Clay	1
Total	100

1. Originates from the estate
2. Purchased from outside the estate

replanting at a density of 2700 plants/ha, using shorter (less bushy) varieties. The process of renovation began 6 years ago and is expected to continue for another 4 years. The costs, starting in the nursery and continuing until the third year's harvest, constitute a significant increase in the overall costs of production. In traditional coffee growing, plantations are seldom renovated (Table 1). In intensive estates however, replanting is done at a much faster rate, mainly because of early exhaustion of the shrubs, but also because of erosion and landslides.

Pests and diseases
Problems with pests and diseases are reduced to a minimum by maintaining a maximum of biodiversity in the plantations. Coffee rust is limited by severely pruning the shade trees. Pests are controlled by their natural enemies. Recently an exotic pest appeared, the coffee berry borer (*Hypothenemus hampei*), which originates in Africa and which does not seem to have natural enemies in Central America. Harvest losses are from 10 to 20%. To reduce the population, attacked berries are collected by hand at the beginning of the harvest and destroyed. A biological control program was instigated using a wasp, *Cephalonomia stephanoderis*, introduced into Mexico in 1988 from Africa by the local research station, the Centro de Investigaciones Ecologicas del Sureste. This wasp is reared in a laboratory on the estate using the berries attacked by the borer for multiplication. It is hoped that the wasp will establish itself in the plantations. A second possibility

is the use of the entomophagous fungus *Beauvaria bassiana*. This fungus is being produced in vitro in the laboratory, and is being used in trials on the estate.

Animal husbandry

In organic agriculture high quantities of animal manure are used. For this reason the estate includes a number of pastures in its lower lying areas. Approximately 135 head of cattle are kept there. The cattle are multi-purpose. The milk they produce is used to feed the calves, with the surplus being sold. The bulls are the source of meat for the workers and staff of the estate. The animals are semi-stabled, so as to enable the manure to be collected. They have access to green grass throughout the year. As a supplement they receive sugar cane molasses and mineral salt. Higher up, where the buildings are, 12 cows and 35 sheep are kept. These produce both meat and milk, as well as manure and urine, which are fed into a biodigester to supply biogas for cooking and light. Besides domestic animals a number of wild animals are reared which are indigenous to the area but threatened with extinction. They are released in the nature reserves which are part of the estate. Species include puma, wild boar, pheasant and toucan. For use in the plantation itself, ocelot, grey fox and birds of prey are reared and released as natural predators of rodents.

A problem in cattle keeping are the ticks. The animals are stabled at night to protect them against vampire bats. Damage by the cattle worm (*Gusano barrenador*) is limited through the release of sterile males produced locally.

Mechanization and processing

Despite the often steep terrain the estate has numerous roads, allowing the movement of light motorized traffic. Mechanization of field work is virtually impossible. All work and transport in the field is done manually. The harvested coffee beans are prepared on the estate using the method of wet-processing. The coffee is exported directly to Europe and the United States in different grades. A small portion is sold locally.

Agrotechnical and socio-economic considerations

Considerable labour is required for an organic system—far more than in the traditional and intensive systems (*see* Figure 1). On this estate, a relatively high percentage (25%) of labourers are permanent, living and working on the estate throughout the year. The remaining labour is seasonal, hired mainly for the harvest. Labour costs are an important investment each season, especially in view of the fact that this expenditure is earned back only after the coffee has been paid for by the buyer. An effort to establish a social support system is under way. This system includes nutrition, education and housing facilities, health care, and adequate salaries for the resident labourers of the estate. Its purpose is to integrate organic farming at a socio-economic as well as an environmental level, and to prevent labourers from seeking off-farm occupation.

According to Mr. Peters and his agronomist Mr. Martinez, the organic system they have developed can be adopted by any kind of producer, and is especially suitable for

Figure 1 Distribution of production costs in three different coffee growing systems in the Soconusco area of Chiapas State, Mexico

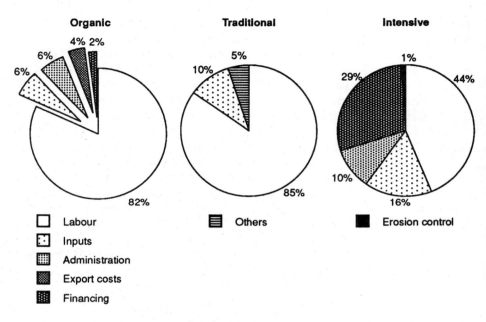

traditional growers. Representatives of Mexico's smallholder organic coffee cooperatives have visited Finca Irlanda for instruction. For wider acceptance it is important that new farmers can convert to organic production while relying on their own family labour. Smallholders cannot afford the use of external labour. Adoption can only be a slow process. The producer must have an opportunity to understand and to accept the new way of thinking, adapting it to his or her local circumstances. When the new organic system is introduced in a hurry, and when it is not a free choice but an imposition, it risks being rejected prematurely.

The cost/benefit ratios of the three systems are compared in Table 3. Net returns to the organic farm are approximately 10% lower than on the intensive estate and approximately 80% higher than in traditional coffee growing. However, the price received for organic coffee is double that of conventional coffee. If future income losses due to erosion and deteriorating soil structure could be calculated, organic farming would probably appear superior to traditional production over the long term.

Summary
Finca Irlanda faces constraints caused by its topography, necessitating strong measures for erosion control and at the same time prohibiting mechanization. It provides an

example of a well established, integrated approach to organic coffee growing, which is both profitable and sustainable over the long term. The organic system compels the estate owner to diversify away from monoculture coffee cultivation, especially into livestock. Because of the diversity of operations throughout the year, labour demand is spread throughout the seasons.

As we shall see below, the organic coffee estate serves as a learning centre for other farmers, who come to see and understand organic coffee cultivation for themselves. In this way the estate serves as a useful tool to the local extension service.

Community Organic Coffee Growing

The remainder of the original Indian population of Mexico is found mainly in the country's southern states of Guerrero, Oaxaca and Chiapas. They live in communities in the mountains, growing beans and maize as their staple foods and coffee as a cash crop. The main struggle of the Indians in the past has been over land. They have been repeatedly dispossessed of their lands, driven out of the fertile valleys into the mountains. Even in the past 30 years they have had to fight new expulsions as the government granted timber concessions to (mainly) foreign companies in the areas where they live.

A common characteristic of Indian communities is their dependence on intermediaries who act as local bosses. These intermediaries control the supply of credit, 'buy' the

Table 3 Cost-benefit ratios of coffee growing under three different management systems in the Soconusco area of Chiapas State, Mexico (1990)

Item	System		
	Traditional	Organic	Intensive
Person-days	160	305	186
Working hours per worker	80	2240	1488
Yield (kg)	460-552	828-920	1150-1380
Average price (US$/quintal) [1]	66	125	66
Gross income (US$)	840 (100%)	2740 (100%)	1782 (100%)
Costs (US$)	614 (73%)	2338 (85%)	1326 (74%)
Gross margin (US%)	226 (27%)	402 (15%)	456 (25%)

1. The international price for non-organic coffee was US$ 78/quintal; Mexico imposes a duty of US$ 12/quintal (1 quintal = 46 kg)

coffee, and supply life's basic necessities. The income of an average Indian family of six is usually far below what is thought to be the minimum for bare survival: US$ 250-450 per year. Families try to organize themselves to improve their situation, but their efforts are often short-lived because they cannot stand up against the vested interests of the local financial and political power groups.

In 1982 farmers from three communities in the state of Oaxaca organized themselves into the Union of Indian Communities in the Istmo Region (UCIRI). Their main aim was to find ways of selling coffee themselves, obtaining a better price for it and so more control over their own lives. In 1986 the Union obtained an export license and began selling coffee directly to buyers in Europe. In 1985 members had decided unanimously to move from traditional forms of agriculture to an organic system. This was partly a political decision, since the move would make farmers less dependent on credit, but it was expected that yields would improve as well. Organic farming became one of the instruments by which communities sought to improve their standard of living. Marketing the coffee as organic earned them a premium price, with some of the profits available for ploughing back into communal activities. Contacts with Fair Trade organizations in Europe supported them in reaching their goals. Today, 37 communities are members of the Union, and more than 3000 families are actively involved in the movement.

The local situation

The Istmo area is mountainous and coffee is grown mostly on slopes. The altitude ranges from 400 to 1250 m. The flatter areas are used for maize and beans. Traditionally, horticulture is virtually unknown in the area, as are dairy cattle. Farmers generally have pigs or chickens around the house. Donkeys or mules are used for transport. A family with five adults to help in picking can grow 2 to 3 ha of coffee. The coffee is grown in a secondary tropical rainforest which has been partially cleared. There is a short but distinct dry period from March until May. The main rainy period is from May to September. Annual rainfall varies from 800 to 1900 mm, depending on location. The soils are of volcanic or granite origin, acid (pH 4-4.5) and poor in phosphorus. The coffee is grown under heavy shade. The trees providing the shade also produce a thick mulch layer. When not eroded, the soil is rich in humus. The exotic coffee berry borer (*Hypothenemus hampei*) recently attacked the coffee in this area.

Organic versus traditional coffee growing

Farmers spend most of their time cultivating their staple foods, maize and beans. When coffee was grown traditionally it did not need much attention. Switching to organic coffee growing means implementing various practices which demand a higher labour input from the farmer. Coffee was usually planted in straight rows up and down the slope, increasing the risks of erosion. Tall varieties were used and little replanting was done. Organic farmers are encouraged to replant with shorter, more modern varieties, such as Catura, Borbon, Mondo Novo and Carnica, which can yield more and are more resistant to coffee rust (*Hemileia vastatrix*). These varieties are planted across the slope. Slashed weeds and pruned branches are used to form rows along the contour lines.

In the traditional system the coffee beans were de-pulped near a stream because of the need for water to wash the beans. The pulp entered the stream, causing tremendous pollution downstream. Organic farmers return the pulp to the field through composting, thereby preventing both pollution and nutrient loss. Other materials used for composting are animal manure, lime and green matter from the surrounding area. Compost is primarily used in vegetable gardens, nurseries and planting holes. Established coffee grown under shade does not give significantly higher yields with applications of compost, unless the soil is poor. The soil is covered with a thick layer of mulch.

The coffee is grown in secondary forest, not all the trees of which have been cleared. The farmers know and select those trees which are known to be beneficial to coffee, such as the leguminous *Inga juinicuil*. Some farmers grow shade trees in their nurseries, transplanting them into the field later. The amount of shade is regulated by lopping, which also intensifies the nutrient cycling.

At present, the Union encourages terracing around coffee trees. Farmers form half-moon shaped terraces on the downhill side of each tree. These allow sedimentation of the soil carried by runoff. Since time is a constraint for most farmers, a bonus for terracing has been introduced by the Union, to be paid on a per tree basis. In this improved and intensified system the grower produces 600-1200 kg/ha of coffee beans each season—an improvement of 30-50% compared with the past. A high level of technology is not required, but commitment and physical strength are. It should be noted that maize and beans are also grown organically by the Union's members, whereas traditional farmers usually use some chemical fertilizer on their maize. When erosion is controlled, there is little difference in yields between organic and traditional farmers. In many communities plots for growing organic vegetables and medicinal herbs have also been established.

Social aspects

The Union has been able to develop its own infrastructure for the transport, storage, processing and export of coffee. This allows members to profit themselves from the added value, which in the past was taken by a chain of local intermediaries, processors and exporters. This development was encouraged through contacts with Fair Trade organizations, which promote direct purchase from smallholder organizations by western buyers. In some countries the coffee is sold as 'socially just coffee', under a special trademark. Such products are sold at a premium, with the profits directly transferred to the producers. These marketing schemes also include help in financing the export and minimum price guarantees.

The profits are put to various uses in the community. For example, the educational system in remote areas is being improved. The Union also runs a public transport system in the mountains and owns a number of shops where members can buy basic necessities. There is a medical insurance system. A local school for agricultural extension workers has been started. In this school, boys from the co-operative's villages are trained, as well as pupils from other areas in Mexico who want to convert to organic agriculture.

Summary

The organic practices adopted in this case study can be classified as 'improved traditional'. A comparison with the estate organic coffee of Finca Irlanda confirms this observation: only a limited number of organic practices have been adopted. Yield levels are between those of estate organic coffee and of the traditional system. (The agro-ecological conditions are more or less comparable.)

Interesting features include maintaining a thinned rain forest by means of shade tree regulation, making compost for seedlings and vegetable growing, and terracing to limit erosion. It is questionable whether soil replenishment keeps abreast with the uptake of nutrients. Intensification without any inputs will lead to depletion sooner or later.

In this case, organic agriculture is clearly part of a larger social movement aimed at restoring peoples' self-confidence and land rights, as well as improved livelihood. It is a direct approach to human resource development. From this point of view it may be considered a success, since it has been widely adopted.

Acknowledgement

Many of the data for this study were supplied by Mr. Peters and Mr. Martinez, and from organic inspection reports.

Source

First published in *Benefits of Diversity: An Incentive towards Sustainable Agriculture,* by B. van Elzakker, R. Witte and J.D. van Mansvelt. Published 1992 by UNDP New York and distributed by the International Alliance of Sustainable Agriculture (IASA), Newman Center, University of Minnesota, 1701 University Avenue SE, Minneapolis MN 55414, USA. Reprinted by kind permission of the authors.

Address

Boudewijn van Elzakker and Rob Witte: AGRO-ECO, Hooghiemstraplein 126, 3514 AZ Utrecht, the Netherlands
Jan-Diek van Mansvelt: IFOAM, Ökozentrum Imsbach, D-6695 Tholey-Theley, Germany.

Can Ecological Agriculture Meet the Indian Farmer's Needs?

Erik van der Werf

Introduction

The Agriculture, Man and Ecology (AME) Programme, Pondicherry, India, promotes socially just, economically viable and ecologically sound land use systems within the Indian subcontinent. The programme is implemented by the ETC Foundation, Leusden, the Netherlands, with financial support from the Netherlands Government. In 1989 a research component started with the objectives of:
• Identifying, qualitatively and quantitatively, the viability of ecological agriculture, both by itself and in comparison with conventional agriculture
• Examining the long-term prospects for ecological agriculture
This paper describes the results of 2 years of field work by the AME Programme.

Methodology

The study covers seven farm pairs, each consisting of one ecological and one comparable reference farm. Due to the limited number of established ecological farms available, a comparative case-study approach was chosen. Ecological farms were selected according to the following criteria:
• No application of chemical fertilizers and biocides
• Deliberate use of ecological farming principles, such as stimulation of diversity within the farm
• Practice of ecological farming for at least 3 years.
   Selected ecological farms were paired with a similar reference farmer using external inputs, namely fertilizer and pesticides. Reference farmers were selected taking into account their similarity in soil type, topography, holding size, cropping pattern, livestock species and numbers, irrigated/rainfed land use, intensity of farming, distance from home to fields, and quality of farm management.
   Data are collected twice monthly on all relevant aspects of the crop and livestock enterprises: inputs and outputs in quantities and money value, total labour requirements and total cash flow. Results are tabulated per farm pair and presented in detailed agronomic and economic interim reports (Sivasubramanian and de Jonge 1990; Narayan

1990; Puspalatha 1992; Srinivasa Reddy 1991). For each year an overall report is published (van der Werf and de Jager 1992; and van der Werf et al. 1992). This paper is based on these reports.

Results

Agronomic aspects
Table 1 gives the average figures for some key agronomic variables for both types of farm over the 2 years of research.

Table 1 Average figures for key variables on ecological and reference farms during years 1 and 2 of research

Variable	Ecological farms		Reference farms		T-test[1]
	Year 1	Year 2	Year 1	Year 2	Year 2
Holding size (ha)	4.4	4.6	2.2	2.7	1.61
% of cultivated area irrigated	71	43	67	60	1.73
No. of crops/farm	9.4	17.9	7.0	12.4	1.96*
Share of gross income from crops (%)	73	78	94	85	0.49
Liveweight units/ha[2]	1.9	1.9	1.3	2.1	0.31
No. of trees/ha	217	226	32	39	1.84
Total external nutrients (kg/ha)	133	50	203	114	1.12
External nutrient dependence of crop activities (%)	42	36	65	54	2.12*
No. of soil fertility improvement practices/farm	4.6	5.7	3.1	3.9	3.13**
No. of plant diversification practices/farm	3.6	4.3	1.6	1.6	5.72**

1. Test of significance of difference between ecological and reference farms during year 2
2. live weight unit = 250 kg
* = significant at 90% probability level (1.943)
** = significant at 95% probability level (2.447)

The number of trees/ha is higher on ecological farms. Tree products and services on ecological farms include fruit, fodder, green manure, nitrogen fixing, fuel and construction wood—mostly in combination. Furthermore, trees are used as windbreaks, for the provision of permanent soil cover and leaf litter, and to recycle nutrients leached to deeper soil layers.

Dependence on external sources of nutrients, calculated in kg/ha, on ecological farms is only two-fifths that of the reference group. Both groups reduced their dependence from year 1 to year 2, mainly by decreasing their imports of nitrogen. For both groups this can be largely attributed to a decrease in the area under irrigation, particularly that cultivated to rice. In addition, the area cultivated to leguminous crops increased.

Dependence on external nutrients for the group of ecological farms during the second year was 25% for N, 34% for P and 26% for K. For the reference group of farms it was 42%, 66% and 58% respectively. For the ecological farms this represents a decrease from the first year, when all three percentages were in the low forties. The reference farms also reduced their dependence, but only in the case of N and P; the figure for K rose slightly. Of the external N-P-K used on the reference farms in the second year, 53%, 49% and 50% respectively were in the form of fertilizers. This compares with first-year figures of 70, 70 and 46%. N and P fertilizers were replaced by manure on reference farms.

On the ecological farms the number of different crops grown was greater than on the reference farms (18 versus 12). In the second year, the diversity of crops grown increased in both groups, but slightly more in the ecological than in the reference group. The ratio between the two types of farm increased from 1.3 to 1.5.

Average nutrient inputs per hectare were considerably lower in ecological than in reference farms (*see* Table 2). This is partly explained by the lesser area under irrigation, where more manure and/or fertilizers tend to be used. Lower imports of external nutrients also contributed considerably.

Table 2 Average inputs of major nutrients (kg/ha) on ecological and reference farms during first and second years of research

Main nutrients (kg/ha)	Ecological farms		Reference farms	
	Year 1	Year 2	Year 1	Year 2
Nitrogen [1]	73 (56)	44 (18)	126 (51)	80 (62)
Phosphate	18 (13)	6 (6)	24 (13)	19 (35)
Potassium	36 (40)	12 (13)	75 (38)	44 (52)

Notes: Figures within brackets denote standard deviation (n–1)
1. Including estimated N-fixation from leguminous crops

Techniques practised for soil fertility maintenance (*see* Table 3) on ecological farms are significantly more numerous (1.5 times) than in the reference group (Table 1). On average, ecological farmers practise somewhat more than four different techniques, whereas their conventional colleagues practise fewer than three.

Table 3 Percentages of farms applying practices for soil fertility maintenance on ecological and reference farms, June 1990 and 1991

Practices	Ecological farms		Reference farms	
	Year 1	Year 2	Year 1	Year 2
Use of bio-fertilizers	0	29	0	0
Deep-rooting crops	100	100	70	100
Green manure[1]	15	0	30	0
Green leaf manure	85	88	70	88
Compost [2]	45	57	0	0
Use of biogas tank effluent	15	14	0	0
Mulching (live)	30	43	0	14
Farmyard manure	100	100	100	100
Night soil	85	100	45	57
Other organic matter	45	43	0	29

1. Excluding trees
2. Of farm or agro-industrial origin

Two ecological farmers used bio-fertilizers partly because the research had increased their awareness of this option. Deep-rooting crops were grown by all farmers, but they were slightly more important on ecological than on reference farms (46% versus 34% of the area cultivated). The same is true for the use of farmyard manure. Green manures were cultivated less during the second year, partly because of the unavailability of seeds. Composting, biogas production and mulching are typical techniques practised by ecological farmers.

Plant diversity techniques practised on ecological farms were significantly more numerous (over 2.5 times) than in the reference group (Table 1). Multi-storey cropping, selective weeding, cover crops, and on-farm tree nurseries were found only on ecological farms (Table 4). Trees in agriculture, whether in the form of hedges/shelterbelts, multi-storey cropping or other forms of agroforestry, were much more important than in the reference group. Multiple/relay cropping increased in the reference group over the study period, but hedges/shelterbelts decreased.

Table 4 Percentage of farms applying practices for creating plant diversity on ecological and reference farms during first and second years of research

Practices	Ecological farms		Reference farms	
	Year 1	Year 2	Year 1	Year 2
Mixed/intercropping	85	100	45	88
Multi-storey cropping	30	43	0	0
Agroforestry/alley cropping	55	86	45	14
Selective weeding	30	43	0	0
Cover crops	45	71	0	0
Hedges/shelter belts	100	10	55	43
On-farm tree nurseries	30	43	0	0

Economic aspects

Ecological farms have a marginally higher gross income/ha than reference farms. However, this is counterbalanced by higher variable costs per hectare, resulting in a slightly lower average gross margin per hectare. These differences can largely be explained by:
• The generally lower rate of return on variable costs realized from livestock (compared with crops), which are more important on the ecological farms, combined with
• The better rates of return achieved by the reference farms for both crop and livestock enterprises.

The returns per person-day are similar for ecological and reference farms. Taking into account differences in the area irrigated, the number of person-days per hectare in both groups is comparable for both irrigated and dryland cultivation.

The key economic variables for the 2 years of research are compared in Table 5. The gross income per hectare, the variable costs per hectare, and the gross margin per hectare all declined in real terms during the second year of research. This is in part a result of the decrease in the area under irrigated high-income-earning crops, which was accompanied by a decrease in cropping intensity (from 1.65 in year 1 to 1.47 in year 2) and lower yields in certain crops (rice). In addition, the total holding size was included in the study.

Comparing the two years, it is striking that, in spite of the decrease in gross margins per hectare, the farmers were able to maintain their returns per person-day. This implies that cultivating rainfed land can be as profitable as cultivating irrigated land.

Total variable costs for crops per hectare were similar for ecological and reference farms (*see* Table 6). As both farm groups had a similar cropping intensity, around 1.47, during the second year, costs per cultivated crop were also comparable.

Table 5 Averages for key economic variables on ecological and reference farms during the first and second years of research

Variables	Ecological farms		Reference farms	
	Year 1	Year 2	Year 1	Year 2
Gross income (Rs/ha)	20430	13110	18340	12270
Variable costs (Rs/ha)	9810	6270	6830	12270
Gross margin (Rs/ha)	10620	6850	11515	7190
Returns/person-day (Rs)	32	31	32	35
Person-days/ha	346	162	333	207
% of produce sold	57	47	52	57
Assets (Rs/ha)	85480	87600	80000	95900

Note: annual inflation rate during the study period was approximately 10%

Table 6 Breakdown of variable costs for crop activities in ecological and reference farms during first and second years of research

Variable costs	Ecological farms		Reference farms	
	Year 1	Year 2	Year 1	Year 2
Total (Rs/ha)[1]	4905	4181	5592	3947
Breakdown (%):				
Seeds	17	13	14	24
Manure	24	20	17	15
Fertilizer	-	-	18	9
Agrochemical	-	-	5	4
Paid labour	55	35	43	44
Other	4	32	3	4
Total	100	100	100	100

Note: Paid labour includes wages, and animal and mechanical labour
1. Per ha = per hectare of area studied

Seed costs were greater in the reference than in the ecological group. Manure costs, on the other hand, were greater in the ecological group. However, the reference group spent an average 13% more on fertilizer. Taking inflation into account, both ecological and reference farms spent around 40% less on fertility management in the second than in the first year. In the ecological group this resulted in a lower positive nutrient balance—a variable which did not change that much in the reference group.

The changes in the figures over the 2 years can be explained largely by differences in practices on individual farms. It is too early to speak of any trends. Fertilizer costs on reference farms were influenced by the decrease in irrigated area. Taking into account the inflation rate of approximately 10%, the decrease in total costs per hectare was approximately 23% for ecological farms and 36% for reference farms.

Analysis at crop level

In all the six pairs in which both farms cultivated rice, production under ecological practices was greater than under conventional agriculture. As illustrated by Table 7, an average ecological farm harvested about 50% more paddy per hectare than its reference counterpart. However, differences within pairs varied considerably, ranging from 7% to 119%. Differences within the group were also considerable. For both groups, yields for the second year were lower than for the first. The decline was greater for the reference than for the ecological farms. Comparing nutrient inputs with yields, it can be seen that total inputs in year 2 were higher on ecological than on reference farms. This contradicts the findings for the first year. The increase in nitrogen inputs on the ecological farms in year 2 did not result in an increase in yield.

Table 7 Average yield (kg/ha), average inputs of N, P and K (kg/ha) and average nutrient balance at field border for N, P and K (kg/ha) on five ecological and reference farms cultivating rice during first and second years of research

Yields, nutrient inputs and nutrient balances (kg/ha)	Ecological farms		Reference farms	
	Year 1	Year 2	Year 1	Year 2
Paddy yield	4822	3916	3953	2628
N input [1]	60 (34)	114	93 (44)	86
P input	9 (3)	25	22 (10)	9
K input	43 (27)	58	45 (28)	64
N balance [1]	−68 (68)	14	−10 (76)	6
P balance	−7 (8)	12	8 (15)	0
K balance	−60 (60)	−24	−46 (57)	−11

Note: Figures in brackets denote standard deviation
1. Including estimated N-fixation from leguminous crops

Table 8 shows the average per hectare yields of the five most frequently cultivated crops. The yields of rainfed crops such as sorghum, finger millet and sesame are greatly influenced by the total rainfall and its distribution over the growing season. The figures shown should therefore be considered as indicative only.

Table 8 Average yields (kg/ha) of selected crops on ecological and reference farms during first and second years of research, and Karnataka State averages, 1990-91

Crop	Ecological farms		Reference farms		Karnataka average
	Year 1	Year 2	Year 1	Year 2	Year 2
Rice (paddy)	4822 (5)	3916 (6)	3953 (5)	2628 (6)	3165
Sorghum	845 (3)	722 (3)	560 (1)	649 (4)	725^2
Finger millet	ND	$470 (3)^1$	$650 (1)^1$	$490 (2)^1$	1200^2
Groundnut	640 (3)	788 (4)	1019 (5)	564 (6)	822
Sesame	ND	481 (4)	ND	441 (3)	338

Notes: Bracketed numbers denote N
ND = No data available
1. = Excluding irrigated cultivation
2. = Average for total farm area, with and without cultivation

For sorghum the average yield on reference farms was over three times as high as on ecological farms. This was due entirely to the remarkably high yield (9450 kg/ha) achieved by one reference farm— the only farm cultivating sorghum under irrigation. If this case is omitted, the average for the reference group falls to 649 kg, comparable to the figure for the ecological group.

The yield of finger millet in the ecological group was much higher than that of the reference group. Again, this was influenced by a single farm, cultivating 0.54 ha of finger millet under irrigation. Without this case, yields in the two groups were comparable.

Sesame yields on ecological farms ranged from 165 to 933 kg/ha, while on reference farms the range was narrower, from 264 to 750 kg/ha.

Discussion and Conclusions

The case study approach and the limited number of cases studied mean that great care is needed in drawing conclusions. In each group studied, the cases range from fully market-oriented to quasi-subsistence farmers, from small to large, and from fully irrigating to cultivating dryland crops only. Furthermore, there are considerable differences in results between the two years studied.

Despite this variability, a number of farming practices have been identified in which the groups studied differ significantly.

Agronomic aspects

Besides differing in their use of chemical fertilizers and pesticides, the two groups differed significantly in four other agronomic aspects.

On ecological farms, a significantly higher number of different crops was grown. In the first year of research it was 34% more, for the second year 44% more. Ecological farmers chose to cultivate more crops in order to create diversity and so enhance stability. This accounts for the larger share of livestock in gross farm income on ecological farms. It is too soon yet to see whether this expectation of greater stability is actually met.

Ecological farms were some 34% less dependent than reference farms on external nutrients for their crop enterprises. Their lower use of external inputs did not prevent them from obtaining yields and gross margins per hectare that were comparable on average to those of the reference farms. Again, this implies that the ecological farmers were more efficient in their internal recycling than their reference colleagues. The mechanisms responsible for this were not examined in detail by the study, but two hypotheses may be advanced. The first is that the leaching of nutrients from the topsoil is less marked on ecological farms owing to the greater importance of deep-rooting species (both annuals and perennials). The second is that recycling through livestock is better in the ecological group, as these farmers pay more attention to the management of manure and urine. In addition, it is known that losses through leaching and volatilization/denitrification are greater for chemical fertilizers than for organic manures. Finally, in both years ecological farmers cultivated more nitrogen-fixing crops than their reference colleagues.

In both years, ecological farmers practised nearly 50% more techniques for improving soil fertility. The additional techniques they used included composting, (live) mulching, and the application of night soil and other organic matter. Not only were soil fertility techniques used more frequently by ecological farmers, but also more extensively and more efficiently. For example, deep-rooting crops were grown on all the farms studied, but on ecological farms they accounted for 46% of the gross cropped area, a quarter of which was under trees, whereas on reference farms they covered only 34% of the cropped area, of which only one-ninth was under trees. Recycling through livestock was also applied on all the farms studied, but was more efficient among ecological farmers, a number of whom collected their cattle urine in addition to applying farmyard manure, and paid greater attention to the effectiveness of storage as well as to the timing and amounts of field applications.

Ecological farmers applied around 2.5 times more practices for managing plant diversity than did reference farmers. The additional practices they used included multi-storey cropping, the use of hedges and shelterbelts, the use of on-farm tree nurseries, and other agroforestry practices. These techniques resulted in more intensive land use and better soil cover. All farmers practised multiple and/or relay cropping and both groups had a similar cropping intensity (defined as the ratio of gross cropped area to holding size), but on ecological farms there was more, and more intensive, mixed cropping and intercropping.

Yields showed no significant differences between the two groups, varying considerably within the groups as well as between years. In one year it is the ecological group that achieves the higher yield for a specific crop, the next year it is the reference group. However, paddy yields were higher on ecological than on reference farms in both years (22% in year 1, 50% in year 2).

In agriculture, 2 years of research is too short to reach firm conclusions. However, the agronomic evidence collected to date suggests that the performance of ecological farms is as good as that of conventional farms, with the added advantages of lower dependence on external nutrients and greater diversity in both crops and cropping practices.

Economic aspects

Despite the differences in agronomic approach noted above, the two groups showed no significant differences for the major indicators of economic performance.

In both years, gross income per hectare was higher in the ecological group—11% in the first year and 1% in the second. However, in the ecological group variable costs as a percentage of gross income were higher than in the reference group—50% compared with 40%. As a result the gross margin per hectare of the reference group was slightly better than that of the ecological group, by 8% in year 1 and 5% in year 2. Taking into account the huge differences within groups, these figures are not significantly different. However, they can be explained in part by the mix of enterprises in the two groups. The greater importance of livestock on ecological farms leads to a higher percentage of variable costs spent on livestock. However, the rate of return on these costs is considerably lower than for crops, approximately 1.5 versus 2.6 Spending more on the livestock enterprise decreases the overall rate of return.

It is commonly assumed that ecological agriculture requires more labour than conventional agriculture. Interestingly, this assumption does not hold for the ecological farms in this study. If the number of person-days per hectare required for each group is adjusted for differences in the relative importance of irrigation and for cropping intensity, the labour requirements are comparable for the two groups.

Returns per person-day differed considerably between the cases and over the two years. For both groups they were on average at least twice as high as the returns to unskilled, male agricultural labour off the farm.

The structure of variable costs differed for the two groups. As mentioned earlier, expenditures on livestock were higher among ecological farmers. As regards variable costs for crops, ecological farmers spent about 22% on soil fertility, whereas reference farmers spent from 24% to 35%. In the reference group the amounts spent on fertilizers were more heavily influenced by changes in the area irrigated than they were in the ecological group. Reference farms spent 4 to 5% of variable costs on agro-chemicals.

Extrapolation

The data presented in this study are the first available comparing ecological and conventional farming in a developing country. Although 2 years of research are too few on which to base firm conclusions, some extrapolation is possible to the national level.

The data suggest that ecological farms can perform just as well as conventional farms, even though they use no imported chemical inputs. They can produce similar levels of output, supplying the farmer with similar returns to labour. Extrapolated to national level, this means that ecological agriculture does not put food security at risk in the short term. Nor does it do so in the long term, for ecological farming practices may be expected to slow down soil erosion and the depletion of soil fertility. In addition, the lower dependence on exteral inputs associated with ecological farming is likely to have a positive influence on foreign exchange reserves.

The practices of ecological farming can be used to increase the efficiency of conventional farming. This is particularly true of internal nutrient cycling, improved manure management, the greater use of nitrogen-fixing species, and the inclusion of trees in the farming system.

References

Narayan, B. 1990. A report on ecological farming in South India: Economic analysis. ICSIM, Bangalore, India.

Pushpalatha, A. 1992. Ecological farming in South India: An agricultural comparison, 1990-1991. AME, Pondicherry, India.

Sivasubramanian, K. and A. de Jonge. 1990. Sustainability analysis of ecological agriculture in South India. AME, Pondicherry, India.

Srinivasa Reddy. 1991. A report on ecological farming in South India: An economic analysis. ICSIM, Bangalore, India.

van der Werf, E. and A. de Jager. 1992. Ecological agriculture in South India: An agro-economic comparison and study of transition. LEI/ETC Foundation, The Hague, Leusden, The Netherlands.

van der Werf, E. , G. Keshav Rao, A. Pushpalatha and Francis Xavier, A. 1992. An agro-economic comparison of two years of research in ecological and conventional agriculture in South India. AME, Pondicherry, India.

Source

Not previously published.

Address

Erik van der Werf, ETC Foundation, P. O. Box 64, 3830 AB Leusden, The Netherlands.

An Economic Assessment of Rice-fish Culture in the Philippines

M.P. Bimbao, A.V. Cruz and I.R. Smith

Introduction

Rice (*Oryza sativa*) is the staple food of 90% of Filipinos. Their second most important food is fish (NSCB 1988). Average per capita consumption of rice during 1980-82 in the Philippines was 88 kg (FAO 1985) while that of fish was 41 kg (BFAR 1984). A large proportion of the fish consumed comes from overfished marine stocks, from which no increase in yield can be expected (Pauly and Chua 1988).

Technologies to increase rice and fish production are needed urgently. Rice-fish culture, producing such fish as the Nile tilapia (*Oreochromis niloticus*) and the common carp (*Cyprinus carpio*) among other freshwater species, in addition to the rice harvest, could help improve the nutrition and livelihood of low-income groups (dela Cruz 1988).

Rice-fish culture is a relatively new farming system in the Philippines, introduced only about 15 years ago. Most studies on it have dealt mainly with the technology itself, providing detailed acounts of trench construction, fish stocking density in monoculture and polyculture systems, the use of supplementary feeding, and other aspects of production. In contrast, information on the economic feasibility of rice-fish culture is sparse (Temprosa and Shehadeh 1980; Maclean 1986). For example, only 4 out of 74 studies on rice-fish culture conducted by the Freshwater Aquaculture Center of Central Luzon State University for the period 1974-1987 covered economic aspects (Sevilleja 1988).

The production and area of rice-fish farms have not yet entered the country's official statistics. The government's first Rice-fish Culture Programme (known locally as 'Paly-Isdaan') was officially launched in 1979 (Arevalo 1987) but was hampered by the widespread use of high-yielding rice varieties that needed heavy use of fertilizers and pesticides (Banzon 1971; Arce and dela Cruz 1978). Moreover, about 80% of the fish produced in Philippine rice farms are consumed by the farmers' households and do not reach markets (Tagarino 1985).

The profitability of rice-fish culture as opposed to rice monoculture has already been indicated by the costs and returns analysis of nationwide field testing (Arevalo 1987) and by on-station experiments and trials with farmer cooperators conducted by the Freshwater Aquaculture Center, Muñoz, Nueva Ecija, using the partial budgeting technique (Arce and dela Cruz 1978; dela Cruz 1980).

This paper compares the results of various costs and returns studies. It also discusses the constraints to more widespread adoption of rice-fish culture.

Materials and Methods

Three case studies of costs and returns to rice-fish production in irrigated areas of the Philippines were carried out from the late 1970s to 1987 (Table 1). Cases 1 and 3 present the results of nationwide field trials conducted by the Philippine Department of Agriculture. Case 1 (NFAC, n.d.) provides no details on the data used to derive costs and returns. Case 3 data on production were taken from a report of the rice-fish culture programme, while those on costs were based on Arevalo (1987). Case 2 refers to 53 rice-fish culture farms studied by Tagarino (1985) in Central and Southern Luzon, two regions which together contribute 26% of total national rice production. Details regarding the raw data were not provided. The fish used throughout were tilapias: *Oreochromis niloticus* and *O. mossambicus*.

Profitability and productivity indices were derived from the three case studies. These may be compared across production systems, together with the costs and returns. All prices are given in Philippine pesos (P) at the time of the studies. Constant prices, used to compare net profits from different years, were estimated using a consumer price index, with 1985 as the base year. Prevailing exchange rates at the time of the studies were P 8.50 and P 20.00 = US$ 1.00 for cases 2 and 3 respectively. Case 1 was undated.

The inputs contributing significantly to total production costs were identified, as also were the outputs contributing significantly to total returns. This forms the basis for calculating the combination of enterprises that maximizes revenues. This information is useful for deciding on resource allocations (Doll and Orazem 1978).

Profitability indicators were used to compare the operating efficiencies of rice monoculture and rice-fish culture. They included the net profit/returns (NR), the profit margin (PM), and the rate of return to operating costs (ROC). Net profits/returns were estimated as the difference between total costs and total returns. Profit margin is the ratio of net profit to net sales. The rate of return to operating costs is defined as the ratio of net profit to operating costs (total variable costs). The value of alternative investments foregone is expressed as the cost/benefit ratio (Gittinger 1972), estimated by dividing the incremental benefits of engaging in rice-fish culture by the incremental costs. The normal decision rule applied for planning purposes in the Philippines is to accept only those projects with a ratio greater than 1 (NEDA 1984).

Productivity indicators were used to measure the opportunity cost of inputs used in an alternative production activity. Included here are total productivity (TP), which is the ratio of total output to total input; specific productivity (SP), which is the ratio of total output to a specific input; and net productivity (NP), which is the ratio of net product attributed to a factor to the input of that specific factor (Villegas 1977).

Results and Discussion

We found that rice-fish culture is a more profitable and productive farming system than rice monoculture (Tables 2 and 3). The shift from rice monoculture to rice-fish culture improved NR, PM, and ROC by an average of 40%, 10% and 14% respectively. The cost-benefit ratios for cases 1 and 3 (wet season) were 1.75 and 3.23 respectively.

The TP indices in cases 1 and 3 show that resources are used more productively in rice-fish culture than in rice monoculture. The SP and NP indices of major inputs that are common to both systems show that labour, fertilizer and pesticides contributed more to total revenue in rice-fish culture, by 21%, 27% and 36% respectively for SP and by 21%, 33% and 40% respectively for NP.

No conclusions can be drawn as to which season is more suitable for rice-fish culture. The profitability and productivity indices in case 2 were higher during the dry than during the wet season, in contrast to case 3, where they showed better returns during the wet

Table 1 Information on three case studies of rice-fish culture in the Philippines

	Case 1	Case 2	Case 3
Institutional support	National Rice-Fish Culture Coordinating Committee of the National Food and Agriculture Council, Department of Agriculture	Philippine Council for Agriculture and Resources Research and Development, International Center for Living Aquatic Resources Management	Department of Agriculture, Department of Natural Resources, National Agricultural and Fishery Council, Central Luzon State University
Years of study	Late 1970s (precise details not available)	1991 (wet season) 1992 (dry season)	1986 (wet and dry seasons)
Culture systems	Rice monoculture and rice-fish culture	Rice-fish culture	Rice monoculture and rice-fish culture
Species used	*O. niloticus*	*O. niloticus, O. mossambicus*	*O. niloticus*
Location and sample size (No. of farms)	Throughout the Philippines (precise details not available)	6 provinces in 2 regions: Central Luzon: Pampanga, 9; Tarlac, 7; Bulacan, 4; Nueva Ecija, 17 Southern Luzon: Leguna, 7; Albay, 9	25 provinces in 12 regions (550)
Source	NFAC (n. d.)	Tagarino (1985)	Arevalo (1987)

Table 2 Average costs and returns (P/ha) to rice monoculture and rice-fish culture in the Philippines

	Case 1		Case 2			Case 3		
			Season			Season		
			Wet	Dry	Wet		Dry	
	R	RF	R	RF	R	RF	R	RF
Returns:								
Rice	6200	5658	6825	7083	17500	17500	17500	17500
Fish	6200	8108	9249	10137	17500	21900	17500	21900
Costs:								
1.Variable								
Labour	2193	2313	915	812	4885	4966	4883	4802
Seeds	108	108	128	198	300	270	300	270
Fertilizer	672	672	777	980	1237	1237	1062	1062
Pesticides	580	580	206	171	1462	1324	1462	1324
Fingerlings	-	750	1681	1380	-	1000	-	1000
Feeds	-	0	458	374	-	600	-	600
Screens, bags	-	220	-	-	-	62	-	12
Subtotal	3553	4643	4165	3915	7884	9459	7709	9070
2. Fixed								
Interest	81	81	-[1]	-[1]	225	225	225	225
Land amortization	510	510	-[1]	-[1]	580	580	580	580
Tax, irrigation fee	18	18	-[1]	-[1]	864	864	708	708
Depreciation					200	200	200	200
Subtotal	609	609	-	-	1869	1869	1713	1713
3. Miscellaneous	303	303	460	562	-[2]	-[2]	-[2]	-[2]
Total costs	4465	5555	4625	4477	9753	11328	9422	10783
Net returns	1735	2553	4624	5660	7747	10572	8078	11117

Note: R = rice; RF = rice-fish
1. Included under miscellaneous
2. No data available

Table 3 Economic indicators for rice monoculture and rice-fish culture in the Philippines, a comparison between three case studies

Indicators	Case 1		Case 2		Case 3			
			Season		Season			
			Wet	Dry	Wet		Dry	
	R	RF	RF	RF	R	RF	R	RF
Profitability:								
Net returns (P/ha)[1]	1735	2553	4624	5660	7747	10572	8078	11117
Net returns (P/ha)[2]	45	66	68	95	77	105	80	110
Rate of return[3] (%)	49	55	111	145	98	112	105	123
Profit margin (%)	28	31	50	56	44	48	46	51
B/C ratio		1.75				2.79		3.23
Productivity:								
1. Total	1.39	1.46	2.00	2.26	1.79	1.93	1.86	2.03
2. Specific:								
Labour	2.83	3.51	10.11	12.48	3.58	4.41	3.58	4.56
Fertilizer	9.23	12.07	11.90	10.34	14.15	17.70	16.48	20.62
Pesticides	10.69	13.98	44.90	59.28	11.97	16.54	11.97	16.54
3. Net:								
Labour	1.79	2.10	6.05	7.97	2.59	3.13	2.65	3.32
Fertilizer	3.58	4.80	6.95	6.78	7.26	9.55	8.61	11.47
Pesticides	3.99	5.40	23.45	34.10	6.30	8.98	6.53	9.40

1. At current prices
2. At constant prices, 1985 = 100
3. To operating costs

season. One possible explanation is the difference in study area: case 2 covers the major rice-producing provinces in Central and Southern Luzon, which give above-average rice yields. A further complication is that the PM and ROC ratios for wet-season rice-fish culture were lower than for rice monoculture (Table 4). This implies that the additional economic benefits derived from rice-fish culture are somehow reduced or eliminated

Table 4 Economic indicators for rice monoculture and rice-fish culture in the Philippines, averaged over three case studies

	Rice	Rice-fish	
		Dry	Wet
Relative importance of cost components (%):			
Labour	50	31	36
Seeds	3	3	2
Fertilizer	13	17	13
Pesticides	15	8	9
Fingerlings	15	8	9
Feeds	-	7	5
Screens, bags	-	0	1
Relative output (%):			
Rice	100	75	75
Fish	-	25	25
Profitability:			
Net returns (P/ha)	67	100	81
Return to operating costs (%)	68	89	66
Return to gross sales (%)	39	47	38
Productivity:			
1. Total	1.68	2.10	1.83
2. Specific:			
Labour	3.33	8.45	6.06
Fertilizer	13.28	14.02	14.86
Pesticides	5.60	21.54	12.75
3. Net:			
Labour	2.34	5.55	3.82
Fertilizer	6.48	7.02	7.74
Pesticides	5.60	21.54	12.75

1. At constant prices, 1985 = 100

during the wet season. Our results are consistent with the recommendations found in the literature concerning rotation schemes (dela Cruz 1980; Huat and Tan 1980; Pullin 1985).

The costs analysis for rice-fish culture shows that labour, fingerlings, fertilizer and pesticides are, in that order, the major production inputs. The returns analysis shows that the contribution of rice and fish to total revenue is the same in both the wet and dry seasons, with rice contributing an average of 75% and fish 25%.

Over 15 years after its introduction, rice-fish culture is still at the experimental stage, with field testing and verification directly managed by researchers and extensionists. Technological problems, such as pesticide application, the availability of fingerlings and inadequate water supply, and social constraints, notably poaching, have prevented widespread adoption. Perhaps the most serious barrier to adoption is lack of motivation: most farmers have yet to be convinced that the additional inputs, management and risks required to incorporate fish production into rice farming systems are worth the returns they can expect. These problems must be resolved if rice-fish culture is to expand in the Philippines (Pullin 1985; Tagarino 1985; Chaudhuri 1985; dela Cruz 1988). It is hoped that this paper will help in this process, in which information to influence farmers' attitudes appears to be just as important as technological advances.

References

Arce, R.G. and C.R. dela Cruz. 1978. Improved rice-fish culture in the Philippines. In: Proceedings, International Commission on Irrigation and Drainage. ICID Second Regional Afro-Asian Conference. Technical Paper No. 10.

Arevalo, T.Z. 1987. The rice fish culture programme. Paper presented at the First Fisheries Forum, held at the Bureau of Fisheries and Aquatic Resources, Quezon City, Philippines, 27 March 1987.

Banzon, M.A. 1971. Status of the rice-fish production programme. Unpublished report of the Chief, Rice Fish Production Programme Section, National Food and Agriculture Council, Ministry of Agriculture, Quezon City, Philippines.

BFAR. 1984. Fisheries statistics of the Philippines, Vol. 34. Bureau of Fisheries and Aquatic Resources. Department of Agriculture, Philippines.

Chaudhuri, H. 1985. Rice-fish culture. Paper presented at the International Rice Research Conference. International Rice Research Institute, Los Baños, Laguna, Philippines, 1-5 June.

dela Cruz, C.R. 1980. Integrated agriculture-aquaculture farming systems in the Philippines, with two case studies on simultaneous and rotational rice-fish culture. In: R.S.V. Pullin and Z.H. Shehadeh (eds), Integrated agriculture-aquaculture farming systems. ICLARM Conference Proceedings 4. International Center for Living Aquatic Resources Management, Manila, and Southeast Asian Regional Center for Graduate Study and Research in Agriculture, College, Los Baños, Laguna, Philippines.

dela Cruz, C.R. 1988. Rice-fish farming: A potential contributor to rural socio-economic upliftment in the Philippines. Paper presented at the National Rice-fish Workshop, Wuxi, China, 10-13 October 1988.

Doll, J.P. and F. Orazem. 1978. *Production economics: Theory with applications*. Grid Inc., Ohio.

FAO. 1985. Rice: Selected aspects of production, trade and price policies. Economic and Social Development Paper 54. Food and Agriculture Organization, Rome.

Gittinger, J.P. 1972. *Economic analysis of agricultural projects.* Johns Hopkins University Press, Baltimore.

Huat, K.K. and E.S.P. Tan. 1980. Review of rice-fish culture in Southeast Asia. In: R.S.V. Pullin and Z.H. Shehadeh (eds), Integrated agriculture-aquaculture farming systems. ICLARM Conference Proceedings 4. International Center for Living Aquatic Resources Management, Manila, and Southeast Asian Regional Center for Graduate Study and Research in Agriculture, College, Los Baños, Laguna, Philippines.

Maclean, J. 1986. Who's working in rice-fish culture? Naga. The ICLARM Quarterly 9 (4):37.

NEDA. 1984. Project development manual. National Economic and Development Authority, Manila, Philippines.

NFAC. n.d. Rice-fish culture 1: Production of tilapia in net enclosures and rice paddies; 2: Primer in paddy culture of fish. National Rice-fish Culture Coordinating Committee, National Food and Agriculture Council, Ministry of Agriculture, Quezon City, Philippines.

NSCB. 1988. The Philippine food balance sheet CY 1973 to CY 1986. National Statistical Coordination Board, National Economic and Development Authority, Manila, Philippines.

Pauly, D. and Chua Thia Eng. 1988. The overfishing of marine resources: Socio-economic background in Southeast Asia. *Ambio* 17 (3):200-206.

Pullin, R.S.V. 1985. Time to reappraise rice-fish culture. ICLARM Newsletter 8 (4):3-4.

Sevilleja, R.C. 1988. Rice-fish farming development in the Philippines: Past, present and future. Paper presented at the workshop on Rice-fish Farming Research and Development, International Rice Research Institute, International Center for Living Aquatic Resources Management, and Thailand Department of Agriculture, Ubon, Thailand, 21-25 March 1988.

Tagarino, R.N. 1985. Economics of rice-fish culture systems, Luzon, Philippines. In: I.R. Smith, E.B. Torres and E.O. Tan (eds), Philippine tilapia economics. ICLARM Conference Proceedings 12. Council for Agricultural and Resources Research and Development, Los Baños, Laguna, and International Center for Living Aquatic Resources Management, Manila, Philippines.

Temprosa, R.M. and Z.H. Shehadeh. 1980. Preliminary bibliography of rice-fish culture. ICLARM Bibliographies 1. International Center for Living Aquatic Resources Management, Manila, Philippines.

Villegas, B.M. 1977. *Managerial economics.* Revised edition. Sinag-Tala Publishers, Manila, Philippines.

Acknowledgements
The authors are grateful to Mr. Jay Maclean, Dr. Daniel Pauly, and Dr. Roger Pullin for their valuable comments in the preparation of this paper.

Source
First published 1990 as ICLARM Contribution No. 534, in The Second Asian Fisheries Forum, edited by R. Hirano and I. Hanyu, published by the Asian Fisheries Society, Manila, Phillippines.

Address
M.P. Bimbao, A.V. Cruz and I.R. Smith, ICLARM, MC P.O. Box 1501, Makati Metro, Manila, Philippines

A User Perspective on Rice-fish Culture in the Philippines

C.R. dela Cruz, C. Lightfoot and R.C. Sevilleja

Introduction

Research on rice-fish production in rice fields began in 1974 at the Freshwater Aquaculture Center of the Central Luzon State University (FAC/CLSU), Philippines. This research effort produced the concurrent rice-fish culture technology, nationwide field testing of which was initiated in 1976 by the then Ministry of Agriculture and Ministry of Natural Resources (de la Cruz 1980). Some 38 technicians were trained to take charge of field tests. From October 1977 to March 1978 promising results were obtained, and a pilot phase followed in May 1979. An additional 78 technicians were trained. The areas used and production attained during this phase are presented in Table 1. After an impressive start, reaching a peak of over 2000 families, adoption declined once the programme had ended in 1986. The area fell to 185 ha and the number of farms to 550.

Those promoting the technology attribute the decline in adoption after 1982 to several factors. First, the irregular delivery of irrigation water, which is often not deep enough for fish to survive, means that the new system is too risky for most farmers. Second, many farmers still prefer to use high doses of insecticides and not raise fish, because they consider it necessary to achieve the highest possible rice yield. This is despite an alternative protection regime of soil-incorporated Furadan or Curaterr 3G (Carbofuran), which has been proved safe for the fish (Arce and dela Cruz 1979). Third, farmers have often not been able to stock large enough fingerlings. The limited growing period available for fish raised in combination with short-duration, high-yielding rice varieties results in small-sized fish (<100g) at rice harvest (Arce and dela Cruz 1979). Fourth, the fact that rice-fish culture is a relatively new technology and that farmers lack experience of it and exposure to it also constrains adoption. Most farmers are accustomed to rice monoculture. The income derived by larger rice farmers is high and stable enough, such that diversifying with fish does not seem attractive. A shift to rice-fish means more work and higher costs (Campos 1985).

A revival of rice-fish farming is now being considered by the Department of Agriculture. It is therefore important to find out from the users themselves why rice-fish adoption declined. This paper attempts this task. The study was done in Guimba and Muñoz, Nueva Ecija. A rapid rural appraisal technique was used. Information was obtained by interviewing 18 farmers, 8 of whom were cooperators in rice-fish on-farm trials, 4 were spontaneous

Table 1 Total area and production levels achieved during the National Rice-Fish Culture Pilot Implementation Programme, 1979-1986

Year	Total area (ha)	No. of farms	Average area per farm (ha)	Yields (kg/ha)	
				Rice	Fish
1979	193	428	0.45	4965	115
1980	249	446	0.56	5150	208
1981	497	1141	0.44	5015	155
1982	1397	2284	0.61	5010	174
1983	759	1237	0.61	4450	164
1984	424	932	0.45	3900	152
1985	607	1177	0.52	4300	119
1986	185	550	0.34	3850	140

Source: Arevalo 1987

adopters and 5 were non-adopters. A brief socio-economic profile of these farmers follows, before we describe the technology itself and the users' assessment of it.

Profile of Users and Non-Users

Table 2 presents a profile of rice-fish technology users and non-users. On average, spontaneous adopters were older and so more experienced in rice farming. They had larger farms, averaging 5 ha. However, they owned only 35% of this area, with the balance either rented or mortgaged. Their larger farm size suggests that they earned more than the cooperators and the non-users, a hypothesis borne out by their higher production capital. This meant they could afford the risk of trying out new technology. The spontaneous adopters and members of their families devoted more time to their farm enterprises than did the cooperators and the non-users.

The Rice-fish Technology

Rice-fish farming encompasses several systems: concurrent production, rotational production, and small separate ponds within the rice farm. Moreover, there are further options within both concurrent and rotational systems (Figure 1). A concurrent system is one in which rice and fish are raised simultaneously in the same or in adjacent spaces,

Table 2 Socio-economic profile of rice-fish technology users and non-users

Item	Users		Non-users
	Cooperators	Spontaneous adopters	
No. of respondents	8	4	5
Age (years)	48	57	47
Household size (No. of people)	6	5	4
Years in school	9	10	10
Years experience in rice farming	22	35	28
Area of farm (ha):			
Owned	2.2	1.7	1.8
Rented	-	3.0	-
Share-cropped	0.3	-	-
Mortgaged	-	0.3	-
House lot (ha)	0.1	0.2	0.1
Rice production (t/ha):			
Wet season	4.5	3.8	4.3
Dry season	5.4	5.7	4.9
Crop production capital (US$/farm)	678	1551	513
Labour devoted to farm operation (person-days):			
Farmer	153	239	221
Family	53	303	73

while in a rotational system they follow one another within a prescribed time interval, usually a year (dela Cruz and Lopez 1980). In a 1-year cropping cycle, concurrent and rotational systems may be combined.

Figure 2 illustrates a 1-year rice-fish culture cycle, together with the calendar of activities. This is the concurrent rice-fish system currently being reassessed in farmers' fields in the Philippines. Trials with farmers are being conducted in paddies of $300\,m^2$ with raised dikes. The dikes are approximately 50 cm wide at the base, 30 to 40 cm at the top and 40 cm high, so as to contain water up to 20 cm deep. Each paddy has a fish refuge, which may be one of two types—the trench refuge and pond refuge. The trench is from

0.3 to 0.4 m deep and 0.5 to 1 m wide. The pond is located at one end of the paddy and occupies 10% of the area, with a water depth of 0.75-1 m (*see* Figure 3).

Figure 1 Classification of rice-fish culture systems

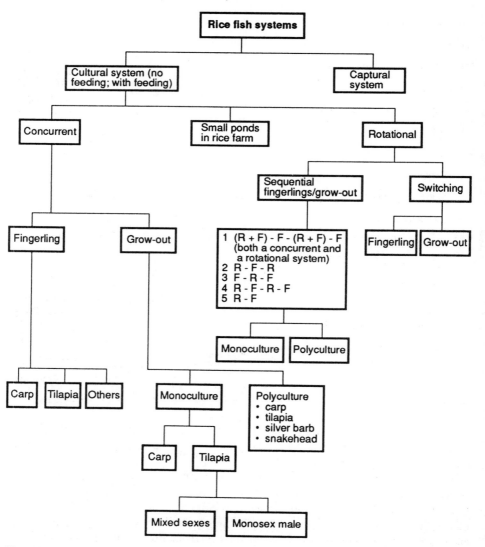

Note. These systems do not include crops and/or animals raised outside the rice-fish environment

Figure 2 Rice fish culture cycle and calendar

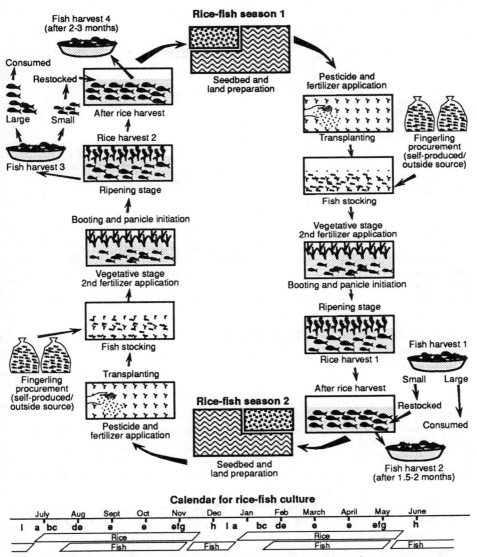

Calendar for rice-fish culture

a Land preparation, first rice-fish season: ploughing/harrowing/levelling/manuring; trench/pond refuge b Seed fish procurement c Transplanting/fertilizer application d Fish stocking e Rice + fish culture f Field draining/fish harvest g Rice harvest/followed by restocking fish in rice field h Fish culture in rice field I Fish harvest/land preparation for first/second rice-fish season

Figure 3 Rice-fish field layout

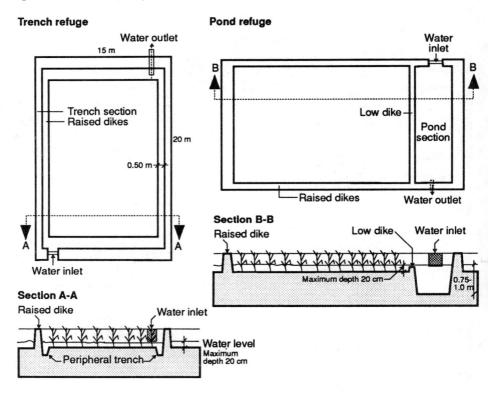

The paddies are prepared for rice transplanting. Fertilizer is applied two to three times: one basal application during transplanting and one to two applications of top dressing during vegetative growth. The first application consists of 200 kg/ha of 16-20-0 and 50 kg/ha of urea. The same amounts are applied in the second application, but may be split into two.

Seedlings of IR rice varieties (such as IR 46 and IR 64) are transplanted at 25-30 days old. Farmers apply either Machete EC at the rate of 0.6 kg or 2-4-D at 17.4 kg a.i./ha for weed control 5 days after transplanting. For insect control, Furadan 3G is applied during the last harrowing at the rate of one bag (16.7 kg) per hectare and Parapest or Cymbush EC sprayed at the rate of 0.4 kg a.i./ha and 500 ml/ha respectively.

Water level in the paddies is gradually increased 1 week after transplanting, reaching 15-20 cm at vegetative growth. Partial draining is done during spraying of pesticides.

Tilapia (*Oreochromis niloticus*) is the main fish species raised. It is stocked at 10-14 days after transplanting, at 5000/ha in the paddies with trench refuges and 5000-7500/ha in those with pond refuges. A stocking size of 15-25 g is recommended (dela Cruz 1980), but is rarely observed. The fingerlings usually available are 5-10 g. Whenever available, rice bran and other local crop byproducts are given as supplementary feed. Fish are harvested from paddies with a trench refuge about 1 week before rice harvesting, giving a culture period of 70-80 days. With a pond refuge, the culture period can be extended much longer, and this allows the stocking of smaller fingerlings (5-10 g). However, the testing of pond refuges has only just begun. Results at the FAC indicated an average yield of about 100-200 kg/ha and a maximum of 293 kg/ha within 90-120 days using the concurrent system (dela Cruz and Lopez 1980), while initial experiments with pond refuges have yielded 396 kg/ha in 150 days (dela Cruz and Sevilleja 1990).

Users' and Non-users' Assessments

It is obvious from the replies of informants, shown in Table 3, that the test cooperators and spontaneous adopters are fully aware of the benefits of rice-fish farming. To some degree, even the non-adopters realize these. This is surprising, since in the past lack of adequate information was frequently given as a reason why non-users were not practising rice-fish culture.

Through rice-fish farming, users raised their income from US$ 143 to US$ 576/ha per year; rice production increased by 3.7% per crop; and vegetables from the banks of the raised dikes provided 425 kg/ha of food or US$ 170/ha of cash.

None of the test cooperators or spontaneous adopters felt that the technology was difficult to implement. Some of the non-users shared this belief.

Users were able to modify the technology as necessary to suit their circumstances. One of the four adopters, having initially followed the technology as introduced, made two major modifications. He raised the tilapia stocking rate two or more times above the recommended level of 5000/ha. He said that marketing fish in his locality was easier if these were sold small. He also practised a rotational system, raising rice and fish at the same time but in separate areas, instead of the recommended concurrent one. He had realized that continuous cropping with rice tends to exhaust the zinc content of the soil, a deficiency common in the irrigated fields of his area. Through the use of a rotational system, switching areas from rice to fish and back again, he was giving the soil time to rest. Another user located his rice-fish farm in a higher lying area than the surrounding paddies, so that at the rice harvest he could drain all the fish into a large pond where he could grow them further to a larger size.

Fifty per cent of the cooperators were not satisfied with the growth rate and size of the tilapia at harvest in the concurrent system. They thought they would be able to improve the size of the fish by themselves, after the project was over. Three of the eight cooperators

Table 3 Users' and non-users' assessments of rice-fish culture

Criteria	Cooperators								Adopters				Non-users				
	1	2	3	4	5	6	7	8	1	2	3	4	1	2	3	4	5
Technology easy to apply	Y	Y	Y	Y	Y	Y	Y	Y	Y	Y	Y	Y	Y	Y	Y	Y	Y
Additional cash affordable	Y	Y	Y	Y	Y	Y	Y	Y	Y	Y	N	Y	Y	Y	Y	Y	N
Poaching is a problem	N	N	N	N	N	N	N	N	Y	N	N	N	Y	N	Y	Y	Y
Bird damage is a problem	Y		Y							Y				Y			
Bigger dikes not a problem in harbouring rodents	N	Y	Y	N	Y	Y	Y	Y	Y	N	Y	Y	Y	N	Y	N	Y
Bigger dikes mean more space for other crops or pasture, so more income	Y	Y	Y	Y	Y	Y	Y	Y	Y	Y	Y	Y	Y	Y	Y	N	Y
Trench/pond refuge increases income	Y	Y	Y	Y	Y	Y	Y	Y	Y	Y	?	N	?	Y	Y	?	Y
Trench/pond refuge is costly	Y				Y	Y	Y		N	N				N	Y		Y
Satisfied with yield and size of tilapia	N	Y	N	N	Y	N	Y	Y	Y	Y	Y	Y	?	Y	?	?	Y
Would switch to common carp/faster growing fish	N	N	Y	Y	?	Y	N	N	N	Y	N	Y	?	N	?	?	Y
Using pesticide not a problem	Y	Y	Y	Y	Y	Y	Y	Y	Y	Y	Y	Y	Y	Y	Y	Y	Y
Believes fish help in pest control	Y	Y	Y	Y	Y	Y	Y	Y	Y	Y	Y	?	Y	Y	?	?	?
Cost of pumping water not a problem	Y	Y	Y	Y	Y	N	Y	Y	Y	Y	Y	Y	N	N	Y	N	Y
Irrigation water is adequate									Y	Y							
Use of family labour is effective with rice-fish	Y	Y	Y	Y	Y	Y	Y	?	Y	Y	Y	Y	Y	Y	Y	Y	Y
Income is greater with rice-fish	Y	Y	Y	Y	Y	Y	Y	Y	Y	Y	Y	Y	Y	Y	?	?	
Rice increases in yield	N	Y	Y	Y	Y	Y	N	Y	Y	Y	Y	?	Y	?	?		?
Farmer can modify technology to suit conditions	Y	Y	Y	Y	Y	Y	Y	Y	Y	Y	Y	Y	Y	Y	?	?	?
Will continue with rice-fish after project	Y	Y	Y	Y	Y	Y	Y	Y	Y	Y	Y	Y	Y	N	?	?	?
Will expand rice-fish area	Y	Y	Y	N	Y	Y	Y	Y	Y	Y	N	Y	?	N	?	?	

Note: Y = yes; N = no; ? = don't know

wanted to try common carp, if fingerlings were available. All the four adopters, on the other hand, expressed satisfaction at the size of their fish, since marketing small-sized fish was not considered a problem. Two of the five non-users also expressed satisfaction at the size of the tilapia they saw at harvest on other people's farms.

As regards the capital required for initial investment, none of the cooperators considered it beyond their means, but one of the users did. Three non-users agreed that the technology was affordable. Of the cooperators and adopters, only one felt that pumping water to sustain fish culture in the paddies was too costly; three of the non-users felt the same way. Half the cooperators felt the provision of fish refuges to be costly, but no adopters saw it that way and only one non-user did.

Surprisingly, none of the informants considered the use of pesticides as a deterrent to the development or expansion of rice-fish farming. Aside from the recommended methods for the proper use of pesticides, the cooperators and adopters devised their own precautions for avoiding fish mortality.

Poaching was acknowledged as a problem by only one of the cooperators and adopters. However, their rice-fish paddies were located close to their houses at the time of the survey. They knew poaching would be a risk in the future, when their rice-fish paddies were further away. Four (80%) of the non-users expressed a fear of poaching. Predation by birds was also identified as a problem by 4 of the 17 informants.

Conclusions

Overall, the assessment of rice-fish technology derived from this rapid rural appraisal was positive. This has encouraged us to continue. Not only did all the rice-fish farmers interviewed see the benefits of the new technology, but they also demonstrated a willingness and ability to modify or improve the system to suit their own circumstances. The farmers are also willing to expand their rice-fish areas, converting to this use those areas of their farms that are low-lying and/or waterlogged. We are now better informed about the constraints that research can address, such as fingerling size and the riskiness of the new system. Our experience confirms the growing body of opinion worldwide that user participation in on-farm research can facilitate technology generation and speed up adoption. It also justifies the continuation of current participatory on-farm research efforts devoted to the development or reappraisal of rice-fish technology in Indonesia, India, Thailand and the Philippines.

References
Arce, R.G. and C.R. dela Cruz. 1979. Yield trials on rice-fish culture at the Freshwater Aquaculture Center. *Fish. Res. J. Phil* 4 (1):1-8.
Arevalo, T.Z. 1987. The Rice-Fish Culture Programme. Paper presented at the First Fisheries Forum for 1987, a seminar on Developments in Integrated Agriculture-Aquaculture Farming

Systems, held at the Bureau of Fisheries and Aquatic Resources, Quezon City, Philippines, 27 March 1987.

Campos, A.C. 1985. Rice-fish culture in the Philippines. In: Trinh Ton That (ed.), *Rice: Progress assessment and orientation in the 1980s*. Proceedings of the 16th session of the International Rice Commission, 10-14 June 1985, Los Baños, Laguna, Philippines. International Rice Commission Newsletter, Vol. 34 (2). FAO, Rome, Italy.

dela Cruz, C.R. 1980. Integrated agriculture-aquaculture farming systems in the Philippines, with two case studies on simultaneous and rotational rice-fish culture. In: R. Pullin and Z. Shehadeh (eds), Integrated agriculture-aquaculture farming systems. ICLARM Conference Proceedings 4. International Center for Living Aquatic Resources Management, Manila, Philippines.

dela Cruz, C.R. and E.A. Lopez. 1980. Rotational farming of rice and fish in paddies. *Fish. Res. J. Philipp.* 5 (1):39-52.

dela Cruz, C.R. and R.C. Sevilleja. 1990. Evaluation of pond refuge systems. In: Rice-fish farming systems research project. Final report to the Asian Development Bank. International Center for Living Aquatic Resources Management, Manila, Philippines.

Source

This paper was presented at World Aquaculture '90, June 10-14, 1990, Halifax, Nova Scotia, Canada. Reprinted by kind permission of the authors.

Addresses

C.R. dela Cruz and C. Lightfoot: ICLARM, MC P.O. Box 1501, Makati Metro, Manila, Philippines
R.C. Sevilleja: Central Luzon State University, Nueva Ecija 3120 Philippines.

Further Reading

Alcorn, J.B. 1989. An economic analysis of Huastec Mayan Forest Management. In: Browder J.O. (ed.), *Fragile lands of Latin America: Strategies for sustainable development.* Boulder, Westview Press.

Barbier, E.B. 1990. *Economics, natural resource scarcity and development: Conventional and alternative views.* London: Earthscan Publications.

Barde, J.P. and D. Pearce. 1991. *Valuing the environment: Six case studies.* London, Earthscan Publications Ltd.

Chambers, R. and Conway, G.R. 1992. Sustainable rural livelihoods: Practical concepts for the 21st century. IDS Discussion Paper No. 296. IDS, Brighton.

Conway, G.R. and E. B. Barbier. 1990. *After the green revolution: Sustainable agriculture for development.* London, Earthscan Publications.

Dixon, J. A., D. E. James and P. B. Sherman (eds). 1989. *The economics of dryland management.* London, Earthscan Publications.

Ekens, P. (ed.). 1986. *The living economy: A new economics in the making.* London, Routledge.

Ellis, F. 1988. *Peasant economics: Farm households and agrarian development.* Cambridge University Press.

Elzakker, van B., R. Witte and J.D. van Mansvelt. 1992. Benefits of diversity: An incentive towards sustainable agriculture. New York, UNDP.

ILEIA. 1991. Assessing low-external-input farming techniques: Report of a workshop. ILEIA Newsletter 1 and 2.

Kotschi, J. (ed.) 1990. *Ecofarming practices for tropical smallholdings.* Tropical Agroecology 5. Weikersheim, Verlag Josef Margraf.

Kotschi, J., G. Weinschenck and R. Werner. 1991. *Ökonomische Bewertungskriterien für die Beurteilung von Beratungsvorhaben zur Standortgerechte Landnutzung in bäuerlichen Familienbetrieben.* Forschungsberichte des Bundesministeriums für wirtschaftliche Zusammenarbeit, Band 99. Cologne, Weltforum Verlag.

Pearce, D., E. Barbier, A. Markandya. 1991. *Sustainable development: Economics and environment in the Third World.* London, Earthscan Publications Ltd.

Prinsley, R. T. (ed.) 1990. Agroforestry for sustainable production: Economic implications. London, Commonwealth Science Council.

Schramm, G. and J. J. Warford (eds). 1989. *Environmental management and economic development.* World Bank/Johns Hopkins University Press, Baltimore.

Senanayake, R. 1991. Sustainable agriculture: Definitions and parameters for measurement. *Journal of Sustainable Agriculture* 1 (4): 7-28.

Swinkels, R.A. and S. J. Scherr. 1991. Economic analysis of agroforestry technologies: An annotated bibliography. Nairobi, ICRAF.

Toledo, V.M. 1990. *The ecological rationality of peasant production. In:* M.A. Altieri and S.B. Hecht (eds), *Agroecology and small farm development.* Boston, CRC Press.

Winpenny, J. T. 1991. Values for the environment: A guide to economic appraisal. London, HMSO.

Checklist of Criteria for Assessing Agricultural Technologies

Productivity
- Does the technology meet farmers' needs in kind?
    - Does it improve food availability, quality and security?
    - Does it sustain or improve the availability of secondary products (fuelwood, building materials, medicines, gifts, etc)?
- Does it meet farmer/household needs for cash (or exchangeable products)?
    - Is there a market for the products?
    - Are prices high enough?
- Is enough land available to produce sufficient for farmer/household needs?
    - Quantity
    - Quality
- Do labour requirements fit farmers' labour resources?
    - By gender
    - By season
- Do farmers have access to the necessary inputs?
    - Are inputs available?
    - Are inputs affordable?
- Do financial requirements fit farmers' cash resources and needs for cost-effectiveness?
    - By different cost components (nutrients, pesticides, hired labour, transport, etc)
    - By season

Security
- Does the technology minimize the risk of
    - Crop failure (pests, diseases, drought, waterlogging, etc)?
    - Financial failure?
    - Health hazards?
    - Non-availability of external inputs?
    - Inappropriateness of exotic species?
- Does it allow sufficient management flexibility?
- Is it based on the use of local resources (genetic resources, knowlege, skills, etc)
    - Are these resources under the control of farmers?
- Does it reduce dependence on information, subsidies, credit from outside the farming system?
- Does it avoid conflicts between interest groups?

Continuity
- Does the technology maintain/enhance soil quality?
    - Soil life
    - Soil fertility (macro- and micronutrients)
    - Nutrient balance (macro- and micronutrients)
    - Structure
    - Water-holding capacity
- Does it recycle nutrients?
- Does it prevent/reduce soil nutrient loss?
    - Soil cover
    - Complementary root structure
    - Water conservation
- Does it enhance/maintain perennial biomass (grasses, shrubs, trees, animals)
- Does it use water efficiently and safely?
    - Water use efficiency of crops
    - Overpumping
    - Drainage
- Does it enhance diversity?
- Does it reduce toxic effects on people and resources?
- Does it enhance human health?
- Are maintenance costs (ecological and economic) affordable?
- Does it recycle capital?
- Does it have neutral or positive effects on systems beyond the farm (watershed, village, downstream areas, nation, etc)?
    - Use of non-renewable resources
    - Pollution of air, water, soil
    - Production of greenhouse gases

Identity
- Does the technology integrate well within the existing farming system?
    - Agro-ecologically
    - Socio-economically
    - At household level
    - At gender level
    - From a developmental viewpoint
- Is it possible to introduce the technology given the existing infrastructure (credit, roads, transport, extension support, etc)?
- Does the technology fit/strengthen the culture of the farming population?
    - Social organization
    - Religion or values
    - Tastes and preferences

- Perceptions of social justice
- Can it be easily understood by farmers?
- Is it consistent with government policy?
     - Does it generate employment opportunities (on-farm, off-farm)?
     - Does it contribute to regional/national food security?
     - Does it contribute to foreign currency reserves?
- Does it benefit poor/powerless groups (men, women)?

Adaptability
- Has the technology already been practised by small-scale farmers (if so, with what results)?
- Does it bring rapid, recognizable returns?
- Does it allow experimentation/adaptation by farmers?
- Can it be easily communicated to other farmers?
- Can knowlege/skills required be easily transferred to farmers through training?

Guidelines for use
This is a checklist, not a 'should' list. People working with this list should feel free to give high or low values to different criteria, or to add, delete or change criteria as they see fit.

This checklist of criteria was prepared during ILEIA workshops.
ILEIA. 1991/2. Assessing low-external-input farming techniques: Report of a Workshop. ILEIA Newsletter 1 and 2.